FERAL CITIES

ADVENTURES WITH ANIMALS
IN THE URBAN JUNGLE

TRISTAN DONOVAN

CHICAGO
REVIEW
PRESS

Copyright © 2015 by Tristan Donovan
All rights reserved
Published by Chicago Review Press Incorporated
814 North Franklin Street
Chicago, Illinois 60610
ISBN 978-1-56976-067-3

Library of Congress Cataloging-in-Publication Data
Is available from the Library of Congress.

Cover design: Rebecca Lown
Cover photo: Chacma baboon group raiding apartment building, South Africa.
  Cyril Ruoso/Minden Pictures
Interior design: Jonathan Hahn
Illustrations: Tom Homewood

Printed in the United States of America
5 4 3 2 1

**To my wonderful parents,
John and Maria Donovan**

CONTENTS

01

HOT TUB SNAKES

On the Trail of Rattlesnakes in Phoenix

Bryan Hughes lives a double life.

Much of the time he is a mild-mannered web designer, tinkering with computer code and honing the look and feel of websites. But there's another Bryan, one his IT colleagues are only dimly aware of: Bryan, the rattlesnake catcher of Phoenix, Arizona. "I don't tell anybody in my tech life what I do with the snakes, really," Bryan tells me as we drive down Piestewa Freeway. "I'd rather not have people think I'm weird or something. There was a snake in the parking lot at work one day, so I went and caught it. All my coworkers' jaws were wide open. They had no idea. They thought I was going to die."

We've been driving the highways of Phoenix for a few hours now, circling the fast-growing city's patchwork of sprawling new developments and oven-hot Sonoran Desert, where columns of tall saguaro cacti reach into the sky like spindly fingers. From the back of Bryan's truck comes the sound of angry hissing from a rattlesnake that, thankfully, is securely stored in a bright red tub that was once a pool pellet container.

We're killing time, waiting for a call. We've been waiting all morning, hoping that someone, somewhere in this city of more than four million people is going to have a rattlesnake encounter. So far, all we've done is release one of Bryan's previous catches—a light brown-and-yellow southwestern speckled rattlesnake. It had slithered into someone's backyard to drink from the swimming pool. Now it gets to make a new home in a remote corner of one of the city's large desert parks.

As we head down the freeway, I ask Bryan what got him into rattlesnakes and to found Rattlesnake Solutions.

"Dinosaurs," he says, after a brief think. "That might have been the start.

"I really loved dinosaurs and bugs as a kid. When I was five, my grandma gave me a little 35mm camera. I got some ants and put them into all the spiderwebs in the yard and took pictures of them. They were the worst pictures, but I put them on a board and then got all the adults in the neighborhood together in grandma's living room and gave a talk about spiders. So I was kinda born to do this kind of stuff."

The young Bryan soon discovered that the problem with dinosaurs is that they're extinct. "So when I got done reading all the dinosaur books, I got started reading the reptile books and it was just fun. I'd go out and catch them a lot. I just haven't grown out of it, I guess. It's like people who have Lego when they're young and grow up to be architects—same kind of thing."

And being a snake catcher in Arizona is about as good as it gets for a reptile fan like Bryan. "I really love my job doing design, but I like doing this more. It perplexes my peers—they think I'm just doing pest control, like I'm going out spraying for termites or something. But there's lots of excitement, and I love the snakes. When I was a kid, I couldn't dream that I would have the entire city of Phoenix looking for snakes for me."

Trouble is, not many people like snakes, let alone rattlesnakes. In fact, they are hated.

Bryan tells me about the rattlesnake roundups of Texas, where people catch the reptiles by the thousands by pumping gasoline into snake burrows to force them out. "It's the most disgusting practice. They gather ten or twenty thousand of them and take them to a big festival under a tent, and people pay to come," he says. "If you're a kid you can pay five bucks and you can decapitate a rattlesnake or skin them alive—they hang them up by their head and rip their skin off. It's awful, and if it was any other animal there is no way it would be legal."

Rattlesnakes, he tells me, don't deserve their bad reputation. They are social animals that give birth to live young. They even have friends. "They will prefer to sit next to a particular snake and not another one. If you put them all in a room they will always find each other to hang out, and they can recognize siblings, that kind of stuff. They're mothers, not just things crawling around, pooping out eggs at random."

And although they are—of course—venomous, rattlesnakes use their poison defensively. When people get bitten, says Bryan, it's usually because they were trying to be macho. "They're often people who say 'I grew up on a ranch,' people who hold the snakes up by the head and take selfies or say they are protecting their kid by whacking a rattlesnake with a spade, but that's dangerous.

"People build up these imaginary threats because in a city the biggest threat is your favorite coffee shop running out of dough-nuts. I try to tell them to walk away and have a mutual respect for their foe. That works well because that gives them a good story to tell their buddies at the bar." Teenage girls are the worst, he adds. They encourage their boyfriends to do stupid things because they want rattlesnakes killed.

Rattlesnakes do seem to make people go a bit crazy. Bryan tells me of the time a rattlesnake was seen on the grounds of a school in Mesa. "The janitor pulled out a handgun and shot it. They were all freaking out about the snake, but what about the janitor with the gun? Does anyone care?"

Another time the cops called Bryan after an iguana, probably an escaped or released pet, was found in downtown Phoenix. "It was kind of funny. There were these three cops there, one of them has a gun drawn, and there's this baby iguana up on a mailbox, hissing," he says. "It jumped off the mailbox and this cop ran like a little girl, like tippy-toe running away. I caught it and found a sanctuary for it."

Just then, Bryan's cell phone rings. I listen in, my fingers crossed for a rattlesnake.

"Is it rattling?" asks Bryan. A pause. "OK. I'll be there very soon. Just keep an eye on it." He hangs up, turns to me and says: "We've got a rattlesnake."

Bryan punches the zip code into his GPS and hits the accelerator. It feels like we're in the Batmobile and the searchlight has just been switched on.

The journey that took me to Phoenix began more than five thousand miles away, back home in the United Kingdom. For months British newspapers had been filled with strange tales about London's red foxes.

There was the sleeping IT worker who turned over in bed to cuddle his girlfriend, only to find a fox that had gotten in through the cat flap and snuggled up to him. Another man found himself having a standoff with one of the reddish-brown creatures over a stick of garlic bread. After trying, unsuccessfully, to frighten the fox by waving the stick at it, the man threw the bread at the animal, which promptly grabbed it and left. Then there was Romeo, the fox found on the seventy-second floor of the Shard, the UK's tallest skyscraper. The tower was still being built at the time, but the fox had climbed up the stairs and managed to survive by eating scraps of food left behind by construction workers.

Some stories were worrying rather than cute. In south London a couple fought with a fox in their living room after it entered their home and attacked their cat. In Hackney, a fox entered a Victorian terrace home and mauled two nine-month-old babies.

Almost everyone I knew in London had a fox story, from the fox that goes begging for food at summer BBQs in Clapham to the group living next to a gas reservoir that use my friend's garden as their toilet. The stories got me thinking about my time studying ecology at university in the 1990s. Neither the course nor the academic journals had much time for the city, which seemed to be regarded as a nonhabitat, devoid of wildlife. As a Londoner, that always seemed wrong to me. Sure, much of the British capital is a landscape of road, brick, and concrete, but the city of my childhood certainly wasn't lifeless.

In the local park there were gray squirrels edging out the last of the native red squirrels. Then there were the pigeons that sometimes joined me and other passengers for a ride on the London Underground. Not to mention the sooty mice scurrying between the tracks, whose disappearance always told you when a train was coming.

Then there were the flying ants that would swarm from improbable nests in the concrete and brick of the housing estate I grew up on. They would emerge in such numbers that you couldn't go outside without getting hapless ants in your hair or, if you were really unlucky, your mouth.

But the headline-grabbing foxes with their distinctive bushy tails seemed new. City foxes were rare sights in my childhood, yet today they are everyday sights in most British cities. Their presence seems like a direct challenge to the very idea that cities are "our" space. People talk of cities as sterile, barren places somehow divorced from nature—places that wipe out the wild as they grow, gobbling up the land like asphalt-skinned monsters. And yet here were foxes, brazen foxes, wandering through the streets of one of the world's biggest cities, climbing skyscrapers, entering homes, and digging dens under garden sheds.

It made me wonder if we had it wrong. Maybe our cities are

more wild and alive than we think. And if they are, what about the animals that live there? Are they thriving or dying in the concrete jungle? Why are some animals victims of urban expansion while others are urban survivors who seem as at home on the streets as we are? This book began as a search for answers to these questions about what lives among us, whether that be London, Los Angeles, Mumbai, or Nairobi. But it soon became clear it couldn't stop there.

Cities are possibly the most exciting, most surprising, and least understood ecosystems on the planet. They are places where much of what we think we know about the natural world doesn't apply. Places where our own love-hate relationship with wild animals flings open the door for the unexpected. Places that may even be changing the animals within it, just as the shift from country to city changed us.

The red foxes of London seemed like a good place to start looking for answers to these questions and, as it turned out, the city fox has a long history.

The first urban fox was spotted in 1930s London. The British capital was expanding fast, rolling out suburbs in every direction, swallowing villages, farms, and entire towns as it went. By the end of the 1930s, London was four times the size it was ten years earlier. And it was in this period of rapid expansion that the city fox emerged.

The foxes didn't so much move to the city as have the city built around them. Within a few short years they found themselves marooned in a new world of semi-detached houses, freshly laid roads, and fenced back gardens. By the 1940s foxes were common enough in south London for the government to attempt to eradicate them by hiring hunters to chase them through the leafy new suburbs. It didn't work.

Forty years on, London's foxes were still outsmarting the urban hunters, and when the British public turned against the idea of wearing fox fur, the city hunts fizzled out. By then having urban foxes was not just a British phenomenon. Red foxes could be found in cities across the world, from Zürich and Melbourne to Toronto and Hakodate in northern Japan.

Central to their success was their adaptability. "They can tolerate a wide range of environments. They are very adaptable," ecologist Dawn Scott tells me when we meet at her office in the University of Brighton. Dawn has been tracking foxes in the English seaside city to learn more about their urban lives. "They are renowned for being cunning and they've got such a variety of diet—they can survive off everything—and that makes them a good urban exploiter."

One thing cities aren't short of is food. From garbage bags filled with leftovers to roadkill and compost heaps, cities offer a varied menu for hungry foxes. Dawn's GPS-tagged foxes even go for dinner on Brighton's pebble beach. "They pootle around the seafront, and if there are any places where they deal with fish they go and scavenge there," she says. "I've also had people reporting them on Brighton Pier, eating ice cream or whatever else has been dropped by people that day."

Plenty of people feed them too, some by hand, and this helps explains why urban foxes are now comfortable enough with us to not worry about being seen and will venture into homes or hassle Londoners for their garlic bread. "We have records of people encouraging them into their kitchens and houses, and that can lead to foxes exploring other houses," says Dawn. "If you hand feed a fox, then it associates hands with food. And because they explore with their mouths and tend to snap and grab because they are opportunistic animals, they tend to go in, grab something, and peg it off.

"If you combine hand feeding and grabbing with running off, there could be an instance where a fox goes up and gives someone's hand a test with its mouth that could be perceived as an attack."

The bountiful supply of food also makes the life of the city fox noticeably different from those living in rural areas. Like us, foxes live in denser populations in cities than in the countryside. In rural England there's roughly one fox per square mile, but cities cram in as many as fourteen into the same space.

The size of their territory shrinks too. "We've had some very, very small home ranges in Brighton, and we think one of the things that affects the size of their range is human feeding," says Dawn. "So if you have a suburb where you have got two or three people who are feeding foxes, that means the home range isn't very big as they only need to go and visit those two or three gardens. But in the next suburb, if nobody is feeding them, the range will be bigger."

The city does have dangers, though. Dogs are a problem, so foxes often avoid yards with pet dogs on the loose. Roads are a big killer, but the ever-adaptable fox has devised a solution for that. "We found that foxes delay crossing the main busy roads until the middle of the night and are more likely to cross at two or three o'clock in the morning," says Dawn.

Disease is another problem, and infections can be devastating for dense populations of urban foxes. In spring 1994, Bristol's foxes experienced a major outbreak of mange, the disease caused by the same skin-burrowing mite that gives people scabies. When untreated it can cause itching so severe that animals have chewed off their own tails. Mange spread fast in Bristol, taking fox after fox. When the disease finally fizzled out two years later, more than 95 percent of the city's foxes were dead. Yet, bad as the outbreak was, it also demonstrated the resilience of the red fox. Today, fox numbers in Bristol are back to the levels seen before mange struck.

Foxes, it seems, are as at home in cities as in the countryside, capable of altering their behavior to fit in with the demands of urban living. But, I wondered, are these charismatic scavengers one-offs or just one of the most visible examples of how wildlife is adjusting to life in cities across the world?

And that's how I ended up five thousand miles away from home in Phoenix, looking for urban rattlesnakes.

Fifteen minutes after Bryan got the call, we arrive at the entrance to a gated community in Scottsdale. The homes are huge, done out in a Pueblo Revival style with sandy stucco walls topped with curved terracotta roof tiles. Next to the homes lies a patch of undeveloped desert dotted with spiky green bushes and tall cacti.

"It's probably going to be a western diamondback—it's the most common snake here," says Bryan as we turn into the driveway of the house with the rattlesnake.

A woman is waiting for us. "It's in there," she says, pointing at the garage. Bryan opens the back of the truck and gets out an empty red bucket and his snake hook—a long metal stick with a smooth U-shaped hook at one end.

We enter the garage. In one corner is a coiled-up dusty gray rattlesnake with its head raised and ready to strike. Diamond-shaped patches of darker gray run along its back, and its underside is a patternless egg white. Its tail points upward and is rattling manically.

At the opposite corner of the vast garage are a young man and a terrified-looking woman with frizzy hair and a high-pitched voice. She's brandishing a garden rake as if she expects the snake to fly across the garage at any moment. You could probably fit a bus in the space between her and the snake.

Bryan glances at the snake. "It's a western diamondback," he says.

"Wow! Look at the face. He's angry," says the woman with the frizzy hair.

"He thinks you're predators and are about to eat him alive," explains Bryan as he flips the lid off the bucket.

He moves in, snake hook at the ready. The diamondback rattles even faster.

"Oh, crap! Oh my goodness!" squeals the woman. "He is so big! Oh my God!"

Bryan stretches his arm out and twists the hook so it slips underneath the snake's body. He carefully lifts the snake into the air and gently tips it into the bucket before slapping on the lid. We've been here less than ninety seconds.

"That's awesome!" says the man.

The high-pitched woman looks stunned. "That's it?" she asks.

"That's it," confirms Bryan.

"What you going to do with it?" she asks, putting down the rake.

"I'm going to let him go," replies Bryan.

"Not around here," says the woman, staring at the hissing bucket.

"No, but I do have to release him within a mile. But he won't come back. This is the scariest thing he has ever experienced. He thinks he is dying right now—he thinks that something has eaten him. So even if I put him right outside, this garage was a near-death experience and he won't come back in."

Reassured, she recounts the discovery of the snake. "He was on my son's clothes. I pushed it, and then I saw it was moving, and then I freaked out."

"Did you leave the garage door open?" asks Bryan. She nods.

"This is a cave," says Bryan. "If you're a snake and you see this thing, it's a cave. It's a nice way to get out of the sun. Rodents will come in too, sometimes, and the snakes will track them into here."

"The bobcats!" exclaims the woman suddenly. "What about the bobcats? They poo! Do you pick up bobcats?"

"I wouldn't worry about the bobcats," says Bryan.

"But they are in my swimming pool," she says, excitedly. "I cannot swim. I cannot swim. They're wicked. A mom and two children. With the snake here and the bobcats in the swimming pool—all kinds of poos!"

"The bobcats will just run off if you go outside. They don't attack," says Bryan.

We return to the truck and load the trapped snake in the trunk. As we leave, Bryan explains that situations like this are typical. "See all these rocks?" he says, as we look at the front yard. "They are like the perfect habitat—it's what the rattlesnakes look for."

We look at the untouched desert right next to the house. "It's amazing that someone who lives here is so shocked. They should have seen a rattlesnake before, but they get shocked because they are not from here. They are shocked, shocked, that there is a snake in Arizona."

They're not alone, or even the worst. One time a lady called Bryan because a hawk was in a tree. "She was the perfect mix of town, animals, and ignorance all in a bundle." It seems as if people have a mental block when it comes to urban wildlife. We move to the city and expect it to be free of bugs, snakes, carnivores, and just about everything else too. Even, it seems, when the land right next to our homes is untamed desert.

Snakes show up all over the Phoenix area, though, not just on the edge of deserts. A couple of days before I arrived, Bryan picked up a diamondback from the parking lot of a hotel in downtown Scottsdale. "He had been living in this hotel parking lot for years and years. The gardeners say they've seen him numerous times. He didn't rattle, didn't bother anyone and then one day they were like you've got to get rid of him. I don't know what to do with him. I can't put him in the desert—he is old, he'll just crawl around and die, and no one wants him as a pet because he is a big, old, ugly diamondback. He is old and crusty and his color is fading."

Then there was the hot tub. "It was in the spring. The guy opened his tub for the first time since winter and there's a gopher snake lying half in, half out of the hot water. I got there an hour later and he was still lounging in there, like 'Yeah? What do you want? I'm in the hot tub.' I felt bad taking him out of there. He seemed pretty happy."

Hot tub snakes aren't that unusual. "In the summer I get calls in the night from super-drunk people, really drunk people, who've gone out to the hot tub. A lot of almost successful dates people have had have been interrupted by a snake in the hot tub."

Rattlesnakes tend to be found close to desert parks, but sometimes they end up in more urban places. "There's this one area where there are still rattlesnakes that come in from the desert deep into the city because there's this old drainage canal," says Bryan. "If it rains there are these torrential floods that just go through the city, and that's when these diamondbacks get washed into those neighborhoods."

For the most part, though, it's the gopher and king snakes that have really taken to the city. "King snakes especially, they love golf courses. The snakes that are more generalist than the rattlesnakes do well at adapting to the city. Gopher snakes and king snakes can be found throughout the city. I've caught them in downtown Phoenix.

"Some of them do better in the city than they do in the wild. In Paradise Valley there are consistently larger, healthier, and older gopher snakes than out in the desert because they are eating roof rats and living in these lush backyards and swimming in the pools. They are doing pretty good there."

Another city success is the night snake. "They get into pipes a lot, so if someone in the middle of the city calls me and says there is a snake on their bathroom counter, I know exactly what it is," says Bryan. "It's weird because they are specialists but they've figured out how to live in the town very well. They eat lots of bugs, and in the city there's new, exciting bugs like cockroaches and crickets for them to eat. They also do well because there's no predation pressure."

Phoenix's city parks, which by and large are just patches of preserved desert surrounded by buildings, also work well for snakes. "The snakes that are there are eating the rats that are eating the granola, garbage, and rotting bananas that hikers throw on the ground."

····᠉·•

After releasing the western diamondback we head to Anthem, where Bryan's booked to check a house for rattlesnakes. Fifteen years ago, Anthem consisted of little more than a handful of show homes thirty miles north of Phoenix. Today, it covers nearly ten square miles and around twenty-five thousand people live there.

"It's a planned community. They planned an entire town, complete with schools and stuff, and then just built the entire thing at once, sold it, and incorporated it as a town," says Bryan on the drive there.

When we arrive I see what he means. Anthem has an unreal feel about it. The countryside around it is desert, but the town center is an expanse of neatly clipped lawns kept on life support by an army of sprinklers and small, man-made lakes. It clashes so much with the dusty wilderness around it that it looks as if it's been airlifted in from North Carolina.

The problem with plunking lakes and lush grassland in the desert is that it doesn't just attract people, it also draws in the local wildlife. "They made this huge city park and lots of people use it, but at night you don't want to go there because there's tons of animals there," says Bryan.

Among the animals that have taken to the streets of Anthem are javelinas, also known as collared peccaries. They look like wild pigs but evolved separately and are about as closely related to pigs as they are to hippos. At night, packs of javelinas roam the streets of Anthem, tipping over garbage cans, feeding on people's plants, and digging into the soil for tubers. They may be vegetarians but they can cause problems. Sometimes they chew through irrigation hoses, quench their thirst at backyard swimming pools, or take shelter under mobile homes.

They also hate dogs. Really hate dogs. In the wild, dogs and coyotes are their main predators, so when javelinas encounter a dog they turn aggressive. And, as some Anthem residents have discovered while walking their dogs, their sharp teeth can deliver a nasty bite.

Between 2003 and 2013, the number of reported incidents involving javelinas in the Phoenix area quadrupled. The Arizona Game and Fish Department puts most of that down to urban expansion bringing more people and their dogs into contact with the animals.

Rattlesnakes turn up in Anthem too. "One woman had been feeding rabbits in her backyard, giving them little baby carrots and stuff," says Bryan. "She went out there one day and there was a rattlesnake. It had eaten all the baby rabbits. She lost her mind at that, but it's like don't feed the rabbits—that's why the rattlesnakes are here."

The family at the home we're visiting in Anthem has spotted a couple of rattlesnakes in the past week. The first was found coiled on their front porch late at night. The second was seen a few days later slithering along the driveway at about ten in the evening.

Bryan reckons the snakes were just passing through. September's a busy time of year for rattlesnakes; they are preparing for winter, so they tend to move around a lot.

He checks out the front and back yards, poking leaf litter with his snake hook, checking inside the outdoor BBQ, and looking for holes in the decorative rocks by the pool that could make a nice spot for a resting snake. Nothing.

He spots a woodpile and knocks it several times with his hook to see if a snake is in there. Again, nothing. The fencing around the backyard also looks secure, and there are no snake tracks in the gravel or wood chips, either. The house is rattlesnake-free; the snakes were just passing through.

It looks as if the Scottsdale rattlesnake is all I'm going to see. But then, as Bryan drives me back to my hotel, his phone rings again. There's a snake in Paradise Valley.

We arrive at the house to find a gopher snake that has gotten itself wedged in the hard plastic sprinkler cover in the front lawn. It looks much like a rattlesnake, with black diamond-shaped blotches running along its otherwise gray-yellow body, but without the distinctive rattle at the end of its tail.

The similarities with rattlesnakes are not lost on gopher snakes, which specialize in hunting small mammals. When threatened they coil up just like rattlesnakes and rapidly shake their tails in the hope of fooling their foes. But this gopher snake is in no position to fool anyone thanks to the pale pink sprinkler cover that is stuck almost exactly halfway along its body, which is about four feet long.

Bryan heads over and starts feeling the snake, which—fast as lightning—bites his hand. Bryan shrugs it off and continues trying to figure out how to get the snake free. A few seconds later blood starts seeping from the bite in his hand.

"He got you in the finger there," says the man who called in the snake. "Yeah, it happens. I get bitten a lot," says Bryan, prodding the snake carefully. "I'm trying to determine if he has something in him or not, like food."

The man's teenage daughter comes out of the house to watch and spies Bryan's bleeding hand. "He's bleeding. Snakes are venomous," she says.

"It's OK. He's not," says Bryan.

He stares at the trapped snake. "He is just really stuck in there."

"I wish he would bite you again so I can see it," says the teenage girl. Maybe Bryan was right about teenage girls and snakes.

Figuring that freeing the snake is going to be a challenge, Bryan asks the man if he can take the snake *and* the sprinkler cover away.

The man looks unsure and starts fumbling around for a reason why not having the sprinkler cover would be a big problem.

"His guts are all squashed up in there, and if you don't do it right it can really injure him more," explains Bryan. "So I'm going to try and cool him down so he is calm and is less tense, put some cooking spray around the hole and see if I can squeeze him out. His ribs are stuck."

"Does it have bones?" asks the man.

"Yep, it's a vertebrate," says Bryan.

The man relents and lets Bryan take the sprinkler cover away with the snake. Bryan's hand is still bleeding but he's relieved: "I was really hoping that that guy wasn't going to get too upset that I needed his lid. About the time he asked if they have bones was about the time I was thinking he might just say, 'Why don't you kill it and give me the lid back?'"

After loading the snake into the truck, Bryan washes out his wound. "It's easy to get infections from the bites," he says. "I wouldn't have handled a rattlesnake as cavalierly as that. If a gopher snake bites me, who cares? But a rattlesnake? It'll be a whole different situation."

He wraps a bandage around his hand. Spots of blood start to show through. He glances at the bucket where the gopher snake is now locked away. "Moves pretty quick, doesn't he?"

A few days later the snake, aided by copious amounts of grease, will work its way out of the sprinkler cover, fine except for a few broken ribs. The man will get his sprinkler cover back.

We resume the journey to my hotel, and as we near it Bryan tells me about another member of Phoenix's wildlife. "There's this species of scorpion—the Arizona bark scorpion. If you went to a desert and flipped over some rocks, you'd see a few. Here in the city, they are everywhere, scampering up the walls. If you find a flower pot that's wet or a garbage can and tip it up, there will be three under it, every time. They are all through the city and that's always been the case."

As we pull into my hotel he adds: "At your hotel tonight, go outside and look around the walls and you'll find North America's most venomous scorpion crawling all over them. Sleep tight."

02

VOODOO CHICKENS

Miami's Chicken, Snail, and Snake Invasions

"Where we're going today, it's what people call the hood," Jill Turner informs me as we set off.

Jill handles community outreach for Miami's Neighborhood Enhancement Team, and the area in question is Little Haiti. In the 1990s it became notorious after being engulfed in street battles between rival drug gangs armed with AK-47s and Tec-9s. Things have improved since then, but there's no escaping the signs of poverty. Even the bright, upbeat Miami sunshine can't bleach that away.

We drive past pastel-colored homes with doors and windows shielded by iron bars and front yards populated by aggressive-looking dogs and sofas that have seen better days. At one point our route is blocked by parked police cars, lights still flashing, and officers searching for suspects. Later we pause by a house to work out where to go next, only to notice we've pulled up alongside a car surrounded by shady looking men talking to someone inside the vehicle. It looks for all the world like we've interrupted a drug deal.

17

We glance at them. They don't look pleased to see us. We quickly move on.

But we're not here for trouble. Or drugs. We're here for the chickens. Miami is full of them. There are thousands of feral chickens roaming the city streets, and it's the job of the Neighborhood Enhancement Team to round up nuisance poultry.

As we drive, Garry Lafaille, the team administrator, tells me that the main complaint about the birds is that they rip up people's gardens. "Those two little legs are very powerful—they will tear apart the garden within minutes," he says. "That's how it all came about: people started to complain and now we are their security among other things that we have to take care of." He shows me the list of complaints the team is responding to today. Each comes with a brief summary of the problem. "Roaming chickens." "Too much chicken." "Chickens roaming on the sidewalk across the street."

We head to the first complaint site, where chickens and roosters have been hanging out in large numbers on a vacant lot. There are usually a couple dozen birds wandering around here, says Garry as we enter the road. He scans the street. "Look to the right," he says. "Two. Two, right in there." Sure enough there's a chicken and a rooster strutting around. The pair clock the team's white truck and run. "They've seen us coming," says Garry, as the birds vanish into the undergrowth of the lot.

It turns out that Miami's street chickens have gotten wise to the team. "They are very intelligent little creatures because now they recognize us," he says. "When they see us coming they crow and—*boom*—they start spreading and running. In the beginning they didn't run as much. We'd corner them, capture them. But now when they see us coming, they start running, start flying. It's like they can see us a mile away now."

I glance back over at the lot. The chickens are long gone.

Thwarted, we head to the next address. This time, Garry has a plan. As we approach the problem area, he slows the truck to

a crawl, rolls down the window and starts calling: *Kik-kik-kik.*
Kik-kik-kik. Kik-kik-kik.

It's a trick he learned on the job. "There was an old lady who
did not realize I was there. She came out with the corn and goes
kik-kik-kik, kik-kik-kik and starts throwing the corn. The chickens
hear it and they start flocking. So I thought I will do that since
maybe they will think that it's feeding time and, sure enough, even
if they don't run to us, they stand up and move around just to see
what's going on."

He leans out of the window. *Kik-kik-kik, kik-kik-kik.* Warily, the
chickens roaming the street stir. We get out of the truck. Soon there
are about half a dozen chickens on the street, where the rest of the
team are already waiting, armed with the Miami chicken catcher's
tool of choice: large green fishing nets.

We eye the chickens. They eye us back.

"We've got a little competition going on where we see who
catches the most," says Garry as he gets out his own net. Jill's
the scorekeeper. At the moment, Vernon, a neighborhood service
worker with shoulder-length dreads, is the reigning champ with
fifteen catches to his name.

Then, suddenly, one of the roosters across the road lets out a
shrill cry and the chickens start heading for cover. "They're sending
a warning," says Jill. The team members fly into action. Vernon
closes in on one, net held aloft ready to strike. The bird veers left
and dives through a small gap in a wooden fence. "Aw! He's gone,"
says Vernon in frustration.

The other chickens have followed the rooster's lead, moving off
the street and into gardens and behind fences. Calls and clucks ring
out as if the birds are well aware that the city employees cannot
enter private property uninvited to remove them. Defeated again,
we return to the truck and head to the next location.

The Neighborhood Enhancement Team isn't the city's first
attempt to tackle the chicken problem. Before them came the
Chicken Busters, but the program was scrapped in October 2009

as part of a drive to clear the city's $118 million deficit. For a while the chickens were left to it. The streets were theirs. Then, in summer 2012, City Commissioner Michelle Spence-Jones had a firsthand encounter with a rooster during a public meeting at Little Haiti Soccer Park.

"The commissioner came to the meeting, and there was this rooster standing there by the glass door," recalls Garry. "Every time she was about to say something, the rooster would just stand there and start crowing. It would not move. It was not afraid of humans—it just stood there and it was funny because whenever she started to say something, the chicken starts singing. Basically that was the day that the message was being sent." Soon after, the city revived its chicken-catching program.

Our third stop is Northeast Eighty-Second Terrace. Judging by the complaints list, it's something of a chicken hotspot, with three separate complaints made in just one day. "There are chicken everywhere around, make too much noise," reads one. It's no exaggeration. There really are chickens everywhere, hopping in and out of garden fences, pecking at dirt, and clawing at lawns.

Vernon, fishing net at the ready, homes in on a rooster. It flees down the sidewalk, heading between a metal fence and a large pile of twigs and leaf litter topped with a shabby cream sofa. Garry quickly closes in from the other side of the makeshift corridor.

The bird squawks, clucking agitatedly as the two close in on it. Then it leaps into the air, flying straight over the rubbish pile and narrowly missing Jill's head. "*Waah!*" she yelps, ducking. The rooster lands in a nearby garden, but its escape is quickly foiled by team member Wilfredo, who manages to shepherd the bird into the corner of the garden's fencing before scooping it up in his net.

Grins break out. Success at last. The captive bird is placed inside a plastic box and loaded onto the truck. Later it will be taken to a farm on the outskirts of Miami, where it will spend the rest of its life away from city streets. But it's just one bird among many, and time is running out. Come midday, the birds will take to the shade and all hope of catching any more will be gone.

As we head to the next location, I ask Garry why chickens are roaming the city as if it's a free-range farm. The answer lies in Miami's long history of immigration. "They were brought here," he says. "I'm Haitian. The Haitians, the Spanish, the Cubans, the Puerto Ricans, we all share this one point in common with chickens—they do the fighting of the chickens, the cockfights. So they will feed them and raise them for that.

"There's another thing about the cultures," he adds. "They believe that if they have a live animal, kill it, butcher it, and eat it, it's more fresh, and sometimes they will keep the live animal in the backyard until they want to eat it and sometimes the chicken gets away. Now, they reproduce like there's no tomorrow—a mother will lay about twelve eggs—and it goes on and on, the cycle repeats, and before you know it we have thousands running around."

The final ingredient in Miami's chicken problem is religion. "In Haitian culture you have the Voodoo religion and in the Spanish the Santería religion," says Garry. "They all use the chickens for rituals. Sometimes they don't kill them, they will just let them loose, and people don't touch them because they think they might be part of a ritual." But sometimes the chickens are killed. "After one sacrifice, the head was left downtown," recalls Jill. "I had to go get the head. Miami-Dade County collects the dogs. We collect animals when they are dead."

Given the role chickens have in ritual, illegal cockfighting, and food, removing them doesn't go down well with some residents—as I soon discover. Our final stop of the day is a run-down house with a backyard full of chickens and wiry kittens. We head in to see if there's a way the birds can be flushed out of the yard and into the vacant land next door where they can be caught. Moments later, a Haitian man in grubby clothes appears. He is visibly angry.

"YOU THERE! GET OFF MY PROPERTY!" he yells. "YOU COME HERE! I DON'T WANT YOU ON THE PROPERTY!"

Garry tries to calm things down by introducing himself, but the man's not having any of it. "YOU WANT TO BE MAD WITH ME? I'LL BE MAD WITH YOU!" he shouts, before turning on Vernon. "I SEEN YOU, I SEEN YOU A WHILE BACK. YOU CUSSED ME!"

"I ain't cussed nobody," replies Vernon, who really doesn't seem the cussing type. "I DON'T CARE!" grunts the man.

Garry tries again. "We're here to serve. We've got a job to do for the city—you're a citizen—and we're going to get them," he explains, gesturing at the chickens digging up the yard. "The chickens, they get into the bush, they ransack the place. That's why we're here."

"THEY DON'T DO THAT!" snaps the man as a rooster claws at the dirty soil behind him.

"OK, they don't do that to you. All right. Sir, you take care," says Garry, winding up the conversation. We head back to the truck, stepping over roaming kittens while the man watches to make sure we move on. "They pulled that same move last time," says Vernon. "They're not the owners."

Does that happen a lot? I ask. "Oh yeah," says Garry. "We've gone out to areas and gentlemen will come out and say, 'What is it that you're doing? Don't touch my pets.'"

But times are changing. Little Haiti is gentrifying, and a divide has opened up among residents over the chickens. "There was no tendency of reporting your neighbor for having chicken in the backyard, because it was a normal thing," says Garry. "Now it is an issue, because people are really in tune with taking care of their homes, making them look beautiful, but with chickens running around that's not going to happen, because whatever you plant, once they get in, within minutes you have mayhem."

I ask Garry if he thinks the team is winning the battle against the chickens. "I would more or less say that we win, because we have chickens to last us our careers," he says with a smile. "At least until the public themselves come to a consensus of we don't want this. But right now you have a portion who are feeding them, nurturing them, raising them, thinking that they are pets. You have some who don't care until it becomes a nuisance, and others who think that we're crazy because we are messing with the chickens. So right now we're just keeping people quiet by addressing those chickens that make a lot of noise."

"In other words," Jill interjects, "we're putting a Band-Aid on the wound."

Miami may have a love-hate relationship with its urban poultry, but there's another religious import that is proving a universally unwelcome addition to the city's fauna: the giant African land snail. They might be slow but they are the stuff of nightmares. Fully grown, these gastropods measure eight inches long and boast an insatiable appetite for calcium that means they will happily eat the stucco walls and plaster of your home.

Giant house-eating snails would be bad enough but, explains Mark Fagan of the Florida Department of Agriculture, it gets worse. "By the time they are six months old, they start laying a hundred eggs a month," he tells me. They are also hermaphrodites—both male and female at the same time—and capable of impregnating themselves if the mood takes them.

OK, so they are giant hermaphrodite house-eating snails that breed fast. No, says Mark, it's worse than that. "It's also a human and animal health threat. We have confirmation from the Centers for Disease Control in Atlanta of the presence of *Angiostrongylus cantonensis* in them. That's rat lungworm disease."

I don't know what rat lungworm disease is, but it sounds terrifying. It doesn't take long for Mark to enlighten me. "It's found in the feces of rats. The snail will consume the feces, and in it is a tiny parasitic nematode that begins its life in the snail, eventually emerging as an adult in the slime of the snail. That's why we tell people *do not* pick up snails with your bare hands—always use some kind of plastic or latex glove because that tiny little nematode, you are not going to see it. And what do we all do in Florida on hot humid days like today? We wipe the sweat from around our eyes and our mouth. Do that and you've just introduced the worm into your body."

I ask what happens next, but I don't think I want to know. "That worm will make its way to the bloodstream, eventually making its way up to the meninges, the protective membranes covering up the brain. At which point it will expire, and that could cause a rare form of meningitis known as eosinophilic meningitis.

"There's no cure for it," he adds. "Some people recover on their own. Others have to be hospitalized. It all depends on your own health status. But it can also cause other neurological issues like blindness, deafness, loss of gait, inability to perform normal every-day duties. That's why it's such a danger."

So far the only confirmed victim has been a dog in Kendall. "It was a very heavily infested property, and the dog was diagnosed by the veterinarian as having eosinophilic meningitis. What we believe is the dog got curious about a snail, was sniffing it, and got a nem-atode in its nose."

So we're dealing with giant potentially deadly hermaphrodite house-eating snails that breed fast. Nope, it gets worse. It turns out they are a threat not just to residents of Miami but also to Flori-da's economy and the national security of the entire United States. "They eat five hundred different crop plants, and that includes everything we grow in the state of Florida," says Mark. "We provide this nation's food from October through May. When you think of Florida, you think of sandy beaches, swaying palms, and Mickey Mouse ears. You don't think of agriculture, but agriculture is second only to tourism economically. This snail threatens Florida's agricul-ture. It can doom it, put an end to it."

In conclusion, what Miami is facing are giant potentially deadly hermaphrodite house-eating *terrorist* snails that breed fast. No wonder their arrival sparked the biggest pest control operation in the history of the Florida Department of Agriculture. Miami is the front line, and if the snails escape the city and make it into the Everglades and the farmlands, they may become unstoppable.

Mark invites me to come see the war against the snails firsthand at the latest outbreak zone. I head there with Alex Muñoz, director of Miami-Dade County Animal Services. On the way there the threat of rat lungworm plays on our minds. "I'm used to the native animals, whether it's sharks, manatees, alligators, crocodiles, but this . . ." he says, lost for words.

The latest hotspot is in Little Haiti, and as we arrive we watch a team member carrying a clear plastic bag full of snails greet a passing colleague with a fist bump. "I'm not touching that guy with the gloves," says Alex. "He just did the Obama punch. I'm not doing that. I'm not touching that guy's gloves after hearing about rat lungworm. I'm going to do the faraway wave."

The houses in the neighborhood have already been zapped with a powerful molluskicide that dehydrates the snails and boasts a kill rate of at least 85 percent. The job today is to go house to house to gather up the dead and dying gastropods.

Omar Garcia is the man overseeing the cleanup. In the past week they've found a couple hundred giant African land snails in the area, he says. "We've just turned up, so you've got snails hibernating that are coming up as we agitate the ground and stuff like that. A lot at all stages: neonates, baby size to adult size." A couple hundred is an improvement. "I remember we found over seven hundred snails on one property when I first started doing this in November 2011," he says.

"There's one here, Tristan," calls Alex, who has been rooting through the front yard of the house. "Not that it's going to run away."

Omar offers me a glove so I can join the snail hunt: "One glove enough?"

I think for a second and then my brain screams, "*Rat lungworm.*"
"Er . . . I'll go for two, actually."

We search through the leaf litter, pulling back bushes, finding snail after snail. We pry them off leaves, haul them out of the soil, and pick them from walls, dropping them into clear resealable plastic bags as we go. They may be the stuff of nightmares, but here—dead and dying in their rock-hard vertical brown-striped shells—it's hard to think of them as the terrors they are.

Miami has been here before, says Mark. "The original infestation was back in 1966 in North Miami where I grew up. A little boy brought back three snails from Hawaii, where they are pretty much endemic. He put them in his pockets, got home, put them in a terrarium and, lo and behold, a month later there's hundreds of eggs. So grandma said let's get rid of these eggs and tossed them out the back, not realizing what could happen."

Two years later the North Miami authorities discovered the snails and called in the Florida Department of Agriculture to eradicate them. It took four years and produced a haul of around eighteen thousand snails. This outbreak is far more serious. "It's much more widespread," says Mark. "We've done 137,000 in just over two years whereas they collected 18,000 in four years in the late '60s and early '70s."

The current outbreak came to light on September 8, 2011. One of the department's fruit fly trappers was changing a trap on a house shared by two Cuban sisters on Thirty-Third Avenue in the Coral Way neighborhood. They asked if he could also help with their snail problem. "They had snails on the walls, snails in plants, snails in trees. The snails were everywhere," says Mark.

The giant African land snail was on a watch list of potential threats, so the fruit fly trapper grabbed a few and sent them up to the department's resident snail expert, who confirmed that same day they were indeed giant African land snails. The following morning, the department descended on the area en masse, sending in every one of its fifty-odd South Florida inspectors to hunt for snails. In house after house, they found snails by the hundreds.

The area became known as Core 1, a mile-radius zone around the Cuban sisters' home. It was the ground zero of the second snail invasion of Miami. By the end of the year, fourteen outbreak zones had been found throughout the city from Little Haiti and Hialeah to Coral Gables and South Miami Heights. By the start of 2014, twenty-five cores had been discovered.

How the snails got into Miami this time isn't known, but the leading theory is that they were brought there for use in Santería or, most likely, Yorùbá rituals. Yorùbá is one of the traditional religions of Nigeria, the native home to the giant African land snail. The mollusk has a starring role in the faith's creation story. The gist is that the deity Obàtálá used a snail shell filled with loose earth to transform the world from marsh to solid land. Fittingly, he used a chicken to spread the earth around the world.

When Yorùbá believers were brought as slaves to Cuba and the rest of the Caribbean, the slave masters banned them from practicing the religion and insisted they follow Catholicism instead. The result of this forced merger of Yorùbá and Catholicism was Santería. "In the practice of Santería, snails are an important part," says Mark. "They foretell your health, spirituality, and prosperity. But there were no giant African land snails in Cuba, so the Yorùbá practitioners and the Santería practitioners used any common snail that was available. But stricter Yorùbá practitioners use giant African land snails, so there is a theory that Yorùbá practitioners may have brought these in and they got out of control."

There are precedents that support the theory. US Customs and Border Protection once caught a woman coming back from Nigeria at Hartsfield-Jackson Atlanta International Airport who had snails hidden under her dress. Another time a man stopped at LAX was found to have giant African land snails lurking in every pocket of his suit.

In Miami itself, police launched an investigation in 2010 into a Yorùbá practitioner who had convinced his followers that the snails could cure them of their aliments. He held the creatures of over their heads and then cut them so his followers could drink the "curative" mucus. The police got involved after the snail juice drinkers began complaining of violent illness.

It's unlikely, however, that the original source of the current outbreak will ever be conclusively determined. "We would certainly like to say here's definitively how they got here, but in reality we will probably never know," says Mark.

Despite the large scale of the outbreak, Mark is confident the snails will be eradicated. The department's fast reaction and a major billboard campaign urging people to "Look for it! Report it!" seems to be paying dividends. The rate at which new cores are being found has slowed dramatically, and the newest sites seem to have far fewer snails within them. In the meantime, the department is preparing to bring in its latest weapon against the snails: Labradors trained to sniff out snails hidden in the undergrowth that human eyes may miss.

"The awareness campaign means we are getting to them sooner, before they are able to establish a huge population," says Mark. "The idea is we need to get to the point where we are not finding any more snails, dead or alive. Then we still have to go two more years of continuing to survey before we ask for a declaration of eradication. But there's no question that we will reach that point."

Miami is something of a hub for exotic animals. Its tropical monsoon climate ensures that almost anything that gets there and manages to breed will survive. "We've got everything," says Alex. "You name it, we've got it. Just like our culture."

Some, like the giant African land snails, are met with a ferocious crackdown, but others become so established there's little choice but to accept them, and this is what has happened with the iguanas. These lizards, with their outlandish Mohawk-like spines running down their backs, are a common sight in Miami. They especially like the canals. Take a trip along North Okeechobee Road and you can see dozens of them sunning themselves on the banks of the Miami Canal. "They love the canal banks," says Alex as we drive past. "Who goes out to a canal bank? Nobody. So it gives them a green corridor to go up and down."

Most of the iguanas we see lurking on the canal banks are green iguanas, which can grow to six feet long, but there are other types of iguanas in the city too, including the black-and-white-colored Mexican spinytail iguana. "They are not dangerous to humans, but the problem with them is they eat flowers," says Alex. "We have a wonderful botanic garden, which is beautiful and world-renowned, but it's challenged because the iguanas go in there and take care of all the buds."

Like the snails and the chickens, people brought the iguanas to the city. "Some were escaped pets, but most came from our old zoo," says Alex. "We had this little zoo out on Key Biscayne, Crandon Park Zoo, and they had iguanas roaming around. The zoo moved and when they left, the problem spread out and they took over the city."

Today iguanas are so widespread in Miami that people pretty much ignore them. "They are just kind of accepted. A lot of people don't even know that they are not native. They poop and people don't like to look at them, but you can't get rid of them. And when you have pythons to worry about, iguanas are low on the food chain."

Ah, yes, the snakes. The Miami metropolitan area is home to increasing numbers of boas and pythons, which vie with giant African land snails for the title of animal enemy number one. Just a few weeks before my visit, a man in Hialeah discovered a thirteen-foot albino Burmese python living under his shed. Shortly after, a ten-foot-long rock python strangled a sixty-pound Siberian husky to death in a backyard, despite the dog owner's frantic attempts to kill the snake with a pair of garden scissors.

Mercifully, attacks on dogs, let alone people, are rare. But the risk is real, so local agencies and biologists have banded together to form the Everglades Cooperative Invasive Species Management Area, or ECISMA for short. Its mission is wide-ranging. Members patrol for giant African land snails in city parks and battle with the mile-a-minute vine, a fast-growing invasive plant with barbed tendrils that smothers rival vegetation.

Another ECISMA project focuses on the boa constrictors living on the 444-acre Deering Estate in Cutler, fifteen miles south of downtown Miami. Boas have been breeding in Miami since the early 1990s, and ECISMA is trying to learn more about their behavior. To do this they have surgically implanted tracking devices into two boas on the estate—one male, one female.

I meet up with Dallas Hazelton, preserve manager at the estate, and Miami-Dade Parks and Recreation's Jane Griffin Dozier, who are both involved in the boa tracking work. The problem with the boas, they tell me, is that they pose a threat to south Florida's native wildlife, including animals living in the Everglades.

Like the iguanas, the boas came to Miami as pets, says Dallas: "My records of boas only goes back to 1999, but there are undocumented reports of boas dating back to the '70s. At some point it must have been a release or escape. This is the only known breeding population of boas in the United States."

They offer to show me the female boa, so we head into the estate through a gated entrance off Southwest 152nd Street. As we drive in along a bumpy track, I notice that there are homes all along the estate boundary. Dallas says the boas have troubled the residents from time to time. "We had an unfortunate incident a couple of years ago," he says. "There was a neighbor over here, and one of the guards found this dead big tomcat and a dead boa lying right next to each other. The boa had strangled the cat, but in the process the cat had bit up the snake so bad that it died from its wounds.

"The neighbor was putting up signs with a picture saying 'Here's my missing cat, call us if you find him.' Someone had to call her to tell her. She was very upset."

We drive deeper into the forest, the road bordered on either side by dense vegetation punctuated by spindly paurotis palm trees. We stop close to the boa's last recorded location. Jane opens the trunk of the truck and pulls out a large electronic box and a handheld aerial, not unlike an old-fashioned rooftop TV aerial. She plugs the aerial into the box, holds the aerial up, and twists a dial on the box. She turns to face the tangle of bushes and the box goes *bip, bip, bip*. "This way," she says.

We follow her into the forest, fighting with vines that snag our feet as we push through the foliage. *Bip, bip, bip* goes the tracker. We press deeper and deeper into the undergrowth, dodging poison ivy as we go. The *bip, bip, bip* of the tracker seems to get louder with every step.

Adrian Diaz, the Miami-Dade County Animal Services investigator who is with us, asks Dallas if he can pick up the snake when we find her. "No, we don't want to disturb them. We want them to go about much as they naturally do. We don't touch them," says Dallas.

Adrian looks a little disappointed. On the way here he was telling me about his lifelong love of snakes. "As a kid I was never afraid to catch the little corn snakes and garden snakes. Never been afraid—there's just something about them," he explained. "At one point I had them at home and everything. I had a blood python, two Burmese pythons, green tree boas, all sorts of stuff. My wife obviously put an end to that quick."

Bip-bip-bip. It's definitely getting louder.

Around this point it strikes me that before this moment I've never seen a snake outside a zoo. My encounter with the Phoenix rattlesnake is yet to come. I vaguely remember seeing a tail of an adder, Britain's only venomous snake, disappearing into a bush as a kid—or, at least, I think I saw it. In fact, thinking about it again, I was probably just told there were adders there and imagined the rest.

Besides, adders are cowardly snakes, more likely to flee before you find them than bite. Now I'm about to come face-to-face with a wild boa constrictor. I hope I don't panic.

Bip-bip-bip. It's definitely louder. *Bip-bip-bip*. And more frequent. It's starting to feel like the scene in the movie *Alien* where they search the spaceship for the monster using motion trackers. I glance at the palm trees. What if it's in a tree? Boas are capable climbers, I think to myself.

Jane walks forward then turns and moves back. *Bip-bip-bip.* She does a U-turn and moves forward again and then back again. *Bip-bip-bip.* "If there's a burrow here it should be on the ground," says Dallas.

We stare at the ground at our feet. Jane moves back and forth, back and forth. It's definitely here. Right here. *Bip-bip-bip.* A few tense seconds pass, and then the snake slips out from the under-growth right by our feet, slithering as fast as she can. My heart stops briefly.

"There she goes," says Jane. We follow, lurching over vegetation and ducking under vines to keep up with the five-foot-long snake as it slides along the forest floor. It's not as threatening as I imagined and it's clearly keen on getting away from us. It's pretty, too—its body a patchwork of hexagonal yellow, brown, and black scales.

Adrian gets ahead of the snake, takes a few close-up photos as her glassy eyes stare back, and then we let it escape. The boa wastes no time and vanishes back into the safety of the undergrowth.

It turns out that finding them when you're right on top of them is normal. "They are adapted to camouflage themselves," says Dallas. "I think that's why so often I only find them when I'm right on top of them."

As we head back to the road, I ask him what they hope to learn from the tagged boas. "We're hoping to get information that will help us catch them," he replies. "Like where we are likely to find them and at what time of day or year and in what weather."

The data is still being crunched, but the initial impression is that they are going to be hard to catch. "Based on what I've seen, the biggest thing we've learned is that they spend up to 90 percent of their time underground, either in animal burrows or natural small cave features," he says. "This makes locating the non-radio-tagged ones for removal pretty much an impossible task, because the only time you even have a chance at seeing them is that 10 percent of the time that they are above ground."

Afterward I visit another player in Miami's snake control efforts: the fire service. The city's exotic reptiles have changed Miami-Dade Fire Rescue, taking its animal work well beyond getting cats out of trees.

The service has a venom response unit that boasts the United States' largest store of antivenoms, and its expertise is so renowned that it offers its venom services nationally and internationally. The unit also captures problem snakes and other reptiles.

Captain Jeffrey Fobb heads the unit. Moving into reptile control was a logical step, he says: "It started because we're around twenty-four hours, and when people get sacred of stuff they call 911. A lot of these animals, particularly the exotics, are found after dark, and our familiarity with the animals makes us well suited to dealing with it."

When we meet he has just returned from the city's airport. "There was a ball python in a taxi cab," he says matter-of-factly, as if cab-riding pythons from Africa are normal in Miami. Did someone leave it behind or did it crawl in? "It crawled in there at some point. Who knows?" he says. "It was a valuable animal. It had a couple of injuries, so I took it to the zoo to have it euthanized."

Over the years the fire department has collected hundreds of pythons. They've pulled them out of backyard swimming pools, picked them up in people's garages, and recovered ones that got injured while crossing roads. Not that every call out proves fruitful. "I was rung out for a dog turd once—somebody thought it was a snake."

Another reptile Jeffrey deals with is the Argentine black and white tegu lizard. Many of the tegus in Miami are thought to be descended from a bunch imported from Paraguay by a pet dealer in the early 2000s but then released because they had broken tails or other defects. Others may have been escaped pets. Tegus are good at digging, and it is thought that some escaped by burrowing their way out of outdoor enclosures.

"Wanna see one?" asks Jeffrey. He gets a bag from his vehicle and pulls out a tegu, holding it by the neck so it can't bite him. Its bead-like scales form a mixed-up pattern of green-white and black, and its feet end in long, sharp claws designed for digging. The lizard flicks its forked tongue out and glares at us, but thanks to Jeffrey's tight grip it can't do anything.

"I got this one at a trailer park," he says. "There are two trailer parks that are loaded with them, close to a hundred tegus. Animals like this are hard to run down. Snakes depend on their camouflage. These guys are very flighty, very active, and they will bite and it will really, really hurt."

There are probably thousands in the county now, he says. Florida City and Homestead are particular hotspots. "They live anywhere. They burrow under leaf litter, burrow underneath dog houses. There was one in Kendall that we chased for nine months. It finally got caught under a doghouse—it went to sleep and let its tail slip out," he says.

"They are like raccoons without fur but active during the day, so they can frighten your children. They eat anything—prepared food, unprepared food, good food, bad food. They eat whatever they can get. Where they come from in Argentina they are a nuisance animal. They get into people's gardens and fight with their cats over the food they put out." There are even reports that in campgrounds outside Buenos Aires tegus beg people for food.

Yet little is known about their activities in Miami, so the race is on to learn more about their movements and what they eat. "We don't know a lot of things about any of these animals," says Jeffrey. "We don't know how they use the landscape, how they move around, or how often."

I ask him what animal in the Miami area worries him most. "People," he says without hesitation. "Not even the mad ones, just those who get irritated in traffic. Everybody's worried about animals, but animals are less likely to hurt you."

People are also the reason why Miami is dealing with these problems. From dog-strangling pythons and garden-eating iguanas to giant snails and child-scaring tegus, they are all here because people brought them to the city. It may have been accidental, like an escaped pet tegu. It may have been a genuine mistake, such as the grandma who threw away the giant African land snail eggs. But sometimes, as with the chickens, it is very much deliberate.

It also seems unlikely the influx will stop anytime soon. "In the past two weeks, we've probably found around seven new exotic species," says Jeffrey. "You're looking at maybe six years of lag time between the release of the animals and the population becoming evident on any large scale."

Miami's next animal invasion may well already be there, breeding out of sight, just waiting to be discovered as the latest human-aided addition to the city's wildlife.

03

THE GREAT SPARROW MYSTERY

Fighting Starlings in Indianapolis and Saving Sparrows

It's early evening in downtown Indianapolis and Wes Homoya of the US Department of Agriculture is hard at work. He is standing near the Indianapolis Union Railroad Station on Jackson Place, banging together two wooden planks with gusto. Noisy *clack-clack-clacks* echo around the area outside the Romanesque Revival station building.

Wes scans the sky. Far above us are starlings. Lots of starlings. A couple thousand at least. The birds have spent the day searching the countryside, raiding landfills, and combing the streets for food. Now, back in the heart of Circle City, they are determined to bed in for the night. But Wes and his boss, Judy Loven, are here to stop them.

The birds gather in the air, forming a dense cloud that darkens the sky. The cloud swirls and ripples like an ocean wave as the birds circle over potential roosting sites. They fly mere inches from one another. Turning, spinning, and diving in unison to confuse predators like the peregrine falcons that live a couple of blocks away on Market Tower.

That the starlings do not crash into each other is nothing short of miraculous. These starling murmurations are enchanting sights, one of the true wonders of nature, but for Judy and Wes it signals a race against time to stop the birds bedding in for the night.

As the early October daylight fades, the battle for downtown Indy begins. Wes bashes the planks together as the birds swoop down. Most shoot back into the air, back to the safety of the murmuration, but a few dive into the trees next to the station. Wes hits the planks together again, but the panicked birds have decided it is safer in the foliage and stay put.

Wes tries clapping the boards together right under the trees. The starlings don't budge. "They have been a little more aggressive lately," he says. "Normally, all of them would fly on, but we've got a couple that are being really stubborn and want to still come in."

Judy gets out another weapon. A silver laser pen. It's the kind you might see used at a corporate presentation, but this evening it's an anti-starling device. She shoots a five megawatt beam of concentrated green light into the tree and wiggles the pen. The birds still don't move. It's too light for the laser to be effective.

The starlings in the tree are a problem, says Judy. "Trees are where they first go. By November the leaves should be off the trees, and then they won't find the trees that appealing anymore. That's when they head for the buildings, so we wanna make sure we get them out before leaf drop so we don't have a population here that moves onto the buildings." By then there won't be a couple thousand starlings descending on Indianapolis. The birds above us are merely the early arrivals. They are the scouts who will establish this year's roosting spots. Come November, as many as half a million starlings will be here and tens of thousands of them will be looking to set up camp downtown.

Judy and Wes debate whether it is worth getting out the pyros. Firecrackers are another of the USDA's stock of starling deterrents. Judy shows me the launcher, a matte-black handgun, shaped like a revolver. It looks just like a real gun. "Yep," says Wes. "This is the main reason why we communicate with the police department and wear our shiny vests. We definitely want to make sure nobody mistakes us for somebody walking around downtown flashing a gun."

The gun takes two types of pyro. The first are the "screamers" that shriek, whine, and hiss as they spiral through the air, leaving a trail of smoke behind them. Screamers are the pyro of choice when fending off starlings amid the tall buildings of downtown. The alternative is the "banger." "The bangers sound like gunfire, so we try to minimize the use of the bangers," says Judy. "We try to do it more in the open areas like the parks, because somewhere like here we're surrounded by buildings and they echo really bad. But there are times." Enough times for downtown to have permanent signs warning people of "loud noises" on winter evenings and for 911 to be used to dealing with frightened people who mistake the firecracker bangs for shootings in the heart of the city.

Today, however, there will be no bangers or screamers. They decide it is better to stick to wood and laser pens, and hold back the pyros until more starlings arrive for their winter residence. "Over time they habituate," says Judy. "They are already starting to get to the stage where they are not paying so much attention to the clap boards as we would like them to."

She offers me the wooden planks. "Here you go: some USDA government equipment! Don't pinch your fingers."

Inevitably, that's the first thing I do. My wood-clapping skills fall well below those of Wes. When I'm not painfully trapping my fingers, I am making a noise that is more a muted irregular *donk* than the loud, crisp *clack* Wes delivers. The birds in the tree and the sky ignore me. Sorry, Indianapolis.

While I struggle with the two-by-fours, Wes puts the laser pen to use. It is darker now and the beam can now be seen dancing on the leaves as Wes twirls the pen in a figure-eight pattern. A few of the starlings panic and fly out of the tree, flapping their wings as fast as they can.

There are more surprises lying in wait around downtown for these distinctive birds, which stand out thanks to the white flecks and iridescent purple-green sheen of their black wings. There are sound systems on rooftops blasting out starling distress calls. Some buildings are shielded with plastic netting that makes landing difficult. Others have electric wires running along ledges that will zap any birds that step on them. There's even a Mylar balloon with a scary eye pattern filled with helium floating off one building on Massachusetts Avenue. Judy didn't think it would work, but it proved surprisingly effective.

Not that every technique works. One hotel placed an unconvincing model owl on its entrance canopy. None of the starlings were fooled. Even electric wires don't always work, says Judy: "In at least one case they invested in putting the shock track only on a few floors and the birds just moved up to the other floors."

The local birds of prey don't help much either. The peregrines on Market Tower only take down a starling a day on average. Not very many when half a million starlings are flying around.

As dusk becomes night, the cloud of birds departs. They've homed in on another spot in the city, away from downtown with its green laser beams and *clack-clack-clack* of wood.

The victory is temporary. Tomorrow evening the battle to keep the starlings out of downtown will resume. It's a war that will only really be resolved in the spring when the starlings finally leave the city to become someone else's problem. And come next fall, they will be back to joust with the USDA again.

Indianapolis has been facing annual starling invasions since the 1950s and, before the USDA came in, winter in downtown often felt like a scene from Alfred Hitchcock's *The Birds*. Tens of thousands of starlings would gather in parks, on buildings, and on sites like the Soldiers and Sailors Monument in Monument Circle. They would just sit there in the trees at night squawking, recalls Anne Maschmeyer, beautification director at Indianapolis Downtown Inc., which seeks to enhance and promote the city center. "It was just like *The Birds*. People were really freaked out."

What the birds left behind was equally unwelcome: park benches speckled white, office windows smeared with excrement, and sidewalks slippery with waste. Some people resorted to using umbrellas to get from their workplace to their car without getting pooped on. Even the city's Christmas decorations took a beating. "They have an artificial Christmas tree made out of colored lights on the monument each year," says Judy. "The starlings would use those trees of light to sit on and poop too. They are like Scrooge. They don't even like Christmas."

Starling excrement is more than unpleasant to the eye and the nose. For a start, it is highly acidic. Unlike us, birds don't have bladders where the uric acid they produce gets watered down to form urine, since carrying around excess water makes flying harder. The result is undiluted droppings acidic enough to eat away limestone and copper. That's bad news for Indianapolis's historic sites, and even when the waste is power washed away, the high-pressure jets of water also scrape away a tiny layer of the structure, inflicting further damage.

Then there's the disease risk. Starling droppings teem with disease, most notably the fungus *Histoplasma capsulatum*. If the droppings are left long enough, the fungus will produce airborne spores that can cause a potentially fatal lung infection called histoplasmosis. "They did a construction project here back in the '80s, and they tore down trees that had historically been a roost for the starlings," says Judy. "They had bulldozers in and that kind of stuff, and contaminated dust particles went up in the air and blew around the city. More than three hundred people came down with histoplasmosis. We've had private companies come in and clean up the droppings off of buildings, and that has been a hazmat clean up."

There have been more recent cases too. In 2002 thousands of starlings roosted on the Indiana State Capitol, two blocks east of Monument Circle. The limestone statehouse—a grand mix of mock Italian Renaissance domes and pediment window hoods—was an ideal site for the starlings, which prefer Neo-Classical and Gothic Revivalist architecture because of the abundance of crevices and ledges to nest on. Such was the festering mess the birds left behind them that Indiana's Republican leader Brian Bosma and a legislative aide contracted histoplasmosis. A cleanup crew was swiftly brought in after the elected representative fell ill.

By the time Bosma caught histoplasmosis, Indy's USDA-aided fight back against the birds had been underway for two years. Indianapolis had endured the starlings for decades but its patience finally ran out in 2000 when it hosted the NCAA Final Four basketball tournament. "It was evening and downtown was bustling. There were people everywhere," says Anne. "Downtown was so hot with people and excitement. But there was the noise of the starlings roosting in the trees and chattering, and there were bird droppings all over the sidewalk and it was smelling. I just thought, we've got to do something."

She got a group of downtown property owners to pool their antistarling budgets so they could call in the USDA. The USDA soon discovered one reason why the starlings liked downtown. Four and a half miles southwest of the city center lies the South Side Landfill. It turned out that the starlings were spending the day picking through garbage before returning downtown for the night.

Curt Publow, environmental manager at South Side Landfill Inc., says the birds would visit in huge numbers. "We would get hundreds, if not thousands, at any one time and they would get on the power lines and things," he says. "If there were enough birds on the lines that all took off at once, it would cause power outages. Then there's just the waste from the birds. They huddle on equipment and we literally have to scrape the windshield off. It's pretty gross."

So as the USDA began harassing the birds trying to stay downtown, the landfill began frightening them off during the day using shotguns and noisemaking propane cannons. "The propane cannons are automated and run all day long," says Curt. "We've got guys out on litter pickup or other jobs and we just equip them with some of the noise makers so the noises are in random locations all through the day. If you couple that with some actual killing, it's pretty effective."

In downtown lethal force is a weapon of last resort. There are plans in place for plying the birds with DRC-1339, aka Starlicide, a poison that causes kidney failure in starlings. It's effective but delivers a slow and painful death for the birds, so the plan sits gathering dust. "I'm glad we've never had to push it so far that we've had to use lethal," says Judy. "We're going to do everything we possibly can to avoid that."

The harassment efforts seem to be working. In recent years the starlings have roosted along the canals, and when Indianapolis hosted the 2012 Final Four the chicken coop aroma of 2000 was missing. "There's never going to be zero starlings, but we can get it down to a handful here and a handful there—something tolerable," says Judy.

But the birds are nothing if not persistent. "We still do have a handful of birds that are going to be in Monument Circle because they have learned and adapted to what we're doing," says Judy. "On Monument Circle they have some light fixtures that look like candelabras, and the birds have learned to dive down into the candelabras. That's their bomb shelter, so they dive down into there and you cannot get them to leave. They are hunkered down in there and feel protected even if we're firing pyros right next to the candelabra."

What must be galling for Judy and everyone else involved in fending off the starlings in Indianapolis is that the situation was entirely avoidable. As their name suggests, the European starling is not native to North America. Their presence on the continent is the fault of just one man: Eugene Schieffelin.

Born in New York City in 1827, Schieffelin was the son of a wealthy drug industry tycoon and president of the American Acclimatization Society. The society was part of an international nineteenth century movement dedicated to "improving" the

Americas, Africa, Asia, and Australia through the introduction of European flora and fauna.

Schieffelin, a keen theatergoer, thought it would be just wonderful if all the birds mentioned in the plays of William Shakespeare lived in North America. So he ordered sixty European starlings from a supplier in England. When the birds arrived in Manhattan in April 1890, Schieffelin took the caged birds to Central Park and set them free. The following year, he released another forty in the same spot.

In another demonstration of starlings' taste for Neo-Classical architecture, many of them roosted on the nearby American Museum of Natural History. They stayed for three years, breeding and multiplying before starting to spread to the outer limits of the city.

After a decade of building up their numbers, the starlings moved beyond New York, expanding their range faster and faster with each passing year, and—in keeping with their aggressive nature—forcing native birds out of their nests as they went. In 1923, seventeen years after Schieffelin's death, they were spotted in Indiana for the first time. Seven years later the descendants of the hundred birds he imported could be found as far north as Nova Scotia, as far south as the Gulf of Mexico and as far west as the Mississippi.

Biologists of the time thought that would be the limit of the starlings' North American invasion. Mountain ranges and a lack of suitable nesting sites on the Great Plains would, they surmised, block their advance. They had, however, greatly underestimated the starling. Fourteen years later the first starlings were seen in California. By 1970 they were present throughout North America. Today, an estimated two hundred million starlings live on the continent and Schieffelin's name is mud among the pest controllers and farmers who must live with the consequences of his flight of fancy.

As in Europe, the starling is equally at home in cities as in the country, with the ledges and cavities of buildings working just as well for nests as trees and cliffs. Cities also provide plenty of food for these unfussy birds. They eat what we put on bird tables, pick through our garbage, and gorge themselves on the abundant insect life found at sewage plants. And, as seen in Indianapolis, city life becomes even more attractive to them in winter as built-up areas are warmer than the open countryside.

Urban areas also helped starlings to spread. Acclimatization societies brought the starling to Australia in the 1870s, believing they would keep insect pests at bay, only to watch them become a major agricultural pest in their own right. For a while, the birds' progress west was halted by inhospitable desert, but then starlings began using the urban areas springing up along Australia's southern coast as a path west.

In response, the Australian authorities urged citizens in starling-free zones to report any sightings so they could send out squads, armed with shotguns, to defend the area.

⋰⋅➤⋅•●

Schieffelin's fateful decision to bring the starling to North America was not only inspired by the Bard. His other inspiration was the runaway success of an earlier European import: the house sparrow, the oldest bird on the city block.

The house sparrow has a long association with urban living. These pocket-sized birds with their distinguishing chestnut-brown backs, white cheeks and black eye stripes took to living alongside us from the moment we shifted from nomadic wanderers to settled farmers some ten thousand years ago. That's about the same time we domesticated dogs and a good couple thousand years before cats joined the ranks of humanity's favored companions.

The settled life suited the house sparrow. By all accounts they are slothful birds, rarely looking for food beyond a mile from their nests. Even the most adventurous individuals rarely travel more than four miles from their birthplace in their entire life. Not that they needed to roam far after hooking up with us. The crevices and cavities of our buildings proved to be ideal nesting sites, and the grain we gathered, stored, and spilled provided plenty of food. So the sparrow stuck with us, tagging along as we spread out of the Middle East establishing settlements across the landmass of Africa, Asia and Europe. By Renaissance times, sparrows were a daily sight in European cities and towns.

People's attitudes to these avian interlopers were mixed. Some encouraged them by hanging earthenware pots from their roofs for them to nest in, while farmers regarded them as grain-gobbling pests. The Lutherans of Dresden even declared a ban on the birds after some dared to chirp and copulate in church during their sermons. For the poor they were—and, as we'll see, still are—a potential meal, with sparrow pie a favorite among European peasants.

Regardless of human opinion, sparrows were part of the fabric of European life by the time the acclimatization movement emerged, so they became a prime candidate for introduction to the new worlds. And in the early 1850s, a group of New Yorkers imported one hundred British house sparrows. After they were delivered via steamship from Liverpool, England, the birds were set free to go forth and multiply, and that they most certainly did. Those pioneer sparrows and their offspring fanned out from Manhattan, spreading north, pushing south, and driving west. Between 1868 and 1888 their North American range grew at an average of 118 miles per year—nearly three times faster than the American pioneers pushed back the western frontier.

The sparrows stumbled briefly at the one hundredth meridian, the line that divides the moist East of the United States from the arid West and runs along the western border of Oklahoma (excluding the panhandle). But as with the starlings facing the Great Plains, the plucky birds soon overcame that natural obstacle. By 1910 house sparrows had colonized North America. They could be found in northern Mexico, in the cities along the Pacific coast, and in much of southern Canada, where they survived harsh winters by nesting in railroad houses and grain elevators. Come 1917 they had even turned up on the ranches of Death Valley.

The same was happening in South America. Following introductions in Buenos Aires, Rio de Janeiro and Santiago, the sparrow
conquered Argentina, Brazil, Chile, Peru and Uruguay. The birds
even reached Ushuaia, the world's southernmost city on the Argentine portion of the Tierra del Fuego archipelago. The Amazon
rainforest blocked the sparrow's northward advance, but when
Brazil began building the Trans-Amazonian Highway in the 1970s,
the birds followed the construction workers, making nests in the
new buildings and trees lining the 2,485-mile road.

These introductions have made the house sparrow one of the
world's most widespread birds, yet wherever it is found it congre-
gates in cities and towns. Half of the UK's sparrows live in urban
areas, even though these account for less than one-seventh of the
land in Britain. And although they may struggle in the innermost
core of cities, sparrow numbers tend to rise rather than fall with
urbanization.

One reason for the house sparrow's urban success is its lack of
fear. Sparrows may be small but they are brave. While many animals shy away from the unusual, sparrows investigate. This lack of
fear makes them well adapted to city life. They are more willing to
try unfamiliar food and are less frightened by changes to their environment. It's a characteristic that has seen house sparrows adapt to
modern life in surprising ways.

Take the story of Nigel. Nigel was a New Zealand house sparrow
and the most frequent visitor to the Dowse Art Museum in the late
1990s. Several times a day, Nigel—as the employees named him—
would fly over the streets of Lower Hutt, a suburb of the capital
city Wellington, to reach the museum's flat-roofed and white-tiled
building.

The automated doors that guarded the entrance would have
proved an insurmountable barrier for most birds, but not for
Nigel. On reaching the entrance, Nigel would flutter in front of
the electronic sensor to trigger the opening of the glass doors.
Having fooled the outer doors, he would nip through the entrance

and perform the same trick again to cause the second set of doors to part.

After entering the foyer, Nigel would veer right, past the ticket kiosk and artwork, to reach the indoor cafeteria, where he would hop under chairs and pogo along the tabletops eating scraps left behind by clumsy customers. After filling up on breadcrumbs, potato chips, and other morsels, Nigel would exit the cafeteria, going back past the foyer and the sliding doors to reach the outside world, only to return for another raid shortly after.

Nigel was no one-off. Six hundred miles north of Wellington in Auckland, sparrows had cracked the automated door conundrum in a different way. Instead of hovering in front of the doors, they would land on the rectangular sensor and duck their heads to cause the doorway to open so they could reach the Hamilton InterCity bus station eatery.

More than four thousands miles northeast of Auckland, on the Hawaiian island of Maui, the local house sparrows figured out another way to fill their beaks with people's leftovers. Each morning the birds would hang precariously from the rooftops of the largest beachfront hotels so they could spy on the tourists eating breakfast on the balconies below and swoop down to grab the remains as soon as the vacationers retreated to their rooms.

After breakfast the sparrows would go and feed elsewhere, but come midday they were back in position for the lunchtime service. Maui's other birds would only cotton onto these balcony buffets when they spotted the sparrows flittering to and fro from the hotel facade.

Some urban sparrows have even become night owls. In Bangkok sparrows have been seen late at night, eating moths drawn to the bright lights of the city airport. Likewise in Manhattan, sparrows have been spotted close to midnight feeding on insects near the lights of the Empire State Building's observation deck.

But the house sparrow's presence in cities is now under threat. Across the world urban sparrow numbers are dropping fast. In

UK cities their numbers have fallen 60 percent in the past three decades. It's a similar story in Amsterdam, Brussels, Delhi, Hamburg and many eastern US cities. Today the oldest bird on the city block is fading so fast it is now on Britain's Red List of endangered species, a situation unthinkable just a couple of decades ago. The pattern isn't universal—numbers are stable in the English city of Manchester, for example—but the declines are alarming and the cause unknown.

Will Peach of the Britain's Royal Society for the Protection of Birds is one of the people trying to solve the Great Sparrow Mystery. "Quite often if a familiar bird declines, there's a glut of research projects and you will come up with a plausible explanation fairly quickly," he tells me from the organization's headquarters, a lodge house nestled within a nature reserve deep in the Bedfordshire countryside. "It's fair to say that with urban sparrows we've had that initial buzz of activity and, so far, it's still a bit of a mystery."

There is no shortage of theories. Although they eat bread, dog food, and other scraps, sparrows are seed eaters at heart, so some suggested a lack of seed was the problem. But when the theory was tested by supplying seed to the birds year-round, it made no difference.

A lack of the invertebrates that young sparrows are reared on was another explanation. "Where sparrows don't have enough insects they tend to feed their young with bread and peanuts and rubbish like that, and usually you'll see high rates of chick mortality in situations like that," says Will. But when Will and his team tried dishing out juicy mealworms to London's sparrows, it only helped the smaller colonies and did little to aid larger gatherings of the birds.

Others pointed the finger at pet cats and sparrowhawks. Yet cat ownership in London has changed little in the past twenty years, and studies suggest that cats kill more blackbirds than sparrows anyhow.

The case against sparrowhawks seems more convincing. These small birds of prey, which feed on a variety of birds (not just sparrows), are making a comeback in British cities after being almost wiped out by the notorious pesticide DDT. But although sparrow numbers are lower in urban gardens where sparrowhawks are active, that could simply be because sparrows avoid the area or evade capture by hiding in dense vegetation. Equally, there are plenty of places where sparrows and sparrowhawks live side by side, suggesting that sparrowhawks simply don't eat enough sparrows to be the sole cause of the decline.

Wilder theories have also been floated. Some suggested that electromagnetic radiation from cell phone masts could be affecting the birds since there are fewer sparrows in places where there are more masts. But, says Will, these are "also the highly urbanized places where you might expect to see fewer sparrows anyway."

Maybe it's genetic, others suggested. Since sparrows don't travel far, there's little mixing of urban and rural populations of the birds, and city sparrows do have slightly less genetic variation than their country cousins. Trouble is no one knows what, if any, difference that makes.

Architectural changes are a better culprit. Buildings define the urban landscape and have a major bearing on what can and cannot thrive within cities. This theory is supported by a study that looked at how sparrows fare in different areas within English cities. It found that poorer neighborhoods offered more suitable habitat for the birds than the better-off areas. So in Golborne, one of the most deprived wards in London, where the brutalist concrete of Trellick Tower looms over high-crime streets, sparrows should do well. Yet three miles south in Queen's Gate, home to Harrods and the city's super-rich, the sparrow should be a rarer sight.

Like starlings, sparrows have their own architectural preferences. They like houses built before 1945 best—and the more run-down they are the better, because that means there are more holes to nest in. Newer buildings are less welcoming, offering fewer nooks and crannies for nesting. Richer areas also have housing in a better state of repair, and house sparrows are less common in areas where houses have been renovated in the past decade. "If you replace your rotting, wooden soffit boards with PVC, which a lot of people do, the sparrows are excluded," says Will, adding that as property prices have risen, more and more Londoners are paving over their front gardens to turn them into parking spaces, which means there are also fewer sources for the seed and insects sparrows eat.

In short, as our cities improve, the house sparrow loses out.

Few places are undergoing as much development as Nashik in Maharashtra, India. This metropolis of one and a half million people is the sixteenth fastest-growing city in the world. Space is tight and the noise of construction is never far away. New high rises are springing up, and so many people are moving in from the countryside that the city is struggling to build the infrastructure needed to cope with them fast enough.

It's a pattern being replicated across India. The country is urbanizing at breakneck speed, and as ramshackle streets with ramshackle houses give way to office blocks and shopping malls, the sparrow is in retreat.

"In my childhood the sparrows were so numerous," recalls Mohammed Dilawar, who grew up in Nashik in the 1980s. Back then less than half a million people lived there. "At that time in Indian homes you could have sparrows making nests behind the window panes, on top of the cupboards, between suitcases. Even in the homes there were sparrow nests." Mohammed's own family home had sparrows nesting in the canopy of their ceiling fan. "If it was summer and the sparrow nest was there, you would stop using the fan," he tells me.

Did people not object to birds living in their homes? I ask. "We were brought up not to disturb the sparrow nest. In those times hygiene and these issues were not so much of a care. That was the kind of culture of we had in India, a very open culture. A culture where your neighbor could regularly just walk into your home unannounced."

Sparrows were not the only bird that imprinted itself on Mohammed's childhood. "I used to see hundreds of vultures foraging every day and that used to fascinate me—to see these vultures sitting there. Since we did not have access to a lot of other things, my entire childhood was spent seeing sparrows, birds, and vultures."

Today, he rarely sees vultures. The few that are left live on the outskirts of Nashik in tiny groups. The fate of the vultures haunts Mohammed: "The Indian species of vulture went from being the most common raptor in the world to being the most critically endangered bird. It only took ten years, which is faster than the extinction of the dodos."

What he finds saddest is that no one even noticed. "Because of a society that was deprived, we didn't have access to things like television or the mobiles, so when these things came in people got so engrossed in the television and their mobiles they didn't even realize what they were losing around them."

Mohammed figured that if the vulture could go from abundance to near extinction in a few years then so too could his beloved sparrows. So he decided to act. He founded the conservation group Nature Forever Society and launched World Sparrow Day, an international event designed to raise awareness of the sparrow's plight. He persuaded the government of Delhi to make the sparrow the official bird of the Indian capital and started selling tens of thousands of cheap bird feeders and nest boxes to Indian city dwellers who wanted to give the sparrow a helping hand.

Mohammed says the sparrow is like the tiger—a gauge of ecological health. It is the canary in the coal mine, "the ambassador for urban conservation," and its success—or lack of it—reflects how suitable our cities are for wildlife.

"India is one of the most rapidly growing countries in the world," he says. "Most of the population in the coming years is going to be concentrated in urban locations or cities. Now imagine cities of tomorrow that are devoid of nature, devoid of sparrows and other birds.

"A common man in India, from when he is born to the time he dies, might not go outside the city. There are a lot of people in India who find it difficult to get two square meals a day, so you can't expect those people to spend a fortune to go to a national park to see a tiger. For such a population, the sparrow and other birds that stay in urban locations are the only connection between humanity and wildlife."

Mohammed's campaign has made waves. *Time* magazine even named him one of the world's foremost environmental heroes. But many challenges remain.

The time when sparrows could freely nest in people's ceiling fans is being left behind. "Somewhere in the 1990s the culture in India started changing, so from being a very open culture it started becoming a closed culture or a private culture of the type one sees in the UK or the western countries," he says. "Open windows started closing up, and from a culture where you knew everything what is happening in the family of your neighbor, today we are in a culture where you don't even realize who your neighbor is. Because of this closed culture, the homes started getting closed and these sites were lost for sparrows."

The way food is sold in India is another important change, he adds. "During the '80s women used to sit outside their homes cleaning grains and other vegetables, so there was food for the sparrow. Today, women no longer sit outside their homes and clean grain in India. They just walk into a store and buy pre-packed grain. This answers a lot of the reason why the food source for sparrows has gone down."

Another pressure India's city sparrows face is being killed not by cats or sparrowhawks but by people armed with plastic cata-pults that cost as little as five rupees. That's about eight cents. The reason the birds are being hunted is simple: hunger. "In India the cost of fresh fish or meat is very high now. A lot of people cannot afford buying protein over the counter, so they go out and kill wild animals because it's free," says Mohammed, who wants the Indian government to ban people from using catapults in this way. "This problem is increasing in cities because a lot of people who used to live in rural areas have migrated to the cities as laborers, and these people have the skills and knowledge to kill urban wildlife."

As India continues to urbanize, the pressure on the sparrow is likely to grow but, Mohammed says, the fight to save the oldest bird on the city block—a bird whose success reflects the state of the towns and cities we live in—is too important to fail. "When you save a species like sparrows, or for that matter any other wildlife found around cities, you don't only save them, but you save a lot of plants that depend on them. You save a lot of landscapes," he says. "A city becomes healthy if there is a big enough amount of wildlife within. This is something that is very, very important."

The contrasting attitudes to the declining house sparrow and the starlings that invade US cities says a lot about how we view urban wildlife. When house sparrows were abundant in cities, we viewed them as pests and berated them for causing many of the same problems as the starlings of Indianapolis. But now that they are vanishing from our streets, we see them as lovable victims in need of rescue rather than elimination.

It's not a matter of us preferring sparrows over starlings, either. In European cities, starlings have been declining fast too, prompting campaigns to save the birds that cause so many problems in urban America.

It seems we have a love-hate relationship with urban wildlife. We want animals around us, but only if they know their place. We revile them when they succeed at living among us, but we'll miss them when they're gone.

STREET HUNTERS

Living with Boars and Raccoons in Berlin

"Smell! Smell!" says Derk Ehlert, using his hand to waft the air toward his nose. He takes a long, deep breath. "You can smell them. *Mmm. Mmm. Ahhhh.*"

I sniff the forest air, wondering what it is I'm supposed to smell and then it hits: a whiff that brings dank mushrooms to mind.

It's the smell of wild boar.

We're in Berlin. Grunewald, the large forest in the city's southwest, to be precise. It's dusk and the fading light makes it hard to see, but somewhere in the trees straight ahead of us are boars.

Not only can we smell them, but we can hear them too: the rustle of hooves moving through leaves, the snorts of boars snuffling in the soil, and a moist crunching sound. "They are eating all the acorns," whispers Derk in his German-accented English.

More munching noises come from the trees. Then, an abrupt squeal. Something moves in the shadows, but I can't make it out. "A call from the ma," says Derk.

Everything's suddenly silent. The rustling, snuffling and munching has stopped. The boars have realized we're here. "They are freezing," says Derk. "They can smell us."

The silence lasts half a minute and then there's a deep groan, a long, drawn-out *ooooorrrrgggghhh*. We catch a glimpse of a piglet moving away from us into the bushes and then the sound of more movement. The boars are leaving.

We've unnerved them. The boars of Berlin may be used to people, but we're not acting right and that could mean we're hunters, so they've opted to head deeper into the trees and further away from us.

"Hunters behave differently," says Derk. "They sneak up, go off the paths. Hunters, if they want to see the boars, might talk out loud to themselves because for the boars normal, talky people walking along are not a problem. It's the sneaking people with the funny smell that worry them."

More than three thousand of these coarse-haired wild pigs live in Berlin. We may have gone looking for them in Grunewald, but their search for food makes them regular visitors to the city streets. In the suburbs they dig up gardens, tip over bins to get to leftovers, and plough the parks. One time wild boars tore up a Second World War cemetery, uprooting gravestones and causing thousands of dollars' worth of damage.

Another time, they broke through the fence guarding the training field of Berlin soccer club Hertha BSC. Once inside they ripped up the pitch to feast on the roots and grubs below the grass. The club repaired the fence, but the shaggy vandals returned, found a new way in, and churned up the pitch for a second time.

The boars are aided in their search by an amazing sense of smell. Their noses are three times as sensitive as those of dogs, making them capable of sniffing out damp soil from as far as two miles away. Perfect for finding the prime feeding spots in the city.

As Berlin's only wildlife officer, Derk has plenty of experience with the boars. The day before I visited, he had to deal with one that got hit by a car while crossing a busy road. Though the boars usually leave people alone, when wounded they can be dangerous.

In fall 2012 another collision caused a 260-pound boar to go on the rampage in the leafy western Berlin suburb of Charlottenburg. The first victim was an elderly man, who was bitten on the back of his leg. The boar then knocked over an old lady before attacking a young woman who had to scramble on top of a parked car to escape. When a policeman came to the rescue, the boar charged at him, cutting the officer's leg. The injured officer ended up drawing his gun and fatally shooting the animal in the middle of the usually quiet residential street.

The previous day's incident was less serious. Well, for Berliners, at least. "The boar was mortally wounded but still alive, so it was really important it was killed," Derk tells me as we drive throughout Charlottenburg. But taking down an injured boar in a busy city is no easy feat, so Derk called in one of Berlin's city hunters, an elite troop of volunteer huntsmen he has recruited for exactly this kind of situation.

Derk has thirty *Stadtjägers*, as the city hunters are known in German, he can call on. They are some of the area's most experienced hunters and they need to be, for hunting in the streets is a risky business. Not only must they contend with wild boars that often know the streets better than them, but they have to be sure their shots won't hit someone by accident or ricochet off the hard urban surfaces with potentially lethal consequences.

"They have to be really experienced. They have to be very good at dealing with people and their weapons," says Derk.

The risk is so high that the *Stadtjägers*, rather than the city authorities, are the ones who are liable if anything goes wrong. It might sound like a bum deal for the hunters, but there is an upside, as they get to keep the meat of any boars they kill to sell or eat themselves. But even that comes with a caveat. Many of the boars they have to kill are sick or injured, so there's a good chance the meat is unfit to eat. This was the case yesterday.

"They did ultimately kill it and it was a very big animal, but it was not appropriate to be sold because the boar had so much adrenaline going through its blood after being hit by the car that it was no longer edible," he explains through the interpreter who is sitting in the back, helping out whenever Derk's English fails him. "The question then is what do you do with the dead body? It was clear it could not be eaten, but it had to be removed."

Derk ended up loading the dead boar into the back of his car and taking it to a vet to be disposed of. The interpreter, who is sitting right where the dead boar was, eyes the seat warily. "You've cleaned the car since then, right?" she asks, only half joking.

Why don't you get the police to shoot them? I ask. "A good question," says Derk. "For ten years we have been at the police school telling them how to shoot the wild boar, but the police often they don't want to kill them. They ask what can we do? Can we bring the wild boar to the doctor?"

Paperwork is another problem. "If they use their weapon they have to write out why they did it. It's a long form, more than fourteen sides of paper, and then they get an official notice in their file that says they used the weapon. If they then want a different position or a promotion, they have this notice saying they've used their weapon. So even if they are stationed in an area with a lot of wild boars, they prefer not to shoot them because it might ruin their chances of getting promoted."

Even when the police do act, they can make mistakes. "Sometimes they misunderstand the situation. In the spring we had a wild boar that was bearing her young in the middle lane of a street, and a cop came and shot it because he thought it was a wounded animal. It caused a huge scandal in the newspapers." As a result the police usually call in the *Stadtjägers* when there's a boar to shoot and restrict themselves to closing off the streets so it is easier for the hunters to make the kill. On average the police call Derk and his *Stadtjägers* three or four times a week.

While there is a steady stream of incidents needing the help of hunters, most of the calls Derk gets about the boars come from people who have had their gardens invaded or object to the very sight of the wild swine in the city.

One especially irate woman called Derk only a few hours before we met. "She was shocked that at ten in the morning she sees a wild boar when walking in the forest. She says it is a problem because children with bicycles go to the forest at that time. But the forest is a normal neighborhood for wild boars. I told her that it is not possible to abolish the wild boars, that they are not dangerous for the children, and that I have never heard of wild boars eating kids—it is not possible. But she was angry with my answer because she wanted to hear another thing. She wants to hear that the army is coming now."

Berliners are hopelessly divided about the increasingly bold boars. When the city authorities asked almost five hundred residents about their hairy neighbors, most agreed that the boars were a "plague" and said they should not be in the city, yet they also felt that the boars were not a nuisance and were adamant they didn't want them shot.

The muddle of opinions also reflects the German capital's divided past. "The westerners call more," he says. "More than three-quarters of my calls are from former West Berlin. They have a certain kind of demand of the authorities, where they go: 'Do something about this problem I have!' The easterners are more relaxed about it. They may go and talk to a forester to get it taken care of. They don't immediately escalate it to the authorities."

With the city unsure how to respond, it falls to Derk to try to reconcile boar and Berliner. "There are three and a half million people in Berlin and they have three and a half million opinions about the animals," he says. "I am the reverend of the wild. The animals don't need me, but the people have problems, so my job is to talk with the people who are angry about the wild boars."

The boars are not new arrivals. They have been living in the forests and outskirts of Berlin for decades. But in recent years they, like the red foxes of London, have become more willing to venture onto the streets.

"The boars have developed a kind of trust of people. They are not so scared of people any longer," says Derk. "In people's perception there are more now, but that's not true. It is the new behavior that they see because the boars don't mind being out where people can see them now." This newfound willingness to roam among people is something many Berliners have encouraged. Estimates suggest that more than three hundred thousand residents are feeding them, despite the threat of a hefty five-thousand-euro fine for anyone caught in the act.

Another attraction is that the streets are often safer for boars than the forest. In the forests licensed hunters are allowed to shoot boar in designated areas, but once the animals enter built-up areas they face no such danger. The boars have even started moving into the suburbs at weekends during hunting season to avoid hunters before returning during the week when the hunters are back at work.

The streets also offer protection from dogs, says Derk. "In the spring when they have children, some female boars come out of the forest and go into the gardens that don't have dogs or to abandoned houses because there are areas of the forest where people can take the leash off their dogs."

Their journeys into the built-up areas are made easier by the plentiful supply of green space. "The very special thing of Berlin is it is a green city," says Derk. "It's the greenest city in Europe because more than 42 percent of the whole city is green—marsh, woodland, and so on."

This abundance of greenery is, in part, a product of Berlin's tumultuous past. The city's large *Volksparks*, or people's gardens, were created in response to the chronic overcrowding caused by the huge numbers of people who moved to the city as it industrialized in the latter half of the 1800s. Then there are the tens of thousands of allotments that can be found throughout the city, which people use to grow cornflower, lavender, tomatoes, strawberries, and more. During the Second World War, these urban gardens kept food on the plates of Berliners. And where once there was the "death strip," the Cold War no-man's-land that made it easy for East

German soldiers to shoot those trying to reach West Berlin, there is now a park famed for its Sunday karaoke shows.

Berlin's urban planners have also played their part. For decades, the city has sought to link together all of its green space, so that cemetery connects with park, park with canal bank, and canal bank with railroad verge. Although this dream of "coherent greenery" remains unfulfilled, enough work has been done over the decades to create a sizable network of green corridors that wild boars and other animals use to move around Berlin unseen.

Some boars have even used these wildlife highways to reach the heart of the city. One of the routes into the urban core is the S-Bahn railroad. It runs from the southeastern suburb of Treptow-Köpenick to Jannowitzbrüecke station, which lies a short walk from Alexanderplatz—the austere square that was once the center of East Berlin. "It happens two or three times a year because there is a green passage along the railway line. It is like a highway of green gardens along the tracks," says Derk. "It's uninteresting for us to walk there, but the wild boars prefer this place because there's no one there. No people, no dogs."

With even the inner city within the reach of the boars, Derk feels that Berliners are just going to have to learn to share the city with the animals. "Boars are part of life in Berlin," he says. "In the city no one expects the wild boar, but since more than 18 percent of our city is forest it is normal."

The challenge is that people in cities are often alarmed by any sense of wildness, he says: "The wildness is a little bit dangerous, and people like to have all things under control."

. ⋅ ∶ ❯ ⦁ ⦁ ●

Wild boars are just one member of what Derk calls Berlin's "big five," the animals that cause the most complaints. Red foxes and rabbits are also members of this club of troublemakers, as are the stone martens. Also known as beech martens, these weasel-like omnivores are just under half the size of a domestic cat and have fur that ranges from dark brown to a pale stony brown. Traditionally these nocturnal creatures live in forests and mountains, but these days are they equally at home in the cities and towns of central Europe.

Stone martens were first seen in cities back in the 1940s, but unlike the boars and foxes, they rarely get fed by people despite their cute faces. Instead, they have retained their hunter-gatherer lifestyle, seeking out fruit, birds, and rodents to eat. Their diet varies from city to city. In the Polish city of Kraków, birds top the menu with pigeons the prime target, but in Budapest scavenged fruit is the number-one snack.

One problem caused by the urban martens is that they set up homes in attics and empty buildings, since the rock crevices and trees they use as dens in the wild are in short supply. But it is not their homemaking that has secured their place among Derk's big five; it's their obsession with cars.

The martens' car fetish started in the Swiss city of Winterthur, about thirty miles northeast of Zürich. It was 1976 and all across the German-speaking city people were getting up in the morning and finding that their cars, which worked fine the day before, wouldn't start. When mechanics checked the vehicles they found a wide range of damage in the engine compartments. Some of the cars had severed ignition cables or mangled electric cables. Others had sliced up windshield washer tubes or shredded noise insulation mats.

Oddly, none of the damage could be explained by wear and tear. It seemed as if someone was deliberately sneaking around the city at night, opening hoods, cutting cables, and tearing up insulation mats. The mystery was finally solved when a biologist was asked to check the damage and found teeth marks in rubber tubes and hair that proved stone martens were the malicious car wreckers. The discovery only made the mystery more intriguing. Why were the stone martens destroying cars? And why just the ones in Winterthur?

The initial theory was that the martens were eating car parts, but the lack of missing pieces from the scene of their crimes quickly disproved that idea. Some thought the martens might be entering engine compartments because of the warmth, but the tests showed that this wasn't the case either. Others suggested they were resting in the cars, but this was found to be too rare an occurrence to explain the number of attacks. Another study tried to see if juvenile martens were inflicting damage while playing, much like a puppy might try eating shoes before realizing that footwear isn't very tasty. But, again, the evidence was scant.

While the biologists continued to struggle to solve the mystery, something strange began to happen. First, the attacks on cars became more frequent and then they began to spread beyond Winterthur. By the 1990s the stone martens in southern Germany and the French-speaking cities of western Switzerland were also using their sharp teeth to damage cars. Since stone martens live throughout mainland Europe, the steady outward spread of the behavior from Winterthur could only mean one thing: the stone martens were teaching their young to attack automobiles, passing down the ritual from generation to generation.

Since then the car attacks have spread throughout Germany and been embraced by urban stone martens in Austria, Luxembourg, the Netherlands and Poland. Within the past decade, the martens in Budapest have also joined the car frenzy.

Mercifully, the martens do not bite through brake lines, but the damage they do to cars hits people hard in the wallet. In 2007 Germany's stone martens damaged a hundred and eighty thousand vehicles, resulting in a $55 million repair bill. Such is the cost that a mini-industry of anti-marten devices has been created in response to the threat. These protection systems range from high-tech tricks, such as UV lights for the bottom of cars and electric defenses that zap any marten that gets too close to the engine compartment, to more homespun solutions such as using chicken wire to keep the creatures out.

Changes in car design have also helped to keep the problem in check. Many modern cars have engine compartments that are harder to access, which helps to keep the martens out.

On the plus side, at least the scientists have now worked out why the stone marten has turned against the automobile. The clue that cracked the case was the seasonal pattern of the damage. Most attacks take place in the spring and early summer, which is when these normally solitary animals are busy with preparations for their July to August breeding season. In preparation for finding a mate, stone martens become increasingly territorial. They start expanding their range, claiming as much of the city as they can by marking their turf with urine, and start to patrol the boundaries more and more frequently.

It turned out that as part of these territorial patrols, martens were running from parked car to parked car, doing handstands and peeing on the rear axles to signal to any intruding marten that this area has already been claimed. The problem with the martens' plan is that cars move. So when a marked car is taken into another marten's territory, the smell of the rival's urine provokes it into attacking the vehicle.

But although the behavior is now understood, it is a habit of urban wildlife that central Europeans are just going to have live with. "From time to time it's not easy to live with the marten, but on the other side there is no possibility of abolishing them," says Derk. "If you hunt them, they are replaced by marten after marten after marten. We have no chance of a world free of marten."

⋯∴🐾•°

The final member of Derk's big five wild troublemakers is an animal that shouldn't even be in central Europe: the raccoon.

Their presence there is fashion's fault. Back in the middle of the 1920s, full-length raccoon fur coats became all the rage in the United States. The craze started when Ford Model T owners took to wearing the distinctive black and gray coats to keep themselves warm when driving in the winter. In the process, these wealthy car owners turned raccoon pelts from the cut-price choice of frontiersmen to a symbol of aspiration. So when celebrities like the Chicago Bears' halfback Red Grange and teen idol Rudy Vallée adopted the look, Ivy League college students rushed to embrace the fad.

Soon big, thick raccoon coats were everywhere, joining the Charleston and flappers as an icon of Roaring Twenties youth culture. America's new look did not go unnoticed in Germany, where the young fashionistas of the Weimar Republic also adopted the raccoon look. But imported coats from the United States were expensive, so enterprising farmers started bringing raccoons over to Germany so they could breed them for their fur.

One of these fur farmers was Rolf Haag, who lived in the state of Hesse in central Germany. As well as being a farmer, Rolf was a keen hunter, and after becoming familiar with raccoons through his business, he began thinking it would be great fun to hunt them. Trouble was there were no wild raccoons in Europe, so Rolf decided to change that. He contacted the local forest supervisor and persuaded him that releasing these bandit-faced creatures would not only provide good sport but also make the local fauna more interesting. On April 12, 1934, Rolf released four raccoons—two males and two pregnant females—close to the Edersee Reservoir, some fifty miles west of the city of Kassel.

Rolf's release was only the start, and when a stray bomb hit a fur farm east of Berlin in 1945, the raccoons staged their own great escape with around twenty fleeing into the forests. Today, there are around a million descendants of Rolf's quartet and the farm escapees living in central Europe. Most live in Germany, but they have also spread to every neighboring country as well as Hungary and Slovakia.

As in North America, where city raccoons have been around for more than a hundred years, Europe's raccoons are supreme urban adapters, moving into cities such as Kassel and Berlin as well as spreading around the countryside. Derk estimates there are around six hundred raccoon "families" living in Berlin, representing at least a couple thousand individuals.

The city's most famous raccoon was Alex. His moment in the limelight came in 2008 when he moved into the underground garage of the thirty-nine-story Park Inn hotel in Alexanderplatz. After the raccoon was spotted raiding the trash cans of the nearby Burger King, the hotel manager saw a PR opportunity. The manager named the raccoon Alex after Alexanderplatz and informed reporters that while he was very proud the animal had chosen the Park Inn, he wanted someone to get rid of his unusual guest.

It did not take long before Derk got wind of the plan to throw Alex out of the hotel. "About twenty minutes after he sent out the news release, the first newspaper rang me up. What the hotel manager didn't know is that relocating the raccoon is not allowed." Raccoons might not be endangered or even part of Germany's natural wildlife, but the law was clear: Alex could not be removed.

"It created waves the poor hotel owner would never have imagined," says Derk, who thinks Alex came from a group of raccoons that live near the Brandenburg Gate. "There were tens of reporters and television news crews outside the hotel, and they all wanted to film the raccoon. I called up the boss of the hotel and told him that he was not allowed to tell people to come and capture a wild animal—it doesn't work like that."

The hotel had no choice but to let Alex stay free of charge. "Alex ended up staying there for a year and a half before he left for another part of the city to find a wife," says Derk. "But for that year and a half the hotel manager would get calls and cancelations from people who told him, 'You're this bad, bad owner who wants to get rid of the raccoon and I don't want to stay in a hotel run by a killer.'"

As Alex's stay in Alexanderplatz shows, raccoons get by just fine even in the most urbanized areas. A large part of the raccoon's urban success is down to its sharp intelligence and its front paws, which are similar to human hands and allow raccoons to open garbage cans, jars, and refrigerators as well as turn doorknobs and use water spigots. Their cleverness and dexterity also makes them a nuisance as they break into attics through weak points in wood-framed houses, rifle through bins, and use pet doors to enter homes.

Despite the problems, Derk admires raccoons. "I like raccoons. They are so pretty and so intelligent—they are the most intelligent mammals in Europe. They can smell with their paws. Where they come from in North America the streams and rivers they use are muddy so they cannot see, so they use their paws to figure out what is worth exploring more.

"Urban raccoons do the same thing with trash cans. They open trash cans and put their hand on top of it to figure out where to go for the good stuff with their paws."

Raccoons have also turned sewer and storm drains to their advantage. One city where raccoons make the most of the drainage networks is Milwaukee. They are so popular with raccoons as a way of getting around the city that Scott Diehl, wildlife manager at the Wisconsin Humane Society, calls them "the raccoon subway." "They use the storm-sewer system to travel without fear of people and predation, and get in and out through the large sewer grates near curbs," says Scott, who has been helping injured wildlife in Milwaukee for the past twenty-five years.

But adaptable and clever as they are, raccoons do make mistakes, and each year the Wisconsin Humane Society rescues around ten raccoons who get stuck in sewer grates. One of these hapless raccoons was Blake, who got his head stuck in a grate in 2009 while trying to climb out of a sewer in downtown Milwaukee. "Blake misjudged one grate and got stuck," says Scott. "He made a lot of noise. He was screaming and crying. I had to sedate him to get him free."

Although most of the several hundred raccoons the society helps each year have been hit by cars, they find plenty of other ways to get themselves into trouble too. Among the trickiest raccoons Scott has had to rescue was the one found near the top of the Milwaukee County Courthouse. "There were renovation works and scaffolding set up on the outside of the courthouse. The raccoon climbed up the scaffolding overnight and had gotten up into the rafters of this scaffolding shelter. The workers couldn't do their jobs with the raccoon up there, so we were called on."

Scott soon had to play daredevil, trying to catch the raccoon thirty feet above the ground. "We put up an extension ladder and I put on a safety harness and went up. When I got up to the rafters there was a metal apparatus I was able to click onto so I was comfortable that I wasn't going to fall, and then I had to use a pole snare to capture the raccoon before carrying him down."

After bringing down the raccoon, the team set him free a short distance away. "We didn't want to take him so far away that he wouldn't know his neighborhood anymore, so we took him to a nearby green space that evening and released him."

. . ⚫ ⚫

Derk has his own wildlife rescue stories, the most dramatic of which is the time a red fox took a ride on a U8 subway train. "From what people said it was early in the morning and this young fox, he was perhaps worried by people or a dog. He was running through the street and goes down into an underground station where there was a train standing with the door open. He goes in and the door shuts and the train starts moving while he is inside."

After passengers reported the fare jumper, the train stopped at Hermannplatz, a busy commuter station where two of Berlin's underground lines meet. "At first they wanted to shoot the fox but then they decided no, there are people, press, and electronics inside the train to worry about, so they rang me up," says Derk.

"So they bring me up to the station by police car with the sirens going. I went down and it was full of people. People on the gate, policemen, people from the fire service, more than forty people, and they are all in a half-circle around the fox in the train, which was crying."

Derk told everyone to get out and to clear the stairs leading out of the station. "After a minute or two, I went into the train to check on the fox and it runs through my legs, up the stairs and out."

While much of Derk's time is spent dealing with the times people and animals clash, he is happy that wildlife is part of life in Berlin. "It's brilliant to see that we are not alone in cities and most people are happy about that," he says.

The challenge is getting those who object to the wildlife to stop feeling threatened. "It is not necessary to change the way we live. It's a change in how we think, to have a coolness, a tolerance. If people are angry about some animal, maybe they do not know about it. The fox, for example, it is not dangerous for the kids and it is normal to have a fox in the city.

"For example, some people came to me and said children are playing in the playground, and every day a young fox comes there. They wanted me to promise that the fox is no danger. So I said, 'I will make a deal with you. If the danger increases we will shoot it.' Then, they say, 'Oh, well, we don't want you to shoot it. Why don't you just take it away?' I said, 'No, we can't just take it away. Where would it go?'

"The foxes have changed their lives. They have no dens in the soil. They have their dens in the houses or basements. They prefer to look at the garbage and not at the forest."

ROMANCING COYOTES

Looking for Coyotes in Chicago and Los Angeles

Shane McKenzie said I wouldn't be able to miss him, and he wasn't wrong.

From the moment I saw the dark blue Ford Ranger heading toward our meeting spot at Chicago's Cumberland metro station, I knew it was Shane. The huge chrome aerial sticking out of the cab gave it away. It's enormous, held aloft by a four-foot-tall mast. The antenna juts out horizontally from the top of the mast, extending five feet, its length crisscrossed with short metal rods.

"So, you saw the giant antenna," grins Shane as I get into the passenger seat. "It's called a Yagi. That antenna allows us to pick up the VHF signal that the radio collars on the coyotes are producing."

Inside the cab is the bottom end of the mast. It is poking through a circular piece of wood affixed to the underside of the roof. A grubby disc of laminated paper with angles marked out in degrees has been glued onto the wood. Sticking out of the base of the mast is a makeshift metal handle that ends in a skewered golf ball and is used to rotate the antenna from within the pickup. A thick black

71

electrical cable runs out of the mast and into a blue 1970s radio receiver covered in dials, switches, and ports. In an age of GPS the kit looks dated but, then again, the Chicago coyote-tracking project predates the smartphone era.

The man behind the project is Ohio State University ecologist Dr. Stan Gehrt. It started in 2000 back when Stan worked for the Max McGraw Wildlife Foundation, the research charity founded by the eponymous electrical equipment tycoon.

"During the 1990s coyotes started showing up in areas where they had never been seen before," Stan told me over the phone before my meeting with Shane. "There was a lot of concern because, at that time, the idea of coyotes living in or around cities was not common. So in 2000 we got funding to do a one-year study.

"It was basic stuff. We were going to try and catch some coyotes, which we weren't even sure we would be able to do, put a few radio collars on them, and find out if these animals were really living in the Chicago area or just passing through."

Stan remembers being skeptical about the project's future. "The thinking was that there weren't many coyotes to study in Chicago and it would be a very temporary thing. But we were lucky and managed to catch some animals right off the bat and, in the first few weeks, we realized that we were completely underestimating the way that coyotes are using the urban landscape and so the project has never stopped."

Stan didn't know it at the time, but the arrival of coyotes in Chicago was no one-off. All over North America, coyotes were moving to the city. Today there are coyotes in St. Louis, in Boston, in Nashville, and in Washington, DC, to name but a few. Even New York City, once seemingly immune to the coyote influx, has now been colonized by the medium-sized omnivores, which resemble small wolves.

Stan thinks the rapid urbanization of the coyote is due to the collapse in demand for the animals' grayish brown to yellowish gray fur back in the late 1980s. "Obviously we weren't doing research on them before they got here, so it's pretty much speculation, but Illinois is typical of most states in that hunters and trappers can take as many coyotes as they want. There's basically no restrictions.

"So there was this constant removal of coyotes in rural settings that kept the population at a certain level. But at some point in the late 1980s, early 1990s there was a crash in the pelt prices and with it a huge drop in the interest and effort to hunt and trap coyotes."

With the hunters and trappers gone, the coyote population boomed and the resulting overcrowding encouraged many of them to seek a home in the urban sprawl. "Coyotes have a very territorial social system, and as their population builds coyotes are constantly getting pushed out into abnormal habitat. So probably what happened was the rural population grew during the late '80s and early '90s and caused the animals to explore new habitats, and the only habitat that was left that wasn't already occupied by other territorial coyotes were the huge metropolitan areas." The coyote baby boom also coincided with efforts to make America's cities greener, a trend that helped to ease the coyote's transition from rural to urban life.

Since 2000 Stan's project has put collars on hundreds of coyotes in the Chicago area. Shane's job is to spend nights cruising the streets and using the Ford Ranger's aerial to locate the coyotes and record their whereabouts.

"Our nights always start at sundown," says Shane, as he turns onto I-294 and we head toward the suburb of Northbrook to find the first coyote of the evening. "That's when they start moving. They know the traffic patterns—they know the times when it is busy. So they all wait until it dies down and then they come out."

Many of the sixty or so coyotes that currently have collars live in the city's forest preserves, but tonight we're focusing on the more urbane individuals. "The animals we're going to go to tonight are much more comfortable being seen by people and being around cars," says Shane. "There are a few of them where I can sit with the spotlight on them and they just turn their eyes away until I turn away the spotlight and then they just continue on.

"They don't worry at all. I think they know the truck, for when we pull up they start watching us, whereas the ones in the forest preserves will run away right away. They never stick around."

First on the list is Coyote 390. She was collared as a pup back in 2009 and the team have nicknamed her the Northbrook Animal. "She began her life in the Highland Woods area, which is about eight to ten miles away from where she now is," says Shane.

Coyote 390's early life was uneventful. She stuck to the golf course she was born on, found a mate, and had a litter of pups. But then, around the age of three, she was struck with wanderlust and took off to find a new place to roam.

Her decision to pull up stakes was a tense moment for the team. The radio signals sent out by the collars can only be picked up within a mile radius and so tracking down a wandering coyote can be a challenge. "Usually it will take months before we'll end up finding these animals again, but we got really lucky with her—we found her within a week. Her home range now, half of it is forest preserve—the Des Plaines River forms the boundary line for her— the other half is a residential area she uses.

"What's really cool is that she was actually absorbed into another forest preserve pack, which according to Dr. Gehrt is very rare. Usually when an animal comes to a new forest preserve there's already going to be a pack there and they are not going to be too friendly, so she's a special case. She's one of my favorites."

Shane has plenty of stories about the secret lives of Chicago coyotes, tales that have been pieced together from snatches of geo-location data, dissected scats, pathology reports, and genetic tests. "Just recently, we had the oldest coyote on the project— Coyote 125—die on us," he says. Coyote 125 was like some grand old coyote queen. At the peak of her reign, she controlled almost half of the vast Poplar Creek forest preserve. "She ended up settling down with her mate and slowly divvied up her territory until what was once a huge home range became concentrated in these two very small blocks. All she and her mate did was travel between those two blocks. It was almost like she was given a small piece of territory—her little senior living home—within the areas of all these other packs.

"Eventually we found her dead one day. Unfortunately it was summer and the body had already gone through an advanced stage of decomposition, so it was not obvious what did her in. We sent her to the Brookfield Zoo to do a necropsy. I'm pretty sure they didn't find anything abnormal other than old age."

Then there's the Campton Hills Animal, who caught mange— the nasty skin disease caused by the mite responsible for scabies in humans. "He had pretty bad mange a while back," says Shane. "He's actually gotten over it, but he was a very visual animal during the middle of the day when he had mange. He'd just be walking down the streets and in backyards." It is thought the fur loss caused by mange can make it harder for animals to regulate their body temperature and this encourages coyotes to be active in the daytime when it's warmer.

"The residents were very concerned about it. Dr. Gehrt had a lot of conversations with residents who were asking us what were we going to do about it. But we're observers, that's all we are. We're not introducing coyotes, we are just collaring them and following them and watching what they do. Luckily, he started to become less visible as the summer progressed and the calls about him have pretty much tapered off."

As we reach Northbrook, Shane switches on the VHF receiver. It fills the cab with a constant hiss of static, but then, as we reach the intersection between I-294 and Dundee Road, a faint but regular pulse of beeps becomes audible over the white noise. *Pip, pip, pip,* it goes.

Shane pulls onto the verge, grabs the golf ball on the handle, and starts rotating the giant aerial clockwise. The beeps get louder and then quieter. Shane stops and starts turning the aerial counterclockwise. The beeps grow louder and louder and then quieter. He continues swinging the aerial back and forth in ever-smaller increments before settling on the point where the beeps are at their loudest.

"She's on the edge about three degrees or so," says Shane as we look into unlit forest preserve we've parked next to.

This is just the first reading. Shane needs more to calculate exactly where Coyote 390 is. "Typically it takes four different bearings to get an accurate triangulation. You only need three, but one will usually be off at some point. But she could just cross the road right now as we're taking these bearings. It gets very frustrating if she's moving quickly."

We return to the road to relocate the signal from different angles. We race up and down the roads, listening as we go for the telltale pips. We pull into driveways and onto the shoulder, each time scanning the area to get the loudest signal. "We do a *lot* of creeping in front of people's houses like this," says Shane, as he takes the fourth and final reading.

And how do people react to having a dark truck with a whopping great rotating aerial pulling up outside their house? I ask. "I get a lot of people who come out and talk to us. Most are pretty friendly, but every so often you get someone who doesn't believe you and thinks you're listening in to their cell phone conversations."

Shane inputs the four readings into a tired-looking PalmPilot PDA. It crunches the numbers and adds the approximate location of Coyote 390 to the records. "She is somewhere in the trees out there," says Shane, pointing at the dark forest.

We may have found her but she's staying well out of sight tonight, so we move on.

The second coyote on Shane's list is another suburbanite, the Palatine Animal. "She is from an area we nicknamed Melonhead's Marsh. We've got time what with the drive, so I'll tell the story," says Shane as we begin the drive south to Palatine.

"The first female ever caught for the project was Coyote 1 in

March 2000. She was named the Schaumburg Female because she was from the Schaumburg suburb." One day the Schaumburg Female found a mate, another collared animal: Coyote 115. "His nickname was Melonhead, because he had a giant head. Those two had countless litters and so they had to change their home ranges. They gave it up to their kids essentially."

Coyote 1 eventually passed away in May 2010 at the age of nine or ten. "When she died, Melonhead left the area, because they are monogamous animals and the only time in which they will split is when one passes. He left his home range to try and find another mate. But his collar was, unfortunately, dying. He settled down in an area that we nicknamed Melonhead's Marsh."

When the batteries on Melonhead's collar finally ran out, the team tried to capture him again, laying traps around Melonhead's Marsh, but they never found him. What became of Melonhead is a mystery, and unless the team get lucky with a genetic test, they will never know if he ever found love again.

But while the traps never caught Melonhead, they did get the Palatine Animal. She was just a juvenile then. "She grew up in an urban setting, in the city parks not forest preserves, so she's much more comfortable in using the roads and using the residential areas. She's in a residential area, using small city parks and stuff."

This isn't unusual. Coyotes can be found all over the city. They live in cemeteries and parks, hide under tool sheds, sleep in compost heaps, dig dens in the sides of gravel pits, and wander Navy Pier after dark. The project even found one, now deceased, coyote that spent her days snoozing in an elementary school. "Every time I came to look for this female during the day I would find her under a deck at this school," recalls Shane. "So there's little kids running around there, and I know exactly where this coyote is right underneath the deck and they are none the wiser. I'm sure if the school knew they would have her removed right away, but the fact that the animal had chosen to stay in that area with all these people around her is just amazing."

Coyotes are extremely good at concealing themselves, and cities are full of hiding places that are near-invisible to us. "There's a lot of nooks and crannies in the urban landscape that are relatively hidden from people even when people are walking by," says Stan. "In downtown Chicago, believe it or not, there's shrubbery down along the lakeshore and crevices in the rocks that they use. There could be a trash pile somewhere and they would burrow underneath that during the day.

"That's an aspect that's still amazing to me. You put radio collars on these animals and they show us what the landscape looks like to them as opposed to humans. It was quite apparent from early on that there's a lot of features in the urban landscape that you or I don't notice or take for granted, but those little features—a little bush in a parking lot, tall grass, a corner between two buildings—can make a difference to whether a coyote can live there or not."

These easy-to-miss hideaways, together with the railroad tracks they often use to travel around unseen, have helped coyotes go deep into the city. They are so common in downtown Chicago that Lincoln Park Zoo now brings the flamingos indoors every night so the coyotes don't get them.

Coyotes also wander amid the skyscrapers of the city's business district, the Loop. One time a young coyote even walked into a Quizno's in the Loop and decided to cool down in the sandwich shop's drinks cooler. It sat there unfazed by the commotion of the crowd that gathered, until animal control officers came and took it away. Most coyotes in the Loop keep a lower profile, and what they get up to there is unknown; the dense towers block radio collar signals, turning the area into a blind spot for the study.

Coyote 441 is one of those that roams the Loop. She often hangs around Lincoln Park and patrols Navy Pier, but she also makes regular trips into the Loop. "She has a GPS collar, and watching the movements of coyote 441 is amazing," says Shane. "You see how far she travels, going down Michigan Avenue and then into the dead zone in the true downtown area, where all of sudden the points stop and later pick back up on the other side of downtown.

"You've got to wonder, what is she doing? Is she just running straight down the streets? Is there an underground area that she uses? How is she moving from one side of the Loop to the other safely every single night crossing countless roads?"

Traffic may be the biggest killer of Chicago coyotes, but many of them have mastered road safety. "If they want to cross a road that's fairly busy with traffic, they will sit by the road, watch very carefully, and wait for breaks in the traffic," says Stan. "They also understand the direction in which the cars are coming from. If it's a divided highway, the coyote will only focus on traffic oncoming to them—they don't spend time looking in the other direction."

If the median dividing the highway is large enough, coyotes will cross to the median and then wait for gaps in the traffic on the other side too. Others have learned to wait at intersections for the stoplights to change. "They will sit at a corner, literally just like a person waiting to cross," says Stan. "They wait until the traffic stops at the light, and once the traffic stops then that's when they go across. It looks like the coyote is actually looking at the lights and waiting for the red light, but that's probably not happening since they don't really have good color vision. But in any event they still take advantage of the light, even if they are not necessarily watching the light."

In Chicago the animals even cross the busiest roads, including freeways that carry as many as a hundred thousand vehicles a day.

The Palatine Animal is one of these habitual road crossers. "Her range is pretty big," says Shane as we reach Palatine. "When we started, her home range crossed Route 53 and she would go from this side to that. In the past six months, though, she has stopped going to the other side." Today her range is on the east side of Route 53, an area of residential streets and city parks.

Shane turns the receiver on and we listen for pips, but there's nothing. We circle the area, looping round and round the suburb.

Still nothing. "This can be a frustrating time, trying to find the animal for the first round of readings, searching and searching and trying to be careful about the speed you're traveling."

As we patrol, I ask Shane whether he ever imagined he would end up tracking coyotes in his home city when he started his career in wildlife research. "No. It sounds silly, but even throughout college I never realized the size of the coyote population here in Chicago," he says. "When I started on this project I was shocked how many were actually out there and how deep into the city they go. It just blew my mind."

Fifteen minutes become half an hour and there's still no sign of the Palatine Animal. The strip mall with the CVS that we've passed over and over again comes back into view. After the best part of an hour searching in vain, we admit defeat and move on to the next coyote, which lives in Schaumburg.

This time, the signal is there from the moment the receiver is switched on. Shane takes an initial reading and then heads into a residential area to get further readings. Shane sighs as we enter the twisty suburban streets. "One of the hardest things of this job is just learning the ropes, learning the cul-de-sacs," he explains. "Suburban settings can be a nightmare because most of the new ones don't like grid systems. Everything has to be curved so you'll think you're going east and then, all of a sudden, you're turning and you're like 'Noooo! Now I'm going west.' It can be quite a nightmare."

As we drive through the mazelike streets, we pass a man unloading shopping from his car. He doesn't even register the strange truck with the big aerial. The residents are probably used to it by now, says Shane. "We've been here for ten years and a lot of the residents know us, but in other areas people will sit there and point and watch you drive by."

We eventually track the coyote to Hackberry Court, a quiet cul-de-sac that ends in a small roundabout. "There," says Shane in triumph, "old 571."

Between two of the houses there's movement and the unmistakable silhouette of a coyote. Shane flicks on the truck's spotlight, illuminating the yard and revealing the yellow gray coyote. She stops moving and looks toward us.

"She is one of them that doesn't care," says Shane. "As soon as I turn off the light, she will continue with whatever it is she's doing. She's also one of the animals that moves around during the daytime. You find her hanging out by bird feeders a lot."

Sure enough, when the spotlight goes off, Coyote 571 gets back to business and calmly wanders behind one of the houses and out of sight.

Coyotes might be recent colonizers of cities, but it's already clear they are well suited to city life. The death rates say it all. The annual survival rate of Chicago coyotes is twice that of rural coyotes living outside protected areas, a figure that puts the coyote on a par with raccoons and ahead of red foxes when it comes to urban survival.

Yet while raccoons thrive on what we throw away, coyotes usually turn their noses up at the idea of eating trash. Even in Chicago's forest preserves where open-lid Dumpsters make discarded human food readily available, coyotes prefer to eat fresh rather than rifle through the garbage with the raccoons.

"The assumption that many of us made at the beginning of the study was that if coyotes were successful in urban areas it had to be because they were eating our rubbish and things like that," says Stan. "But when we did the diet analysis, we found that human foods were actually a very small component of their diet and many weren't eating any human food at all. We thought that garbage and pets would be the two food items that would be at the top or near the top of list, but they are at the bottom and did not make up a large part of their diet. Diet studies in other cities tend to show the same pattern."

Instead rats, mice, and rabbits dominate the menu, supplemented with side helpings of fresh roadkill and fruit. "They like fruits, but not fruit from garbage—fruit from off the plants," says Stan.

Deer fawns are another target. For a separate study the team has been putting radio collars on fawns born within the Chicago area. Around three-quarters died before adulthood, most ending up as coyote supper.

The coyote's taste for hunting has benefits for Chicagoans. As well as eating rats and mice, their consumption of ground squirrels and woodchucks seems to help prevent these burrowing rodents from damaging golf courses, and there is evidence that coyotes scare away cats and other animals that eat songbirds.

Coyotes are also keeping the city's problematic Canada geese in check. Canada geese have taken to North American cities in a big way, drawn in by grassy parks with ponds and causing plenty of trouble in the process. They irritate people with their noisy honking, ruin parks and lawns, and pollute water with their waste. Their presence in large numbers near airports is especially concerning because of the risk of them getting sucked into jet engines and causing potentially fatal engine failure.

So it is good news that coyotes have a taste for goose eggs. Their raids on goose nests are not enough to reduce the total number of Canada geese in the city, but they do seem to be slowing the growth of the birds' population.

But the coyote has an urban enemy: us. Although coyotes may have learned to cross roads, cars are still the big killer for urban coyotes, and a diet of rats and mice makes them vulnerable to poisoning. In Los Angeles around one-quarter of coyotes die from eating poisoned rodents.

A few get shot. "There have been cases where we believe animals have been illegally trapped in some way and we will find them dead with maybe a .22 in their head," says Shane. "Some animals we collar take off and leave the city, so every so often we will go up in a helicopter and listen for lost animals. They found one way out in western Illinois and the signal was coming from a house. So they knocked on the door and said 'Have you seen a coyote?' The guy is like 'Oh yeah! I've had this mounted for about a year now.' It turned out the homeowner had shot the coyote, stuffed it, kept the collar on it, and had it in his living room, collar still beeping away."

Intentionally or not, we pose the greatest threat to urban coyotes, but on other hand they can be a threat to pets and, to a much lesser extent, people. But while people tend to think the worst of an animal Mark Twain famously deemed "friendless," the risk coyotes pose to pets appears small. Study after study has found that cats, including feral ones, rarely make up more than 1 percent of urban coyote meals and dogs even less.

Of course that's little comfort to those who have their pets eaten by coyotes, and the diet figures do overlook the unknown number of pets that coyotes kill for territorial reasons rather than for food.

"For the most part coyotes living next to people has posed very little risk to people and largely little risk to some domestic animals," says Stan. "Most dogs are fine, but there are the occasional dogs that are taken and then there's a much greater risk to cats. Some people have had to modify their lifestyle because of coyotes living nearby, but most people have not had to make any changes at all."

What is unknown is whether this will change. "This is a natural experiment that is going on. It is something that has never happened before, so we don't know what the outcome may be. We don't know exactly what the coyotes in the cities are going to mean for people in the long run."

One place that may offer some answers is Los Angeles. Coyotes have been living in the City of Angels for decades, and most of the 160 or so incidents in which the animals have bitten people during the past thirty years happened within L.A. County, usually when people are trying to protect their pets.

Officers Gregory Randall and Hoang Dinh of the City of Los

Angeles' Wildlife Program spend their lives on the frontline of where humans and coyotes clash. Gregory is the veteran. He joined the city government in 1989 and in 2002 cocreated its wildlife program. Although he was born into a L.A. family that was well plugged into the city's showbiz industry, animals always appealed to him more than Tinseltown.

"When I was a child I lived up in Hollywood Hills, and wildlife was around all the time—coyotes, deer, everything," he tells me when I visit him and Hoang at their office in Lincoln Heights.

"When I was about nine, dad rescued a roadrunner bird that had been hit by a car and I tried to bring it back to health. I didn't know what I was doing, I just didn't want it to die, and it just continued from there. My fondness for wildlife has just grown and grown and grown."

While Gregory honed his expertise through hands-on experience and a voracious appetite for reading anything and everything about wildlife, Hoang's career started with a zoology degree. "Prior to working here I only read about animals and wildlife," says Hoang, whose family moved from Vietnam to Orange County when he was two. "It's been my interest since I was a kid, but all my knowledge was coming from textbooks, so I'm now getting to see the textbook come to life."

Between them they deal with almost all the wildlife issues in Los Angeles. And with nearly four million people and goodness knows how many wild animals living in the city, the work never stops.

Gregory shows me the software he uses to log the complaints they get. It plots each complaint on a map, but the streets are almost invisible, covered up by thousands of icons representing everything from striped skunks and opossums to coyotes, crows, and red foxes. You can almost hear his PC creaking as it tries to display the cluttered map without crashing.

He scrolls the map over to Atwater Village and, after a pause, the map fills up with miniature skunks. "See all the skunk symbols?

I couldn't understand why this area was so inundated with skunks until I discovered that a trapper was releasing every skunk he caught in this area. The trapper has since been turned over to Fish and Game for violating his permit."

Gregory drags the juddering map south to the coast. The computer stalls briefly, but then the area lights up with raccoon, cat, and squirrel symbols. "This is San Pedro. Their big issue is raccoons," he says.

This time deliberate feeding is the problem. The area has a large colony of feral cats that are constantly being fed by people, and the resulting abundance of food has attracted large numbers of raccoons, squirrels, and other animals. Some of the feeders go to extraordinary lengths to fatten up the San Pedro wildlife. "There's a couple and they drive there three times a week from Barstow, which is really far away—a good four-hour drive—to feed the stray cats that live at the beach at Point Fermin. They've got a cart that they roll with the food on it and feed the cats."

Add to this the food people chuck on the ground, and there's so much free grub around that the local cats and raccoons have given up trying to eat each other, probably because it's far too much effort on a full stomach. "There's a trash bin enclosed by a wall nearby, but people are too lazy to go in so they throw their trash at the bin and miss most of the time. On top of that there are people putting plates down for the raccoons."

The raccoons also raid yachts docked on the gangways. "The raccoons go into the vessels through the portholes, and that's when it is dangerous because the raccoon is cornered," says Gregory. "I went down and the big problem was that people were leaving food in the open in the yachts, so the raccoons look through a porthole, see food, and go in. The people come in and there's like Cheetos bags ripped open and whatever. I recommended that they start closing up the portholes."

Gregory shifts the map over to South L.A. Symbols representing Virginia opossums pop up. They are another source of complaints, often because people mistake North America's only marsupial for giant rats. It's an understandable mistake. They do, after all, look a bit like super-sized rats, albeit ones with scruffy gray coats and white-furred faces topped with Mickey Mouse ears.

Opossums are, however, one of the least troublesome animals, says Hoang. "People blow things so out of proportion. One of the great examples is the opossum, one of the most harmless creatures. Not only are they slow but also they don't attack. When you corner most animals they want to fight back, but these guys it's the last thing they do. At their most desperate moment they just fall over and play dead."

Opossums are found in cities all over North America, but their urban success is rather surprising, for not only will they faint rather than fight, they are short-lived and rarely make it to their second birthday.

But they do have some "superpowers," says Mason Fidino, who is trying to learn more about these understudied urban residents for Lincoln Park Zoo's Urban Wildlife Institute in Chicago. "One is that they have loads and loads of children, and when females are pregnant they often disperse and colonize a new area, so that is a really great way to have a new population start. On top of that they don't really need to eat that good a food to survive," he says.

"They are also just a little bit more cryptic than raccoons. So if someone has their trash tipped over and they don't see who did it, they are going to go, '*Arrgh*, cursed raccoon.' They are not even going to think about the opossum, so the opossum skips through wildlife conflict simply because there are easier things to point the blame at."

But even if they do tip over people's trash, it's hard not to feel sorry for opossums, which have an especially hard start to their short lives. "They have something like twenty offspring, but the females only have thirteen teats," says Mason. "Because they are marsupials they get born really quickly—it takes like two weeks for gestation and then they crawl up into the pouch and clamp onto a teat, so it is a race to get to a teat." As if a life-or-death race to a teat two weeks after conception wasn't tough enough, not all the teats work. "So if they clamp onto the wrong one they are out of luck," says Mason. "It's really hard to be an opossum."

Amid the opossum icons clouding South L.A. on Gregory's map are a smattering of snake symbols. Among them are the rattlesnakes that Hoang once got called out to deal with. "These two juveniles called me and go, 'There are three rattlesnakes in the yard,'" he says. "I'm like, 'No way. Not in that area.' I learned later that they stole air conditioning units from out in the desert and these rattlesnakes came crawling out of them. Talk about karma."

But when it comes to wildlife complaints in L.A., the coyote tops the list. In response, the wildlife program has amassed a large collection of oddball deterrents that clutter its small two-desk office. Gregory shows me a plastic tub filled with what looks like the contents of a child's toy box. "This is the wildlife scare kit I take to community meetings to show people what they can use to deter wildlife," he explains.

He plunges his hand into the tub, pulls out an air horn, and presses the button, letting out a deafening blast of noise. Next, he grabs a rainbow-colored umbrella and opens it up. "You know how animals pump themselves up to make themselves look bigger? Well, you get this and all of a sudden you've just become gigantic to that animal, and if you do this," he says, quickly opening and closing the umbrella, "that really scares them."

The inspiration for the umbrella was, oddly enough, a golden eagle. "I was watching this golden eagle and a coyote. Golden eagles are huge. They can take out an adult coyote. So this coyote comes up to try and take the eagle's prey. The eagle flaps his wings and the coyote is gone. I have never had a coyote stand its ground with this."

He puts down the umbrella and starts rummaging through the container, yanking out cooking pans, a megaphone, and a can wrapped in aluminum foil that is filled with coins. Eventually, he finds what he is looking for. "This one is my favorite," says Hoang

as Gregory hauls it out. "This is something I bought at Wal-Mart,"
says Gregory. "It's a girl's ribbon gymnastics toy, a little spongy thing
with Mylar strips. I went to Griffith Park in an area where people
were feeding coyotes, sat down, and waited for about eight coyotes
to gather around me and then did this." He twirls the ribbons fast
above his head, causing the plastic strips to make a loud whooshing
sound. "The coyotes took off," he says.

Other bizarre animal deterrents are spread over the office. On
one filing cabinet is a Haunted Hedge. "It's a Halloween item. It
was designed to scare trick or treaters, but it works for wildlife too,"
says Gregory as the hedge lets out a spooky laugh.

Over in a corner is a deterrent Gregory hacked together from
different objects—a large kite designed to look like a giant owl. "I'm
always trying to make extra things and adapt two items together to
make another scare source. So I have this owl. Normally, it's just
a kite you hang in a tree that flutters. For animals that are afraid
of owls, like raccoons and skunks, it is very effective on its own.
But what I did is I took part of another device to make it hoot and
light up and added a motion sensor so it reacts more realistically."
He switches it on. The owl's eyes light up and noisy hoots echo
around the office.

"The idea is to create a generation of wildlife that is more afraid
of humans again because the trend has been in the other direction.
From seeing us all the time and from being around us, they are
getting into closer proximity and begging food."

Another example of Gregory's handiwork is a motion camera
encased in foam and painted to look like pale brown rock. But this
isn't for the wildlife; it's to help Gregory catch people who are
feeding coyotes. He has spent the weekend perfecting the camera's
camouflage and today he is going to put it to the test.

After Hoang, who has been working the night shift, heads home,
Gregory and I head off to plant the camera. As we drive, Gregory
tells me that most of the problems coyotes cause start with people
feeding them. The Barstow couple who provide meals on wheels

for San Pedro's wildlife are, he says, not unique. "There was this two-story house in the Hollywood Hills, and the neighbor complained because the guy was feeding coyotes in a very unusual fashion. He said to me 'You're going to have to come out and see it to believe it.'"

Curiosity aroused, Gregory headed over to the house early one morning. "The neighbor says, 'Just wait in my yard.' So it's six in the morning and I'm there down in the bushes, and I could have reached out and petted the coyotes from where I was sitting. Then, I see this platform lowering from the second story with plates of food. Next to that I notice a motion sensor that rings a doorbell in the house to let the man know the coyotes are there so that he can lower the food."

Feeding coyotes is a crime in Los Angeles, and so Gregory headed to the front door to have words with the homeowner. "As I come round to the front door, I see him put peanuts into one of the planters outside and go back into the house. So I knock on the door and as I'm waiting for him to come to the door, I feel this tug and there's a squirrel sitting on my shoe, as fat as can be, holding onto my pant leg. This big, fat squirrel that's been eating all the peanuts.

"The first thing he says to me after he sees my uniform is 'How did you know?' I said, 'How did I know? Look at the squirrel. C'mon!' I asked why he was feeding the coyotes and he says, 'Well, so they won't kill my cats.' He thought if he feeds the coyotes and the other animals the cats will be fine.

"So I write him a notice to comply with the law and, as I'm doing this, a lady walking her dogs comes up and goes, 'Oh, you're not going to give that man a ticket. He's so nice. He feeds all the wildlife in the neighborhood.' It's like, 'You're not helping him, ma'am.'"

Far from making coyotes less dangerous, those who feed them are making them less afraid of people and instilling the expectation that people will give them food on demand, and back in 2008 the actions of one coyote feeder in Griffith Park had serious consequences. "This woman was in this green area near where people had been leaving plates of food for the coyotes," says Gregory. "She was stretching and exercising, and there was a coyote sitting there near her. People in Griffith Park are used to seeing coyotes, so she just continued exercising.

"Anyway, she was texting on her phone, and the coyote came up and bit her on the shin and then went back and sat down. This is what we call notification. It is not an aggressive act. It's the coyote telling her, 'Where's my food?' Coyotes do that to each other, but they don't break the skin because their skin is very pliable and has fur. But in a human that's a very thin area of skin, so it didn't take much to puncture her skin."

The wildlife program has a saying that "a fed coyote is a dead coyote" and that was certainly the case in that incident. After the woman was bitten, three coyotes that had become used to food being provided had to be killed to ensure they didn't bite anyone else.

Not that that stopped the feeder. A year later Gregory got another call. "A guy was lying in Griffith Park with his shoes off and felt a bite on his foot. The coyote had bitten him and gone back and sat down. Another guy chased it off with a stick, and the guy reported it to the Department of Health and Safety, who told us. Then, three weeks later, I get a call from a guy saying, 'I was in Griffith Park and was bitten on my foot by a coyote.' I said, 'Oh yeah. You were bitten three weeks ago.' He says, 'No, I was bitten yesterday.' I was like, 'What the hell is going on? We've got a coyote with a foot fetish.'"

Following the incidents, the Department of Agriculture came in and killed nine coyotes that had been begging for food. The coyote feeder whom Gregory is after today has been dishing out food where Griffith Park meets the upmarket houses of the Hollywood Hills.

As we drive up the twisty roads we get an early sign of the results of the feeder's activities. In the bushes overlooking the road is a coyote, staring down, presumably waiting for its food. It looks at us for a moment and then moves on. We're obviously not the delivery he's been waiting for.

Gregory's theory is that it's not a lone feeder they are after but a coyote feeding conspiracy organized by a woman who is hiring people to go feed the coyotes on her behalf. Conspiracy sounds like an overstatement, but as Gregory points out it really is a conspiracy if the woman is paying people to commit crime on her behalf.

But to secure a conviction, the city needs evidence, and that's where the camera comes in. The first attempt to get the feeder on film came unstuck when a tree branch fell in front of the lens. "So I've got to try and do this again," he says as we stop close to the feeding site. He is hopeful the disguised camera will do the trick. "I spent a big proportion of my weekend making this foam rock to conceal the camera and making sure it matches the rocks in the area."

The guy has already had a ticket from a park ranger, but if he comes back, Gregory hopes the motion camera will catch him. "If he keeps coming back in spite of getting the ticket, he is going to get a felony whether he likes it or not."

We head up a dirt path to a secluded ridge. Gregory scrambles up the side and plants the camera, which he covers in dust and dirt for good measure. "It's a crap shoot, this," he says. "Hopefully we will get lucky."

Trying to stop wildlife feeders is a never-ending battle, Gregory says as we return to his truck. He tells me about one woman who has been feeding raccoons. She has been ticketed, but instead of stopping she has put a tarp over her garage door so the raccoons can come in and feed out of sight.

"It is not legal for me to look into her garage beyond where I can see normally, but you see the raccoons going in," he says. "Because she's already had a warning it's going to end up as a $1,000 fine. We try to start with a written notice because it's hard to be hit with that amount of money. A good amount of people will stop but some are stubborn. It's getting to the point where park rangers are now writing tickets right off the bat when they catch someone feeding the animals because people are argumentative and you really have to hit them in the pocketbook to get them to wake up. It's sad that it has to be that way."

The next job on the list is to head over to Mount Sinai Memorial Park. It has been a regular stop for Gregory ever since a pack of coyotes took down a deer on the grounds of the Jewish cemetery. One of the problems at the park is that people bring food when they visit. "They leave food residue behind, like they leave food for the deceased. I'm sure the cemetery doesn't want to change their policy. I'm sure they want people to be able to come here and do that, but as long as that happens coyotes are going to take advantage of what is left behind."

With the policy unlikely to change, Gregory has begun making regular visits to chase away coyotes that stay during the daytime. As we drive through the grounds, Gregory says you have to look carefully to spot them. "They blend in really well. You'll see something that looks like a rock and it'll be one of the coyotes."

We do a circuit and then, just to be sure, we go around a second time. "Is that rock, flowers, or coyote?" asks Gregory. We drive closer. It's flowers.

But a little further on we see them. Two coyotes snoozing under a tree, almost unnoticeable as they lie flat in the shade. Gregory stops the truck and asks me to wait while he heads off to deal with them. He wanders down the path and then, suddenly, starts running across the grass straight toward the coyotes, waving his arms as he goes.

The head of one of the coyotes shoots up. It looks at the uniformed animal services' officer tearing toward them for a moment and then starts running. The second coyote immediately jumps up and starts running too.

The coyotes race through the graveyard, every so often looking over their shoulders to check if Gregory is still charging after them.

Eventually, they dive into the hedge that hides the Ventura Freeway from view and head out of the memorial park.

Gregory returns, panting. "This is the other thing the cemetery doesn't like," he says, looking at a gravestone where a coyote poop sits next to the words "Devoted wife and mother."

Chasing will only do so much, he says, wishing he had his paint-ball gun on hand to reinforce the message. "Running at them isn't that much of a deterrent, although it is keeping the fear of humans, which is really important. But it really needs to be done in a much more assertive manner. In an hour they will be back. In the same spot probably."

When it comes to the threat to pets, Gregory thinks coyotes often get blamed for crimes they did not commit. "You ever seen those movies where the guy finds the victim and the knife, and then three other people come round the corner and see him with it and say 'That's the guy who did it'? Same thing happens with wildlife. Yes, they do kill cats, but a lot of times wild animals like coyotes and raccoons are nature's vacuums, picking up the dead," he says.

"We had a deer hit by a car by the observatory, and ten coyotes were on that thing right away. Everyone who saw it after was saying the deer was brought down by the coyotes, which wasn't the case. Another time a coyote was seen running down the street with a cat in its mouth. Guy saw a car hit a cat—a coyote came and picked up the cat almost instantly and ran around the corner. A person round the corner saw the coyote with the cat and called it in."

While coyotes may be wrongly accused in some cases, pets left out in yards are vulnerable to them. "The coyotes aren't looking for pets per se, but during the course of their natural hunt for food they are going to come across pets in yards. If a pet is out in the yard while a person is at work, it can't really go anywhere. It's like self-contained food for a coyote.

"So while they are not the target animal, pets in the five- to ten-pound range end up being part of it. People hear about this and, because coyotes are the most vilified animals in North America, it doesn't take much to get people going."

This deep-rooted fear is something unscrupulous trappers take advantage of, telling tales of coyotes killing seventy-pound dogs and leaping over six-foot-high fences. "I had a lady who called me. She had a 120-pound Great Dane and actually believed that the coyote could pick up the dog," recalls Gregory. "We're talking about a dog that's four or five times the size of a coyote. That would be like Supercoyote, a coyote with a great big *S* on his chest. I said, 'Ma'am, the day that happens I'm leaving this job.'"

People should be more worried about getting attacked by their own pets. "There are roughly four million dog bites in the United States every year and between one to five incidents with a coyote per year per state. It's not that many."

Nonetheless, the scaremongering works. Another problem Gregory is dealing with is an area in the west of the city where people hired a trapper who put down illegal snares. "I confiscated the snares and the public is really pissed off at me," he says. "So I was driving through this area one day, just to see what was going on, and this guy who looked like Santa Claus—big white beard, big belly—starts yelling at me. 'HEY YOU, MOTHERFUCKER. I'M TALKING TO YOU.'

"I'm like what the hell? He goes, 'I heard you're the guy who took away those traps, you asshole, blah, blah, blah.' I said, 'Sir, wait a second.' I had one of the snares in my truck and the guy's concerned about his cat getting killed by coyotes. I said, 'You see this? This is what was being set at openings to fences. Any animal can get caught.'

"He went from cursing at me to cursing at the guy across the street who called the trapper and said, 'I'm sorry I yelled at you. I didn't get the whole story.'"

The reality is, says Gregory, that trapping coyotes is not going to solve the problem. Coyotes are not going away, and people who are worried about their pets need to think twice about leaving pets outside and alone or consider building pet enclosures in their yards.

"I try to equate this to if there is crime in your neighborhood and a burglar is arrested that has been burglarizing homes," he says. "That doesn't mean that everyone who would burglarize homes from that point forth goes, 'I'm never going to burglarize on that street because somebody was arrested there.'

"People have a false belief that if the coyote or raccoon or skunk is trapped that that will be it and it will never happen again. That's like believing if you remove a human there will be no more humans. That's just not realistic. In the last two centuries millions of coyotes have been killed by trappers and shot on farms and so forth. Possibly eighty million or more coyotes killed by humans. Have we solved coyotes? No. It doesn't work.

"At some point people have to stop beating their head against the wall and realize there's got to be another way."

06

THIEVES IN THE TEMPLE

Monkey Trouble in Cape Town and Delhi

Jimmy was trouble. An outlaw who grew up among the destitute. An infamous gangster who terrorized the people of Simon's Town, South Africa. A thief. A killer.

Jimmy was also a baboon. His gang? A troop of baboons living on the mountains that overlook the coastal Cape Town suburb.

His life of crime began at Happy Valley Shelter, a local shelter for the homeless that was once a naval barracks. There he mingled with some of South Africa's poorest, joining them in the soup kitchen queue.

Justin O'Riain, head of the Baboon Research Unit at the University of Cape Town, still remembers the first time he saw Jimmy's troop at the shelter. "I'll never forget the first time we went there. We saw these people lining up for their free food. It was like *Oliver Twist*. Everyone was lining up for the food and sometimes they get given stale, leftover food from bakeries or what have you," he recalls.

"That day, everyone was being handed out doughnuts. The humans tried them and went, 'Oh, these are stale' and they, literally, held their arms out and just behind them or next to them was this baboon troop that would go up to each person, reach out their hands and take their doughnuts. So these poor people got leftover food and, when they didn't take it, the baboons got it."

Jimmy got his taste for human food there. Sugar-coated donuts were, after all, far more appealing than the fynbos shrubs he and the other chacma baboons on the Cape Peninsula usually ate. Even if the doughnuts were stale.

Soon the baboons were supplementing their soup kitchen visits by rifling through bins and stealing unguarded food. Eventually, the baboons' presence in the town came to the attention of city authorities. "The new biologist service provider for Cape Town came on board, goes, 'This is ridiculous,' and starts trying to drive the baboons away," says Justin. "Then all manner of war erupts, because the baboons are not happy with this and they fought back. They started raiding more aggressively."

Most aggressive of all was Jimmy. His heists became legendary. He began breaking into houses, smashing windows in the dead of night to access kitchens. He raided the school, the stores, and even the naval base to load up on human food.

Jimmy was no Robin Hood. He stole from rich and poor alike. The Happy Valley Shelter, where he once ate alongside the people, also became a target, and it was there that Jimmy's actions turned deadly. "Jimmy had gone into a dormitory and picked up a bag of sugar from one of these poor people, and the guy was pretty cross," says Justin.

A chase ensued. The man raced after the thieving primate, who bolted out of the dormitory, bag of sugar in hand. "There was an old man shuffling down a ramp, which had quite a steep drop off the edge. Jimmy wanted to get past him in a hurry, so he jumped on the old man and, with all four limbs, pushed off him to change direction and go up an alley."

In the process, Jimmy pushed the sixty-nine-year-old off the ramp's edge. "It wasn't a big fall, but the man was old. He died of his injuries."

What's amazing, says Justin, is that the man's death wasn't enough to bring Jimmy to justice. "Jimmy wasn't killed for that. Jimmy, an inveterate raider who would steal from poor people, wasn't put down for that."

Jimmy followed up that incident by breaking into the home of the navy admiral's wife. "He got into her house and they had a huge fight. She tried to hit him with a broom. Jimmy grabbed the broom and started shoving it back into her. They were tugging to and fro. But even that wasn't enough to remove Jimmy the baboon."

Jimmy finally crossed the line when he found a new gang, a baboon troop to the south of Simon's Town. There he discovered the Black Marlin, a restaurant and tourist hotspot overlooking False Bay. Inevitably, Jimmy couldn't resist the temptation to help himself to some of the Cape Malay seafood curry and grilled crayfish being served to the tourists.

"Jimmy would jump onto tables full of tourists," says Justin. "The tourists would squeal in horror and, of course, it would be the highlight of their stories when they went home, how this baboon jumped on them and how amazing it was. But Jimmy started pushing the envelope. He started nipping them."

In a way, it was good thing Jimmy only nipped people, says Justin. "Baboons have huge teeth and they are immensely strong. They could be killing us every day of every week and they don't. They just never seem to use their amazing weaponry on us. Even when we try to take food back from them, they will give a nip but they never use those big canines like they do on each other."

Nonetheless, nipping was bad enough, so the authorities finally brought Jimmy in. His sentence: death by lethal injection.

Justin was among those involved in capturing him. At first all seemed to go well. Jimmy, greedy as ever, happily entered the trap to scoff the fruit inside. As the notorious baboon ate the bait, the team shut the cage door and knocked Jimmy out with a pole dart.

Then, as they began to carry the cage indoors, Jimmy's troop tried to save their trapped comrade. Bongo, the alpha male of Jimmy's troop, charged at the team, who distracted him by rolling apples in his direction. Bongo stopped, stuffed the apples into his cheeks, and resumed the charge.

The team quickly began chopping up apples and scattering the pieces. Bongo's stomach got the better of his brain. As he scooped up the apple pieces, the team swiftly lugged the cage indoors. Jimmy's crimes ended there.

Jimmy isn't the only one of the 350 or so baboons that live on the Cape Peninsula to go rogue. Combined, these large monkeys, which have dark brown to black fur and downward sloping purple-black faces, have a rap sheet to rival any Old West desperado.

Another notorious baboon was William, the stalker of Scarborough, a small town on the eastern shore of the Cape. "He would wait for one particular woman to come back from her shopping trip," says Justin. "He would be hiding in the bushes, and when she parked her car and had to walk the ten spaces to her house and open the sliding door, he would rush her and steal the shopping."

Even if she made it through the door before being mugged, she wasn't safe. "He would physically remove the sliding door, take it off its runners, and get into the house. He would chase her into a room and then make his way quietly and calmly to the kitchen, open the fridge door, take out the butter, take out the eggs, open the cupboard, and eat the sugar. He shared all our frailties for food: he went for the refined carbohydrates and the protein—the eggs, the sugars, the pastas, and the rices."

One time, when the woman was eight months pregnant, she realized, after being chased into a room by William, that her three-year-old son was alone in the house with the baboon. "She kept trying to come out and he kept charging her. She was deeply traumatized as any mother would be."

After that the family had the door runners deepened to try to stop William from removing the door again. The day after, William broke the casing around the door's window and got into the house again. Like Jimmy, William was captured and killed, despite public demonstrations calling for his release by local animal rights activists.

Other Scarborough baboons have also pushed the boundaries. Some have broken into homes via pet doors or by ripping out windows. In one daring raid a troop scaled the wall of an apartment block to reach an open window. After looting the cupboard and the fridge, they left, taking a large teddy bear and a pink curtain with them.

Similar incidents have happened across the suburbs on the Cape Peninsula. Baboons have mugged shoppers at farmers' markets for their bags, shoved people aside to get to bins, and ripped backpacks off the backs of hikers. Rival baboon troops have even battled for control of food-rich picnic sites.

Little gets in their way, says Justin. "Every kind of door handle, they have cracked. Baboon-proof bins, it takes them seven days to work out how to work the latches. One of the most amazing stories is there was this hole in the eaves of a house, made of soft material like Rhino Board. A baboon worked the hole, broke through the eaves, and then fell through the ceiling into the house."

The most famous Cape Town baboon of all was Fred, the car-jacker. "What would happen is tourists would see baboons on the side of the road sitting there looking quite sedate on a pole," says Justin. "They would stop their car and walk up to take a photo-graph, leaving their car door open or closed but unlocked. Fred would watch you carefully and, if you left your door open, he would just run up and jump into the car, and go through all the bags.

"He got to the stage where if you locked your car but were returning to it and pressed the unlock beep-beep thing, he would hear the noise, know that your car was open and get there before you, push you out of the way and get into your car.

"One of my funniest stories ever is watching Fred and these five men. They stopped their car on the side of the road, got out with their cell phone cameras, and walked toward Fred, who was about a hundred meters down the road. Next thing, Fred sees that all four doors were open so he starts running at them. They panicked and ran back to the car. They just made it. Three in the back, two in the front, thinking: 'Jeepers, that was close.'"

Then Fred opened one of the car doors and jumped in. "The car jiggled and wiggled and then all four doors opened. Two of them fell out of the back onto the ground and the third man was screaming. Fred went through the car, through the glove compartments—he knew how to open all kinds of glove compartments—discovered there was only water and left."

Eventually, Fred's habit of getting into cars with people inside brought his carjacking antics to an end. Fittingly, his final hours involved a car chase. After his capture, the caged baboon was loaded onto a pickup truck that then set off on a forty-mile journey to the veterinarian clinic that would administer his lethal injection. Soon the truck drivers noticed something was up. They were being followed. Behind them was Joss Lean, a filmmaker and opponent of the plan to euthanize Fred. Lean had filmed Fred's capture and was now following the vehicle in the hope of last-minute reprieve.

Unnerved, the drivers ferrying Fred to the vet called in an escort. Meanwhile, the South African campaign group Baboon Matters made frantic last-minute pleas for Fred's release. But it was too late; Fred had gone too far. He was delivered to the vet and put down. A week later the activists who tried to save Fred held a candlelit wake at the Black Marlin restaurant to remember the departed animal outlaw.

Fred's death also revealed just how bad Cape Town's baboon problems had gotten. "When he died we had him X-rayed," says Justin. "He had over seventy two bits of metal in him, seventy-two different pellets: buckshot, birdshot, pellet guns, and more. He had a deeply embedded signature of conflict with people in him."

The discovery of Fred's injuries proved to be a crucial moment in how Cape Town dealt with the baboons. Until then the goal was to achieve some kind of coexistence where people could live alongside the monkeys, with only the most aggressive baboons being taken out. People were encouraged to keep their doors locked and to plant native plants in their garden rather than the exotic plants baboons prefer to eat.

In some ways the plan made sense. The baboons of the Cape Peninsula are unique, cut off from the rest of Africa's baboons by the urban sprawl of Cape Town. What's more, they also appear to play an important role in seed dispersal in the peninsula, much of which is a World Heritage Site, so losing them could put this valuable ecosystem at risk. In light of this the Cape baboons are protected by law.

But what Fred's bullet-peppered body revealed was that those who had to live with the likes of William and Jimmy were simply not going to stand aside as baboons terrorized them in their homes. In fact, attitudes toward those preaching coexistence got so bad that people started pelting them with tomatoes at public meetings.

"The public decided that if the authorities are not going to sort them out, they were going to," says Justin. "More and more baboons were dying terrible deaths at the hands of civilians. They were dying from dogs, from electrocutions, from poisons, and from guns. They were dying from the worst kind of gunshots; air gunshots that just pierce the gut and then cause septicemia over a five-day period, causing massive pain. Also, the public was starting to actively hate not only baboons but also wildlife in general. We were very conscious of that as a very negative consequence of urban conflict."

Thanks, in large part, to Fred's bullet-ridden body, the evidence became convincing enough for animal welfare organizations like the Society for the Prevention of Cruelty of Animals to support a new approach designed to encourage baboons to stay away from people. "It was agreed that it is better to be harsh on the baboons than to allow them to get injured and killed by the public," says Justin. "We reached a point where we said to the activists that if you care for baboons, you must scare baboons."

Today Cape Town has a team that works to scare baboons away from urban areas using equipment such as paintball markers and

bear bangers. Justin's next hope is that at some point the authorities will agree to erect a baboon-proof electric fence around the
national park to keep them out of the urban areas. "No one likes the
idea of baboons being chased with paintball markers, and although
it works, some still break away. Recently they approved the killing
of another baboon in Scarborough who decided he is not scared of
paintball markers and is running into the town. So we've suggested
a fence between the national park and residential area. We've got a
lot of resistance, but I know it's the best thing."

Curbing the baboon conflicts in Cape Town could also make
people richer, says Justin. "There's a lot of talk about how we should
be exploiting the baboons as a tourist asset more than we do, but
you can't do that until you remove the conflict. When people go to
Cape Point they want to see the baboons and that makes millions
of rand. They have a serious tourist value."

The baboons are fun too, he adds. "They are very, very funny,
entertaining animals. They are way better than any carnivore or
antelope because they do crazy stuff in front of you," he says. "They
get on your car, they masturbate in front of you, and if you watch
the juveniles playing it is so like humans in a playground. It's just
that humans and baboons are oil and water—they don't mix."

.·:·**➤.•●**

Justin may call the baboons of Cape Town "the most troublesome
nonhuman primate genus," but there is competition. In India and
Bangladesh, a different urban monkey is causing trouble: the rhesus
macaque.

They are much smaller than chacma baboons, weighing in at just
seventeen pounds compared to South Africa's eighty-eight-pound
monkeys. They are shorter too, measuring around one foot seven
inches tall—about half the height of a baboon. But while they appear
weedier, rhesus macaques are no less troublesome. And, unlike Cape
Town's baboons, which pick on areas close to the national park,
these pink-faced primates venture deep into the urban jungle.

In Delhi and the pink-walled Indian city of Jaipur, there are thought to be tens of thousands of these brown-gray monkeys. They are adept city dwellers. They snooze on rooftops, slide down drainpipes, scamper along overhead electric cables, bathe in public fountains, and clamber up telephone poles.

Some even use public transport. One time a rhesus macaque joined commuters on a Delhi Metro train at Chandni Chowk station. As nervous human passengers watched, he rode the Yellow Line train north, eventually ending up at the underground stop of Civil Lines, where the carriage was evacuated. After a short standoff, the monkey decided it was his stop after all and left the train.

Like the Cape Town baboons, the macaques are not above thievery. Stall owners at Jaipur's fruit market are regular targets, harassed daily by shoplifting monkeys out to steal their wares. Raids often start with a lone monkey that distracts the trader. Then, as the owner chases away the first monkey, the others pile in, grabbing everything they can. Each time the trader chases another away, other members get their chance to steal.

Some carry out muggings, snatching candy from the hands of children and intimidating people by surrounding them until they hand over food. They also get into homes and offices, sneaking in through open doors and windows to ransack kitchens. Some have even broken into India's Ministry of Defence.

Stories about their exploits abound. These tales range from the amusing, like the macaque that repeatedly stole bottles of whiskey from a central Delhi liquor store, to the disturbing, such as a monkey kidnapping a baby through an open window. There are even reports of monkeys stealing intravenous units from patients on stretchers as they are wheeled into hospital so they can drink the liquid in the IV bags.

It's hard to know how exaggerated these stories are, but there's no doubt that some encounters do turn violent. Significant numbers of people in Delhi and Jaipur have been bitten after disturbing monkeys that have broken into their homes. Others have died, often from falling after being chased or frightened by the primates. In 2004 a newlywed woman fell to her death in the eastern Indian city of Patna while running away from a group of monkeys. In 2009 a nine-year-old boy jumped to his death from the third floor of his Jaipur home in a bid to escape.

The macaques' most high-profile victim was Sawinder Singh Bajwa, the deputy mayor of Delhi. It was a Saturday morning in October 2007 and Bajwa was reading a newspaper on the second-floor balcony of his three-story white stucco home in the upmarket Savita Vihar neighborhood in east Delhi. As he read, a small group of monkeys turned up. They had probably come from the grounds of a nearby Hindu temple that was home to around a hundred rhesus macaques.

The Sikh politician grabbed a stick and waved it aggressively at the monkeys, hoping to scare them away. But instead of running, the monkeys lunged at him. Startled, Bajwa stepped backward and fell off the edge of the balcony. He was rushed to the hospital but died the next day from head injuries inflicted by his thirteen-foot fall.

Bajwa's death prompted a swift response from the embarrassed city authorities. For years people had been campaigning for the city to do something about the monkeys, even persuading a court to order the Municipal Corporation of Delhi to act. But little had happened. Despite the sprawling Indian capital boasting as many as 60,000 macaques, the city captured just 225 in 2006. Although that's unsurprising, given that the corporation had employed just one monkey catcher to cover the entire metropolis.

After Bajwa's death, the city stepped up its monkey-catching work. By the end of 2007 it had taken almost four and a half thousand monkeys off the streets—two thirds of which were trapped in the two months after Bajwa's fatal fall.

With monkeys being incarcerated by the thousands, the city found itself with a new challenge: what to do with them. Initially they were housed at a temporary facility, pending transfer to another location in India. But Delhi soon found that the rest of India didn't want them, either because they already had enough monkey problems themselves or because they did not want to start importing troublesome city primates into their area. A few demanded huge sums of money for taking in the macaques.

Eventually, Delhi opened a wildlife sanctuary on the edge of the city as a permanent home for the former street primates. Not that all the monkeys were willing to resign themselves to life in the sanctuary. Several captives scaled the walls of the facility and made their way back to the city.

Delhi also called in help from the langur wallahs, the people who made their living from training Hanuman langur monkeys to perform tricks on the city streets. Rhesus macaques are frightened of these larger, gray-furred and black-faced monkeys, so the city figured they could be used to scare the monkey menace away. Soon langur wallahs became regular sights in the richest districts of Delhi as they patrolled the streets with langurs on leashes and encouraged their performing monkeys to urinate on the walls to keep the macaques away. Delhi Metro Rail even hired one for a month to patrol Kashmere Gate, one of the city's largest stations.

The plan went well until, in November 2012, the Indian government notified the city that using langurs in this way breached wildlife protection laws. The city reluctantly abandoned the langur patrols and found itself having to advise staff to keep their office windows shut at all times to keep the macaques at bay.

If Delhi's response to dealing with the monkeys seems half-hearted, that's because it is. For Hindus, monkeys are more than just monkeys—they are gods. Monkeys of all kinds, rhesus macaques included, are seen as living representatives of Hanuman, the monkey-faced god that gave langurs their name.

Hanuman is an important figure in Hindu scripture. In the Hindu epic of Ramayana, he rescues Sita, the wife of Rama—the seventh incarnation of the supreme god Vishnu—from the demon king Ravana. After searching the land, Hanuman finds Ravana and, backed by an army of monkeys, defeats him in a fierce battle. The subsequent reunion of Rama and Sita came to represent the victory of good over evil in the religion.

One tradition that grew out of his story is that on Tuesdays and Sundays, many Hindus make offerings of grain and fruit to Hanuman at temples dedicated to him. For city-dwelling rhesus macaques this belief means they are welcomed on the grounds of temples and are regularly provided with large amounts of food by the devoted.

As Delhi's wildlife warden told the *New York Times* in 2012: "Some communities in the city feed the monkeys by the carful. They do not give a care about the hungry children on the street, but will feed the monkeys." Deliberate feeding of the monkeys is so common that the Delhi authorities have even argued that the macaques are no longer wildlife and, therefore, not their problem.

Unsurprisingly, the bountiful supplies of food have made cities highly attractive to rhesus macaques. In 1980 only 15 percent of rhesus macaques had any contact with people. Today 86 percent have contact with people. Urban expansion explains some of that shift, but the monkeys are also choosing to live in the cities.

For the monkeys that do leave rural life behind, life is often better, as demonstrated by a study in the city of Dhaka, Bangladesh. Hoping to see how a steady supply of food from people altered the behavior of rhesus macaques, researchers compared the activities of a group of eighty macaques living on the grounds of a pharmaceutical factory in central Dhaka with another group living in a rural area more than forty miles to the north.

The city group was pampered to say the least. Each day a government driver would turn up to deliver four hundred bananas for them to feast on. On top of that the drugs company, Sadhona Traditional Pharmaceutical, would give the monkeys eleven pounds of chickpeas for breakfast before returning in the afternoon with another chickpea meal. Then there were the wild and garden plants in a nearby park that the monkeys could help themselves to. And, as if that wasn't quite enough, visitors regularly turned up to supply the macaques with treats of bread, crackers, and cookies.

Two differences between the Dhaka and rural group stood out. First, the city monkeys rested more than those living in the countryside. The Dhaka troop also socialized more, spending much more time grooming one other and playing with each other. It was as if, thanks to the copious human offerings, the city monkeys had moved beyond the physiological and safety levels of Maslow's hierarchy of needs and could now indulge themselves in the love and belonging stage.

City life also helps monkeys overcome the unpredictability of nature. Between 1999 and 2001 the Indian state of Rajasthan suffered a severe drought that wiped out nearly half of the Hanuman langurs that lived in the Kumbhalgarh Wildlife Sanctuary. Yet two hours' drive away, the langurs living in the city of Jodhpur barely noticed. In 2001 their population had changed little from when the drought began, their resilience credited to their status as a holy species willing to live among people. It seemed that, at least in this case, the city was better at conservation than the national park that had been created to protect the monkeys.

India's urban monkeys may cause plenty of problems but there is another, more frightening animal, that prowls the nation's cities.

THE LION OF HOLLYWOOD

Tracking Leopards in Mumbai and L.A.'s Cougar

It's six o'clock on Christmas Day 2011 and Kanjurmarg East is a ghost town.

Usually, this eastern suburb of Mumbai would be teeming with life at this hour, but instead the shops are shut and the street hawkers have long packed up. The children who would normally be playing outside are nowhere to be seen. Even the local factories are idle, their night shifts canceled. The streets are deserted. Instead the suburb's thirty thousand residents are indoors with their doors locked and their windows shut, too frightened to step outside until sunrise.

The fear set in a week earlier. Dilip Dalvi, a worker at Echjay Forgings, had just finished eating his breakfast in Machine Shop B when he saw something move behind one of the machines. He thought it was a dog, but on looking again he soon realized it was no dog.

Dilip ran as fast as his legs would carry him. As he made for the exit, he screamed at his colleagues: "Run! A leopard has come!"

The workshop dissolved into pandemonium. Workers rushed out of the door and slammed it shut behind them, trapping the beast inside. They hurriedly locked the door and then, for good measure, pushed a twenty-two-pound iron block against the entrance.

From inside Machine Shop B came the sound of angry roars and then loud thuds as the trapped leopard began hurling itself against the door. The workers called the police. The police arrived and asked the forest department to come and deal with the trapped leopard.

Then, as the police and workers drank tea while waiting for the forest department to arrive, the leopard once more threw itself against the locked door. This time, the door burst open. The now free leopard, its spotted fur black with machine oil, let out an almighty roar.

Teacups and saucers crashed to the ground, as police and workers fled in panic. For a brief moment, Dilip found himself right in front of the beast, boxed in by the parked police van. But instead of attacking, the leopard dived under the van, before sprinting over the compound wall and into the surrounding slums.

By the time the forest department arrived, the leopard was gone.

Word spread through the suburb about the leopard at the metalworks. As night approached, people retreated inside and traders packed up early. The few shops that stayed open after dark found there were no customers to serve and ended up closing early too.

After a few days the panic began to subside, but then came a second sighting—again on the factory grounds. The forest department sent out a search party. They found scratch marks on a tree and some scat. It was enough to confirm the leopard had been there, but despite their searching they missed the beast itself. The fear set in again and people, once more, shut themselves away after dark. The panic only faded for good after several more days without a sighting.

Leopards are no strangers to India's cities. In 2007 dozens of people in the city of Nashik chased a leopard through the streets, eventually cornering the animal and beating it to death with sticks and stones. And just a month after the Kanjurmarg East sightings, a leopard ended up on the streets of Guwahati, the largest city in northeast India. It was first seen in the morning, near a crematorium where the funeral for a political leader's son was being held. The police chased the animal away from the VIP-packed funeral, but instead of heading out of the city, the leopard ran toward the busy suburb of Silpukhuri. After evading the police by leaping across several rooftops, the leopard jumped down into the streets below.

Alarmed citizens grabbed iron bars and sticks to defend themselves, and as they tried to scare the beast away, it turned on them. One man had part of his scalp removed by a swipe from one of the leopard's claws. Another was mauled and later died from the severe head and neck injuries the animal inflicted on him. Eventually, the beast was locked inside a shop, tranquilized, and taken to a wildlife sanctuary.

Leopards are even more common in Mumbai. By some measures India's financial capital has the highest density of these endangered cats anywhere on earth. Most of Mumbai's leopards live within Sanjay Gandhi National Park, the forty-square-mile reserve that the city has built itself around. But some have grown used to the busy, noisy streets around them. The stray dogs that roam the slums bordering the park are regular targets, and one of the park's leopards even paid a visit to the five-star Renaissance Hotel that overlooks Powai Lake. Another was caught on security camera entering an apartment block foyer late at night and leaving soon after with a small dog in its jaws.

Attacks on people are rare but not unknown. In 2012 in one of the city's slums, a leopard attacked and dragged away a seven-year-old girl who had gone outside with her mother late at night to go to the toilet. Despite a frantic search through the night, the girl was never seen alive again. The next morning, all that could be found was her severed head.

Although no one was killed or injured by the leopard of Kanjurmarg East, its presence was shocking for a different reason. Most
encounters with leopards in Indian cities are attributed to the animals wandering in from rural areas by accident. But unlike the slum
where the girl was killed or the apartment block where the dog was
snatched, Kanjurmarg East is miles away from the national park.
To reach Machine Shop B, the leopard would have had to navigate
a forest, pass over railroad tracks, and cross large, busy roads. It
would have traveled through a university campus, residential areas,
factory grounds, and a huge slum. The Kanjurmarg East leopard was
anything but a case of a leopard that had lost its way.

What's more, evidence is mounting that India's leopards live
among people far more than anyone imagined.

Vidya Athreya, a biologist at Wildlife Conservation Society–India,
is one of the people studying how leopards use human-dominated
habitats. "When I started working on this ten years back, I had
no clue about leopards living in human-use landscapes, so I also
thought that those leopards were abnormal because that was all I
had learnt over the years from my peers," she says.

Her research began in Junnar, an agricultural region about
120 miles east of Mumbai. The region had been having trouble
with leopards for years. Livestock and pets had been killed and,
on average, about four people were attacked every year. To solve
the problem, the region's forest department began capturing leopards and releasing them in wildlife sanctuaries and other remote
locations. After doing this for a while it asked Vidya to assess how
effective the strategy was.

The findings surprised everyone. Vidya included. "They started
catching a load of leopards and leaving them in the forest, but then
a lot of people were attacked there. There were about fifty attacks.
In a couple of cases the released leopards actually attacked and
killed people near the site of release."

Far from bringing leopards under control, the relocations were
making them more dangerous. The trouble was the relocated

leopards were not from the forests they were dumped in. The unfamiliar territory meant they had little idea of where to find food, there were other leopards to deal with too, and the process of relocation had left them stressed. Lost and hungry in an unfamiliar place, the desperate leopards began to see people as a tempting prey.

"I realized that the animals living in human-use landscapes were living there with very low levels of conflict, and when you start taking them out and leaving them in the forests because we expect them to be in the forests, we're actually messing it up," says Vidya.

"The leopard's home is where it is. It has a social system, mothers, sisters, and aunts all living nearby, and when we mess it up simply because we don't think they should be there we are actually worsening the problem."

The removals didn't solve the problems back in Junnar, either. Every time a leopard was removed, another took its place. These new leopards were often younger and less used to people and, as such, more likely to try attacking someone or their animals than those that had been captured, which, Vidya discovered, hadn't been much of a threat in the first place. "When I was writing down the reasons for their capture, I realized that all these animals were caught just because they were seen or because they had killed a dog. None of them were caught because they killed people."

Vidya's findings brought the capture-and-release program to a swift end, but the results fired up her own interest in learning more about how leopards live with people. "I've always been fascinated by large cats and had tried to do some work in the typical protected area in the forest and stuff. But when I started working on the Junnar study, I realized this was way more fascinating than just a leopard in a forest."

The clash of wildlife, people, and politics proved more complex and intriguing than the usual trips to wildlife sanctuaries. "For me, looking at a BBC documentary on forests, I will fall asleep because it's just so pretty and sterile, but these issues where animals and people are interacting—it's totally stimulating."

One study took her to Akole, a town of twenty thousand people some thirty-five miles north of Junnar. There she found leopards living in higher densities than in wildlife sanctuaries. At night the cats would venture close to people's homes, sometimes visiting the same house every few days without ever disturbing the occupants who slept outside. There were even leopards giving birth in the sugarcane fields that lay just three hundred feet from the edge of town.

Yet no one in Akole seemed aware of the leopards, and there were no reports of anyone being killed in the town. The leopards, she found, were attracted to town by the large numbers of stray dogs and pigs that lived off the garbage people were dumping in the open. The pigs and dogs came for the rubbish, and the leopards came for them.

A similar pattern may explain why leopards prowl the slums and fringes of Mumbai and other large Indian cities. "It seems to be that in the last twenty or thirty years the kind of organic garbage that has flooded India has allowed a lot of other life, especially feral dogs and pigs, to take up residence in great numbers and that has lead to more leopards coming there," says Vidya.

In another of her studies, Vidya tracked the movements of Ajoba, an old male leopard whose name means grandfather in Marathi. Ajoba was caught after falling down a well in Takali Dhokeshwar, a village more than a hundred miles from Mumbai. Vidya and her team rescued him, fitted him with a GPS collar, and set him loose so they could follow his travels.

Over the next three months they watched Ajoba travel closer and closer to Mumbai. Along the way he passed through human settlements, crossed roads, and chased stray dogs in the streets. He crossed railroad tracks near train stations and even prowled through an industrial complex on the outskirts of Mumbai before finally settling down in the Sanjay Gandhi National Park. Yet not once on this journey was any sighting of the elderly leopard reported.

The reality is that leopards make no distinction between human and wild habitat, says Vidya. "The question is whose land is it? From the leopards' perspective, it's their land. It's not aberrant, they live here, and with really low levels of conflict, if you leave them alone. Wild animals do not recognize our protected area borders. Nobody has given them a workshop saying 'These are the boundaries and you guys should stay inside there.'"

For much of the time leopards live among the people of India unseen and we only hear about it in the rare moments when their cover is blown or they attack. It's not the leopard in the street that's abnormal, it's the urban leopard seen in the street. "In my research I've found, to my greatest surprise, that there are a hell of a lot of animals living among a hell of a lot of people and this is actually the baseline," Vidya says. "But the media and researchers only look at conflict."

India's cities are not the only ones with big cats, and the world's most famous large, urban feline lives, appropriately enough, in Hollywood. P-22, a mountain lion, lives in Griffith Park, the home of the Hollywood sign, and his discovery was pure fluke.

The park is part of the Santa Monica Mountains, but thanks to the Los Angeles sprawl it is cut off from the rest of the range by the Hollywood Freeway and urban development. Griffith Park's unusual status as an island of natural habitat in an ocean of development had long piqued the interest of biologists. They wanted to find out if animals were traveling in and out of the park when the only safe routes to and fro were a few bridges and underpasses crossing the busy Hollywood Freeway.

To shed some light on this, Miguel Ordeñana, a biologist at the Natural History Museum of Los Angeles, put motion-detecting cameras around the park and the routes over US 101 to get photos of passing animals. Miguel wasn't looking for mountain lions. It was assumed that these secretive animals, which are also called cougars, wouldn't venture across a noisy freeway to get to a hard-to-reach park. Instead, he was on the lookout for deer, coyotes, skunks, and other animals already known to live in Griffith Park.

"It was February 2012," says Miguel. "I check my cameras once every two weeks and I was looking through the photos one afternoon, hoping to see a bobcat as that was the most rare, coolest thing at the time. I went through the photos and was really excited to see a bobcat in there.

"I was really pumped about that and then, all of a sudden, I go to the next photo and see a big mountain lion in the picture. It was a huge surprise. I would never have expected it because, although it is technically possible for it to get to the park, it is just so unlikely. It was just amazing. As soon as I saw it I contacted my collaborators and Laurel."

Laurel Serieys, a UCLA PhD candidate, had been helping out with a National Park Service project tracking mountain lions in the Santa Monicas. Like Miguel, she was shocked by the discovery of a cougar in Griffith Park. "The park is too small for a normal mountain lion gang," she says. "He most likely crossed two freeways to get there, and it is unusual to see a mountain lion crossing a major freeway successfully. In fact, there's only one documented case and that was a smaller freeway. This freeway was ten lanes."

Soon after, the National Park Service trapped the then three-year-old animal so they could give him a radio collar that would let them track his movements. Before setting him free, they did a genetic test that confirmed he came from the Santa Monicas and, in line with the unglamorous naming system the service uses for all the cougars it tracks, they christened him P-22.

The park service has been following P-22 around Griffith Park ever since. One area of keen interest, given his proximity to the city, is his diet, so every week Laurel and Miguel have been heading into the park to check out locations where P-22 was hanging around for long periods to try to retrieve the remains of his kills.

They invited me along on one of their trips. The goal? To visit three suspected P-22 kill sites.

It's a busy, hot Sunday morning when I join Laurel and Miguel at the park. The parking lots are packed and the footpaths are filled with joggers and hikers, but we soon depart from the crowds to head into more rugged terrain.

The trek to the first kill site turns out to be an arduous trip, and I'm soon cursing myself for not following Laurel's advice to get some hiking boots. Sneakers are really not designed for scrambling up rocky hills or getting down steep gullies. Within minutes my jeans and shirt are covered in smears of yellow-beige dirt and my hands are covered in scratches from thorny bushes. Although we can clearly see the skyscrapers of downtown L.A. in the distance, the landscape is wild and unforgiving for unfit writers with inappropriate shoes.

"You're not going to die are you?" Laurel asks me at one point. "I hope not," I reply weakly, before slipping down another slope on my backside. No wonder biologists call the cougars on our doorstep near-urban rather than urban.

"There was one kill that took me four hours to find," says Laurel as we clamber through the scrub. "It was a really hot day, hotter than today. It was my first time out hiking in a while and it was insanely steep and thicker than this. I felt like I was very close to having heatstroke. I told Miguel I was just going to quickly find this kill and then we could meet up and we'll go find some more. Two hours in, he phones up and is like, 'You OK?' I'm like, 'I'm done. I don't think we'll be going out.' But I found it."

After an hour and a half, Miguel calls us over. He has found something. On the ground by his feet are the dusty, dried-out remains of a kill. There are a couple of severed legs and a mess of fur, skin, and bone that was once the animal's rear end. There's also a skull, its jaws locked wide open, frozen in a permanent scream.

"It's a fox," says Laurel, as she puts on her gloves and picks up the skull. "A gray fox."

She looks more closely at the skull, which is covered in small patches of desiccated fur. "Is that a bite mark?" she asks Miguel. "It looks like it's been chewed on. I wonder if a coyote killed it. That would be my guess."

I ask what makes her think it's a coyote kill rather than a P-22 kill. "It could be a lion but coyotes chew on the bones, whereas the lions don't chew on the bones as much. Lions will bite on the head more."

She looks at the skull again. "I don't know if that's just the flesh rotting or an actual bite mark."

There's only one way to tell, so Laurel pulls away the flesh, separating it from the skull. "Hmmm, looks like there is a bite mark. It could be a lion kill, although the lion would probably have eaten more than that. Theoretically, if it was a lion kill the coyotes could have got to it afterward."

As well as the remains of the gray fox, there's a leg bone from a deer. It's been picked clean. "Is that a mountain lion kill?" I ask hopefully. "Ah, probably not," says Laurel. Coyotes again. The evidence from the first kill site has proven inconclusive.

We move on to the next location. Along the way we spot a pack of coyotes roaming along the bottom of the hill below us, just a few hundred feet from the expensive hillside homes overlooking Griffith Park. The next kill site turns out to be within a large garden filled with stumpy cacti and guarded by a metal gate adorned with a sign telling people to stay out. Trespassing isn't an option, so we head off to the third and final kill site.

As we struggle up a steep hill, I ask Laurel what they hope to learn from P-22's leftovers. "A lot of people have misconceptions about what the wild animals are eating," she says. "So it's a general diet study to show that they are eating deer like they are supposed to, even in these very urban environments, and that they're not just picking off people's dogs."

So it's just a myth that P-22 will be feasting on people's dogs? "That's a very commonly held belief," she says. "People will often have the misconception that mountain lions are coming into their backyard and picking off pets when it's more likely to be coyotes or other smaller animals, like owls taking people's cats. But people are always blaming it on mountain lions."

Mountain lions prefer to eat deer and elk. In the Santa Ana Mountains on the other side of L.A., mule deer make up 95 percent of what cougars eat. Coyotes account for another 4 percent of their diet.

Nonetheless, cougar attacks on pet dogs can happen. In 2013 one pounced on a dachshund being walked near the southwestern outskirts of Colorado Springs. The lion grabbed the dog, pulling the still-attached leash out of the owner's hand, before running away and eating it. A few hours later the cougar was caught and euthanized.

Such incidents are distressing and gain a lot of attention, but mountain lions very rarely prey on pets, even when they are readily available. A study of cougar kills in the west of Washington state found that domestic animals, including livestock, formed less than 3 percent of their prey, even though the region examined included residential areas on the edge of Seattle, such as Issaquah. Of the domestic animals that were killed, the overwhelming majority were livestock, with sheep, goats, and llamas alone accounting for more than three-quarters of the victims. Nor was there any indication that the cougars were focusing their hunting in the residential areas, suggesting that domestic animal kills were opportunistic rather than systematic.

"Generally, mountain lions are not even getting close to people's yards," says Laurel. "So for the National Park Service mountain lion survey, the majority of the mountain lion locations they get from the radio collars are a kilometer away from even roads. So despite being in L.A. where there are parks that are very urban, they will just stick to those core natural areas when they can." The few that do enter the streets, like the one that entered downtown Reno in the summer of 2012 and tried—unsuccessfully—to enter Harrah's Casino Hotel, are usually young males looking for new territory after being forced out by older males.

So it's something of a surprise when the route to the third kill site takes us out of Griffith Park and onto a road. After getting our bearings we figure out that the location is up the driveway of a large house. We head up to the front door.

Laurel checks the map again. The site seems to lie right behind the house, although Laurel doesn't think the kill happened in the backyard. "On the satellite images it looks like there's more open space behind the property than we can see from here, but those images are a few years old so it's hard to know exactly what is there."

But there's no way to find out without going through the house, and that's a problem. After all, what is the etiquette for turning up on someone's doorstep, plastered in dirt and dripping with sweat, to ask if you can see their backyard because you think a lion killed something right by their house?

After a short discussion, Laurel and Miguel decide that broaching the subject with the homeowner is best left to a uniformed representative from the Park Service, so we leave empty-handed with not a single confirmed P-22 kill to show for our troubles.

Although today's kills proved elusive, other days have been more successful. "We got a lot more last weekend," says Laurel. "We found a coyote, two deer, and a raccoon."

On the way back, Miguel tells me how he hopes P-22 will make people less frightened about cougars living near cities. "The media likes to make these mountain lions seem very dangerous, but having P-22 right in this very urban area in a small park is a testament to how, even in these urban areas, they are not going to be like a coyote and start asking for food," he says.

⋰⋱•᪥

Although city life hasn't done much to change mountain lions, it has had a profound effect on another potential man-eater. For the past thirty years American black bears have moved into urban North America in a big way. From New Jersey to New Mexico, sightings and complaints about urban bears have soared as new developments encroach on their habitat and the appeal of garbage draws them to the bright lights.

Smart and adaptable, black bears have been making the most of what cities can offer hungry bears. In Colorado Springs one enterprising bear wheeled away a five-hundred-pound Dumpster from the back of Edelweiss Restaurant, just south of downtown. After dragging the German restaurant's Dumpster to a parking lot, the bear gorged on leftover Wiener schnitzel and grilled bratwurst. The bear must have liked its takeaway because the following night it returned to steal another of the restaurant's Dumpsters.

In Anchorage bears have learned how to deal with the electric fences people use to keep them out of their property, avoiding those with three or more electrified strands while stepping through the gap in those with just two wires.

Few places have had an influx of black bears as startling as that seen in the towns and cities near Lake Tahoe. Between 1997 and 2006 the area's bears switched en masse from a rural life to an urban one. Complaints about them in places like Carson City and South Lake Tahoe rose ten-fold and the number of bears involved in traffic accidents increased seventeen-fold. So many bears have moved in that the Lake Tahoe Basin now boasts one of the highest densities of urban black bears in North America and biologists are finding it a real challenge to find bears outside the city limits.

But the bears didn't just relocate. They changed.

For a start, they got fatter. Spoiled by the abundance of human food to eat, the urban bears ended up almost a third heavier than those in the wild. In fact the amount of food on offer in the towns and cities was so great that bears would even stop feeding when there was more food available, despite their need to eat fifteen thousand or more calories every day.

They became less active too. Their home ranges shriveled by as much as 90 percent and even in the buildup to hibernation they remained less active than rural bears. They also became night owls, rarely venturing out until the sun began to set, presumably to reduce their chances of bumping into people. In contrast rural bears are active during the daytime too.

There were odder, less easily explained changes as well. In the urban areas there were more than four times as many male bears than in the wild. Then, there were the females. In the wild the average female bear gets pregnant at seven or eight years old, but in the city they were getting pregnant at four or five. Some were getting pregnant as young as two years old, mere months after separating from their mother.

But if Lake Tahoe's towns and cities sound like a bear paradise of Dumpsters overflowing with free pizza, there's a big downside. Urban bears die young. Of the twenty-two bears tracked by scientists in the Lake Tahoe Basin, twelve lived in urban areas. By the age of ten they were all dead, while six of the rural bears were still alive and kicking.

Vehicle collisions are the main killer, responsible for not only the deaths of many adults but also the high rates of cub mortality among urban bears. An added danger is that bears looking for food in urban areas run into trouble with people and get killed. What's more, the urban bears are dying faster than they can reproduce, making their population reliant on newcomers moving in from the country.

For the black bears of Lake Tahoe, the city is a siren song, luring them in with the promise of a more-than-you-can-eat buffet before sending them to an early grave. It's not the same everywhere. The extreme heat and dryness of the Lake Tahoe area seems to make the city extra attractive for black bears, but in more hospitable climates they use cities differently. In Aspen, Colorado, the bears are nomads. In years where bad weather makes food scarce in the wild they head for the city, but when times are good they return to their natural habitat.

Black bears may be the bear fondest of city life, but grizzly bears, which are brown and about twice the size of the black bear, also dabble, and one of the places they visit is the town of Banff in Alberta, Canada.

"In the summer we've always got bears cruising around," says

Parks Canada's Blair Fyten when we meet on a cold, snowy January morning. "We've got lots of grizzly bears here and a lot of them are very used to people. We have a few grizzly bears that will go right through the town. People see them from their yards."

Three grizzlies, in particular, are regular summer tourists, he adds in a tone so matter-of-fact it hardly feels like we're talking about an animal with such a fearsome reputation. Two are six-hundred-pound males. The other, a female who had three cubs in tow when she last visited. But it isn't garbage that's bringing them to the picturesque national park town.

"Our garbage in the townsite is pretty good. All our containers are bear proof, although every once in a while you get a restaurant that spills some grease or something. So the bears aren't really getting into the garbage, but they might come into town and go for a crabapple tree in someone's yard or to graze down on the golf course."

There's another reason the grizzlies come to Banff, and it's the same reason I'm here. Elk. For years Banff has had a problem with these large herbivores. At its peak in 1999, the town was full of them. "We were getting a lot of elk here, upward of six, seven hundred," says Blair. "They tended to congregate around the townsite during certain periods of the year. One is when they are calving. The cows come into the townsite to seek refuge from predators and have their calves in people's backyards."

But calving elk don't like people getting near them, and in a tourist town of eight thousand residents that can attract enough summer visitors to swell the population to as many as twenty-five thousand people, the chances of someone getting too close are high. "They get very protective of those calves, and so if you happen to step out into your backyard, sometimes the females would get aggressive and actually attack you, strike with their front feet. Then in the fall, the bulls would gather up their harems of cows and they get pretty protective of their cows too. So they would be right in town on the recreation areas and people would be there trying to get pictures, and these bulls would get aggressive and put the run on the people."

Banff didn't always have elk. Their presence is the unexpected outcome of actions half a century ago. In the 1960s Parks Canada had a culling program that wiped out the local wolves and killed many of the local cougars. With their natural enemies gone, the elk population boomed. The elk then ate all the willow trees, wiping out the local beavers. The caribou also lost out to the elk.

By the 1980s, however, attitudes to wildlife had changed. The culling of predators was stopped and the wolves staged a comeback. "The wolves come pretty close to town but stay two, three kilometers out," says Blair. "For some reason they don't come in real close." So the elk responded to the return of the wolf by moving into the town.

And although wolves pushed the elk into town, plants pulled them in. "The town acts as a refuge for the elk, plus there's lots of good vegetation. They come into town and eat on the manicured lawns. They really like the golf course too. And after they've hung out in town for a long period, they become habituated to people."

Sometimes the elk's taste for what people plant in their gardens gets them into trouble. "A couple of weeks back we had a bull elk that got wrapped up in a whole bunch of Christmas lights. He was probably eating under someone's tree that had a bunch of lights on it, lifted his head, and found himself all wrapped up," says Blair.

"We thought there was a risk he is either going to get caught up in a tree and die or get the lights wrapped around his legs, which could cause injuries. So we went in and darted him. We ended up removing his antlers because he was going to be dropping them in two months anyway." The bull's sawed-off antlers, complete with Christmas lights in the shape of candy canes, are still on the floor of Blair's office when I visit.

By the end of the 1990s the elk had become a big problem for Banff. Every year there were more than a hundred incidents involving aggressive elk, including seven where the animals made physical contact with people.

Blair takes me for a tour around town, pointing out places where elk have posed problems. Along the way we pass Central Park, a small park next to the Bow River and on the edge of downtown Banff. "There was a picture that somebody took where there are four or five people standing lined up behind this tree in Central Park, and on the other side of the tree is this huge bull who had gotten them at bay," he says as we pass the park.

The next stop is the outdoor area of the elementary school. It is surrounded by a sturdy metal fence. "We used to get a lot of elk on this little playing field here, so we fenced it all off."

Blair drives a bit further down the street. As we go we catch glimpses through the trees bordering the street of the Canadian Pacific Railroad, which cuts through the town. "We've got elk and deer that are eating the grain that's been dribbled out on the tracks from leaky trains. If a train stops for whatever reason and is leaky, we end up with a big pile of grain there and that attracts bears, elk and deer."

Do they get hit by the trains? I ask.

"Yes, they do. Especially in the wintertime. We've probably already lost eight elk this winter because a bit further down the tracks there's nowhere for them to step off the tracks, so they will run down the tracks and the train will just run them over. They report all the strikes to us so we can go out and find those elk. Sometimes they are still alive and we have to put them down, but we also collect the carcass if we can because it's just going to attract wolves onto the track."

Over on the Fairmont Banff Springs Golf Course there are more fences, this time protecting the putting greens from the elk. "They get tens of thousands of dollars in damage to the fairways from the elk because in the fall, when the bulls are rutting, they will use their antlers to dig up a lot of the turf. If you want to watch bulls in rut, sparring and stuff, this is where you go." In winter, when snow stops the golf, the elk are free to roam, but in the summer the golf course staff chase them off each morning in golf carts and use the sprinkler system to try to scare them off.

Blair takes me to the scene of the incident that was the catalyst for the counterstrike against the elk invasion. It's a quiet backstreet of neat houses, close to a wall of conifer trees hiding the railroad tracks behind them. "I was pretty new to the warden service here and I was the person on call that day," says Blair. "I got a call to go to an incident where a female elk had stomped a little boy in the backyard. The boy got bruised up, but nothing broken, just really scared."

When Blair got there the father was waiting. "The ambulance had come and picked up the boy but the father was sitting in the street, waiting for one of us to show up. His veins are all bugged out on his neck and his fists are clenched and he comes up to me yelling, about this far away," he says, indicating a gap that would have put him and the angry dad nose to nose.

"I thought this guy is going to hang a licker on me. He was saying, 'It's about time we started doing something about these elk.' It was after that that they formed the Elk Advisory Group to come up with solutions."

Core to the eventual solution was a two-part crackdown on the elk. First, a couple hundred elk were trapped and relocated hundreds of miles away. The elk that remained found themselves the target of a daily routine of "hazing," essentially a concerted effort to scare them out of town.

Now each morning and evening Parks Canada patrols the town for elk and frightens away any they find. "We have different techniques for how we haze them. The most basic is just a hockey stick with a garbage bag or a flag tied on the end. You wave the stick and chase them off with that. It works because holding that hockey stick up with a garbage bag on the end, flapping, makes you look bigger."

The hockey stick originated in Parks Canada's daredevil solution to elk raising calves in Banff backyards. "We would go in and grab those calves and move them to a safer location with Mum hot on your heels. So somebody would pick the calf up and run with it, but you had a partner with you who had the hockey stick because that cow was maybe a meter or two behind you wanting to strike you with her feet." As the calf thief ran, the colleague would use the hockey stick to keep the angry cow at bay until the calf had been dropped in a suitable location.

Hockey sticks with garbage bags only frighten elk for so long, however. "Over time they get used to that, but we can up the ante. We have a paintball gun that shoots chalk balls that vaporize into powder when they hit something. We use those to hit the elk to direct them or to hit the trees alongside them to direct them off."

And when paintball guns aren't enough, they turn to rubber bullets. The rubber bullet is a British military invention, developed for use in riots in Northern Ireland as a form of nonlethal ammunition that could be used to inflict pain but no injuries. They proved more dangerous than the British government claimed when it started using them in 1970, resulting in deaths and injury when fired at close range or at the wrong part of the body or in a way that caused the rubber-coated rounds to ricochet off the ground.

"They will penetrate an animal if you hit them in the abdomen instead of the muscle mass, but now they've come out with these rubber bullets that are really pliable and soft. You could get a penetration still if you shot really close into the abdomen." But when used properly it's an effective tool for getting elk to move on. "When we started this program the elk were a little more reluctant to move, but now they know the program. It's 'Oh yeah. Here comes that guy with his stick. Time to get out of here. I don't want to get a rubber bullet in the ass.'"

The same equipment is also used to get rid of grizzly bears. "If we get a report of a bear in the townsite then we do the same thing—we will go out and haze it off," says Blair. When it comes to grizzlies, hockey sticks are out of the picture—it's straight on to paintball guns and rubber bullets backed up with shotguns as the weapons of last resort. But often words and handclaps are all it takes.

"You can get behind a couple of these bears, like the female with the cubs. You can literally get behind her, thirty meters away, and go 'HEY, BEAR! HEY, BEAR!' and clap, and she just keeps moving ahead of you. Once we get her out to a safe area, we've got these little pistols that shoot cracker shells and bangers, and we use those to move the bears."

Bears and some elk have become so wary of Parks Canada patrols that they now move before they've even got the hazing gear out of the truck. "We tend to drive white trucks, and we've noticed that when we're doing hazing on bears they get to know the white trucks are not good, so they see the white truck and move off," says Blair. "The elk are somewhat like that too. You pull up and they see you getting your hockey stick or whatever out of the back, and they are already down the road."

The hazing strategy, combined with regular culls, has been delivering the goods. Today elk numbers in Banff are down to about 270, and the number of reported incidents have slumped from more than a hundred in 1999 to around sixteen a year. Encounters where elk make physical contact with people are down to four or less a year.

Keeping the elk in check also helps lower the risk that mountain lions or bears will end up roaming the streets, adds Blair. "The elk are pulling predators into the town. The wolves aren't coming in, but our cougars definitely come into town to kill an elk, and if you get some kid walking to school who bumps into a cougar or bear with a dead elk, that's a problem."

SINGING A DIFFERENT SONG

Hanging Out with the Parrots of Brooklyn

Just a short walk from Twenty-Fifth Street station in Brooklyn lies the grand archway that marks the entrance to Green-Wood Cemetery. In the 1860s this sprawling burial ground was the second-most-popular tourist attraction in the United States, and every year half a million people would pass through its ornate, brownstone arches. Only Niagara Falls was more visited.

Green-Wood's gothic archway was new then, but it's still a majestic sight. At its center is a tall clock tower topped with an elongated spire decorated with floral sculptures that run up the edges of its pyramidal structure. On either side are two shorter towers with similar spires connected to the clock tower with elaborate flying buttresses. Beneath the buttresses are the entranceway's two arches, each complemented by biblical relief sculptures with titles like "Weep Not" and "The Dead Shall Be Raised."

There's something else, too, right at the base of the clock tower spire: a tightly woven clump of twigs packed into the crevices and punctured with large, smooth holes. And that's where the Brooklyn parrots live.

I missed it at first, too focused on the intricate architecture to see the huge monk parakeet nest crowning the spire. It took Steve Baldwin, founder of the Brooklyn Parrot Society who has offered to introduce me to the borough's parakeets, to bring it to my attention. "See those holes?" he says. "Each portal represents an individual nesting cavity for at least one pair of monk parakeets. The portals normally have two birds, but for those who bore young this year, there will be three."

Monk parakeets are deft engineers. "There are little flowers in the nest that provide inside support, and the monks use that to support some of the weight of the nest," says Steve. "Then, they keep building out from that and the nest is so densely woven that it gets this shape that belongs in the space and is very difficult to dislodge."

So difficult to dislodge that when Hurricane Sandy hit in 2012, the parakeet nest came out the other side unscathed. "They always choose live twigs that are flexible. They don't use dry timber. They take the twigs straight off the trees, fly them over to the nest, and stick them in. Or they hand them to another bird that will work them carefully into the nest expansion area. They are very systematic."

We count the holes in the nest. It's hard to make an accurate count from the ground, but Steve reckons there are fourteen nest holes. Fourteen holes, twenty-eight parrots at least, but probably more. "If there are babies it may be more like thirty-five, thirty-six," he says.

He has counted as many as seventy-five parrots here in the past. "What seems to happen is the flocks build to a certain size, about seventy-five birds, and then something happens and when you next show up it's like half the flock. It's like half splits off and goes somewhere else. Then it takes the rest five to ten years to reach that level of seventy-five and then it splits off again. I think that is what is going on, although it's just suspicion."

None of the bright green birds are around, however. The nest is quiet and still. The birds are out feeding somewhere. "Typically they take off in the morning," says Steve. "They are small but they fly a long way. They can fly twenty miles."

The nest on the archway is the main monk parakeet nest in Green-Wood, but there are others dotted around the vast, hilly cemetery with its impressive views over Manhattan.

As we head into the cemetery Steve tells me how it is thought the parakeets got to Brooklyn in the first place. Before 1993, when the United States banned the import of parrots, monk parakeets were a big deal in the pet trade and Argentina exported them by the thousands. "They were trying to get rid of the parrots because they were pests in Argentina. At first they tried to shoot them, but there was fraud in the program, so they started capturing them in the areas where they were damaging crops and started making money from them as an export crop. Caged birds were popular at the time, and monk parakeets are a very good cage bird. They are the second-best talking parrot and they have all of the attractive, charismatic qualities, but they are also small so you don't have to have a giant cage."

There are two leading theories for how they got free, both of which implicate John F. Kennedy International Airport. The airport is only fifteen miles east of Green-Wood and used to be a major entry point for Argentina's exported parrots. The first theory is that the birds broke out of JFK's quarantine station. "When exotic birds were still coming into the country, they would take the birds into quarantine and keep them there for thirty days to see if they showed signs of Newcastle disease," says Steve. "There may have been an accident at the quarantine station, maybe when attempting to transfer them from one area to another. These parrots are notorious lock pickers, so they can pick the lock on a cage and might have gotten into an air vent and then out." That similar quarantine escapes appear to have happened in San Francisco and Chicago adds weight to the theory.

The alternative suggestion is that Brooklyn's parrots had help from organized crime. "In the 1960s the airport shipping was infiltrated by the mob and they opened up a lot of things so they could pilfer what was in there. It's possible that a crate of parakeets got pilfered one day and the parrots just flew away and there was no record of it. That was told to me by someone who claims her brother worked at the airport at the time, but I can't verify it."

Add to that further releases by people who no longer wanted their pet parakeets, and you've got enough for a breeding population, and with Green-Wood standing out as a prime expanse of greenery in the dense streets of Brooklyn, it makes sense that the birds gathered there.

After wandering through the cemetery for a while, we spy some parakeets. But they are not inside the cemetery. They are across the road, inside a Con Edison electricity substation, where they are busy enhancing the nests they've built on the steel girders and insulator posts. "The parrots love to hang out over there," says Steve, as we watch them through the cemetery gates. "They do tend to prefer manmade structures to trees, and these kind of infrastructures with lots of angles give them a great substructure to build nests on. They really obsess about the quality of their nests."

The parakeets are certainly hard at work. They fly in with twigs held in their orange bills and weave them into their nests before flying out to collect more. One is making adjustments while hanging upside down from a girder, revealing the pale gray breast of its underside. The only breaks they take are to drink from a pool of rainwater that has formed on the flat roof of one of the substation buildings. They remind me of the industrious Doozers from the Jim Henson TV series *Fraggle Rock*, creatures totally absorbed in never-ending construction work.

"Con Edison don't seem to mind that they are here or, at least, I don't think they mind because these nests have been here for many years and nothing's ever been done about them," says Steve. "Maybe that's because to get the nests down they would have to shut down the power to the entire borough and they would have a hard time explaining that. But I don't think they pose a fire hazard. Those insulators get warm, but they don't get hot."

Power companies aren't always this easygoing with monk parakeets, which seem to be drawn to substations and power lines for the extra warmth and because the height offers them unobstructed views that make it easy to spot predators. "There have been culls," says Steve. "There was a cull in Connecticut a few years ago, where they brought in the US Department of Agriculture and killed about 250 of them. The power company was getting very impatient with the parrots because they were removing nests from power poles and the parrots would simply rebuild their nests."

The cull sparked protests, and Steve was among those who rushed to the parrots' aid. "Ultimately, they stopped the cull. Myself and others like me came in and created a lot of headaches for them public relations–wise. The newspapers were writing about this utility company for the first time in, like, twenty years and it was all bad, all about how cruel they were. Nobody wants to be labeled as cruel to animals. I think we Americans can be very, very violent and mean, but when it comes to animals we're very softhearted. Even the very miserly people who wouldn't even give another human being a dime."

Steve, whose interest in parrots started with the African grey parrot he had as a teenager, tells me that he sees himself as a one-man public relations bureau for the birds. "They have such a bad reputation," he says. "People say they are an invasive species and are endangering the lives of people who depend on electricity and that without electricity we would all be savages within a week, so the parrots should be stopped. But knowing what I know about parrots, I knew that while they may be mischievous, they are not like saboteurs or evil. That's why I love Green-Wood because they said, 'We like the parrots, we don't care if they don't belong here. They are here now and they are keeping the pigeons away, so they are doing good work.'"

The monk parakeets, he says, are very much like Americans. "That's something I try to relate to people on the tours I do. Most people who were born in America, their ancestors did not come to America because they wanted to but because they were being kicked out of their own countries, and the parrots had that happen to them. So there's an affinity there."

The birds are very much like the New Yorkers on the streets below them too, he adds. "They talk, they build these crazy structures—it's like performance art or something—and they are outrageously green. That's like a New York thing. You're fabulous! You're outrageous! And you're wearing green when everyone else is wearing brown."

But as Hurricane Sandy proved, the monk parakeets' nests are anything but crazy. In fact, they are vital to the birds' success in Brooklyn, allowing them to shrug off even the harshest winters.

"Monk parakeets are really unusual among parrots in that they build these gigantic stick nests," says Kimball Garrett, manager of the ornithology collection at the Natural History Museum of Los Angeles. "Essentially, all other parrots nest in cavities, so the monks are really different and because of that they do better in temperate and even relatively cold areas. It's about the only parrot that has gained a foothold in the some of the northern cities of North America, and that certainly has to do with these nests, which probably have a more benign thermal environment than just getting into a hole in a tree."

In warmer US cities the monk is just one of many types of urban parrot, and Los Angeles has one of the most diverse wild parrot populations in the country. In the 1990s, Kimball headed a survey of L.A. parrots. He and his army of volunteer bird watchers recorded more than fifteen hundred parrots in the city, made up of thirty-three species that, combined, offered more vibrant colors than a bag of Skittles.

There were mitred conures with their green bodies and red-splattered heads, roaming in flocks of up to a hundred individuals. In downtown L.A. they found yellow-chevroned parakeets that have lurid yellow streaks on the underside of their wings, and, in Temple City, the red beaks and pale blue necks of the rose-ringed parakeets lurking in the sycamore trees. Most numerous of all were the red-crowned parrots, also known as Mexican red-heads. They may be on the verge of extinction back home in northeast Mexico, but more than a thousand were spotted on the streets of Los Angeles.

Regardless of species, most stick to the older neighborhoods. "Where we have the largest numbers of parrots, perhaps not coincidentally, are in areas that used to be orchards of fruit trees and nut trees, many of which were retained when the area was urbanized," says Kimball.

Like the monk parakeets of Brooklyn, L.A.'s parrots have their own unproven, and unprovable, origin stories. One theory is that many found their freedom in the Bel Air fire of November 1961. The fire destroyed hundreds of homes and forced thousands to flee for their safety. It is thought that in the rush to escape the blaze, parrot owners freed their birds en masse so they would not be burned alive in their cages. Soon after, people began reporting sightings of green parrots all over the city.

Another story concerns the bird sanctuary that Anheuser-Busch used to run in Van Nuys. The sanctuary held more than fifteen hundred birds, including many parrots, but at the end of the 1970s the beer maker shut it down so it could expand its brewing facilities. It is thought that some of the parrots may have escaped as they were being transferred to new owners, possibly by using their powerful beaks to pull apart the bars on their cages before flying to freedom.

Yet despite decades of living wild in the streets of L.A., there's little sign that the birds want to follow the example of the European starling and go beyond the city limits. "A great many of them seem to thrive in highly modified suburban and urban habitat as opposed to natural habitats," says Kimball. "They can move out of cities into more sparsely populated areas but, by and large, this doesn't happen."

Access to exotic plants seems to be what keeps them in the city. "The parrots are dependent on a mix of particular food plants that are really only planted where people live, so they are not going to find food in natural areas." These plants include the silk floss tree. "The yellow-chevroned parakeet uses the seed pods from the silk floss tree and encounters the same tree within its native range in South America, so we've kind of reunited them here," says Kimball.

The much-maligned eucalyptus is another favorite. "Ecologists all say eucalyptus are horrible and don't belong here, but they are a magnet for birds. There's a eucalyptus just outside the entrance to the Natural History Museum that's infested with sap-sucking lerp psyllids that create these honeydew combs on the leaves that are candy for birds. For birds, it's the best tree in the whole park."

Our taste for exotic vegetation may allow parrots to thrive in cities, but they are mere amateurs compared with the pigeon.

The rock pigeon is very much the defining bird of the urban landscape, a daily sight in cities the world over from Los Angeles and London to Dubai and Sydney. But unlike the colorful and amusing parrots, the pigeon is rarely loved. We dismiss them as ugly pests, deriding them as little more than "rats with wings." They are birds that peck at the dirt, annoy us with their burbling coos, and stain the sidewalks—and sometimes us too—with their excrement.

We only have ourselves to blame, though, for the city pigeon is our fault, a genetically modified creature born out of our own desires. The street pigeon's ancestors may have been unremarkable cliff-dwelling birds, but for thousands of years we have been molding them for our own ends, turning them bit by bit into birds ideally suited to the city. Like the house sparrow, pigeons began living beside us in the formative years of human civilization, making homes in the holes of the mud and stone homes we built.

People didn't mind. After all, what could be more convenient than having one on your doorstep when you fancied eating pigeon?

Urban red foxes were first spotted in 1930s London. Today, aided by their adaptability, they are found in cities throughout the world, making them one of the most successful urban animals around. COURTESY OF DERK EHLERT

The western diamondback rattlesnake that found shelter in a Scottsdale, Arizona, garage.
TRISTAN DONOVAN

If the cap fits: the gopher snake that got itself trapped in a sprinkler cover in Paradise Valley, Arizona.
TRISTAN DONOVAN

Wilfredo Valladares of Miami's Neighborhood Enhancement Team with a chicken caught in Little Haiti. Just several thousand more to go. TRISTAN DONOVAN

A giant African land snail, the cause of the biggest pest control operation ever launched by the Florida Department of Agriculture.
TRISTAN DONOVAN

Iguanas are so common in Miami that many residents think that they are native to the city. TRISTAN DONOVAN

The tagged female boa that lives on the Deering Estate, fifteen miles south of downtown Miami. COURTESY OF ADRIAN DIAZ

European starlings gathering in the skies around the Chase Tower in downtown Indianapolis. COURTESY OF USDA WILDLIFE SERVICES

Berlin's wild boar problems have led the German capital to recruit a team of city hunters. COURTESY OF DERK EHLERT

Former Park Inn hotel resident Alex, the most famous of Berlin's raccoons. COURTESY OF DERK EHLERT

Coyotes on the run in Mount Sinai Memorial Park in Los Angeles. TRISTAN DONOVAN

A Hollywood Hills coyote waiting in the bushes for feeding time. TRISTAN DONOVAN

A leopard on the prowl at the Aarey Milk Colony in the Goregaon East suburb of Mumbai. COURTESY OF ZEESHAN MIRZA

Tasty gardens and a lack of wolves draw elk to the streets of Banff, Canada. COURTESY OF JAY PRIEST

A group of monk parakeets hanging out in a Brooklyn electricity substation. TRISTAN DONOVAN

Chicago's Bird Collision Monitors find another victim of the city's architecture. TRISTAN DONOVAN

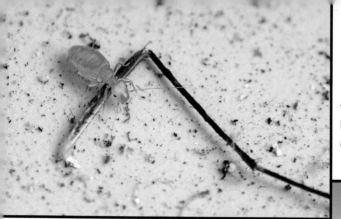

This mosquito leg will keep this book louse well fed for weeks.
MATT BERTONE

Michelle Trautwein searches a lampshade for bugs in a Raleigh, North Carolina, home as part of the Arthropods of Our Homes project.
TRISTAN DONOVAN

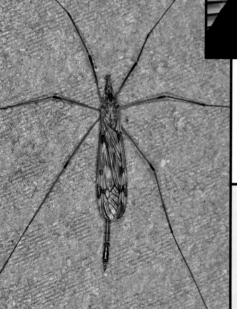

Our lights lure crane flies into our homes, but they cannot survive indoors. MATT BERTONE

Drain flies, also known as moth flies, have turned household drains into their breeding grounds.
MATT BERTONE

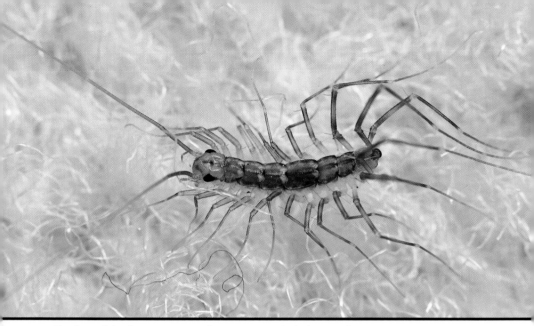

The lion of the home: a young house centipede lurking in the carpet. MATT BERTONE

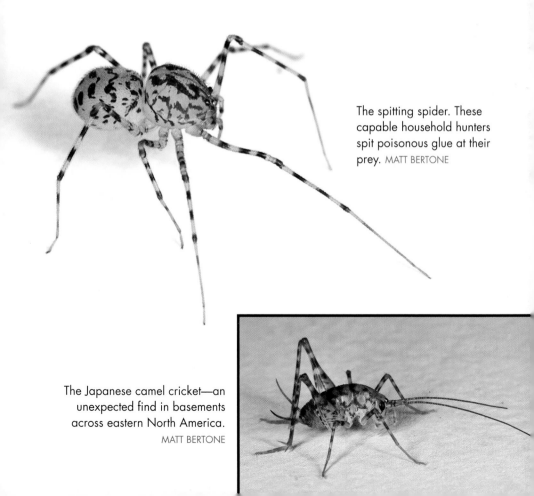

The spitting spider. These capable household hunters spit poisonous glue at their prey. MATT BERTONE

The Japanese camel cricket—an unexpected find in basements across eastern North America. MATT BERTONE

A twig covered in sap-sucking scale insects, which thrive in the hottest parts of Raleigh, North Carolina. MATT BERTONE

Keeping Budapest rat-free: a Bábolna Bio employee laying poison. COURTESY OF BÁBOLNA BIO

American cockroaches might look all the same to us, but there is a big genetic gulf between those found in different parts of New York City. MATT BERTONE

The German cockroach, the Big Apple's most abundant roach.
MATT BERTONE

There were other benefits too. Their nitrogen-rich guano made a great fertilizer as well as proving useful when tanning leather.

Another boon was their impressive homing abilities. We still don't fully understand how they do it, but it seems to depend on a combination of detecting magnetic fields, visual recognition of landmarks, understanding the sun's movements, and smell. While we don't know how pigeons do it, we have been using their homing capabilities for thousands of years; they even spread the news of Ramses III's coronation as pharaoh of Ancient Egypt.

Keen to exploit these useful birds, people began building nest houses called dovecotes to attract them. For the pigeons, it was a good deal. They got protection from predators and bad weather, plus easy access to our farms and the grain and seed that were spilled on the streets. The only downside was the risk of being grabbed if someone opted for a pigeon dinner. But it was worth the risk.

The dovecote spread across the world. The Romans took the idea from Egypt and spread it across Europe. The Spanish and Portuguese took them to South America, and the British and French introduced them to North America.

People also began domesticating the birds, encouraging the breeding of those with useful traits like speed, homing ability, fertility, beauty, and tameness. Over time we molded the former cliff dwellers into something almost new, weeding out the undesirable genes and multiplying the beneficial in much the same way we turned gray wolves into domestic dogs and fostered more productive cattle.

But not every pigeon played along. Some rebelled, abandoning the dovecotes to make their own way on the streets, where the characteristics we bred into them turned out to be powerful assets. Their tameness made them unfazed by crowds of people, enabling them to forage in the busiest parts of our cities, such as London's Waterloo railway station through which a quarter of million passengers pass every day.

Pigeons' speed and agility helped them dodge traffic and escape predators, which they sometimes evade by diving off buildings and using gravity to accelerate to speeds as high as thirty-seven miles per hour before making their escape. Even peregrine falcons can find pigeons hard to catch, thanks to their habit of giving them the slip by zig-zagging through trees and buildings.

Our desire for fast-breeding domestic pigeons gave them the ability to breed year-round, so that a single pair of feral pigeons can produce as many as ten squabs a year. Pigeons also proved themselves to be adaptable birds, making nests out of twigs, paper, and metal wire in locations as unlikely as satellite dishes and neon signs.

They also learn from each other. In Montreal, Canada, researchers caught feral pigeons and taught them how to open paper food containers by using their beaks to pierce and then widen holes. After teaching the birds how to do this, they returned them to streets. Soon the container opening technique began to spread among the pigeons of Montreal, as other pigeons copied the ways of those trained by the researchers.

Contrary to their image, pigeons are also not as dependent on garbage as we imagine, and their reliance on what we throw away depends on where they live. In the English city of Leeds, half of what pigeons eat consists of garbage and food provided by people on bird tables or in feeders, but in the Czech capital Prague, human food is a mere 3 percent of their diet.

In fact many pigeons don't even eat in the streets of the cities they live in. Take the Italian city of Milan. On the face of it, it seems like the kind of place where pigeons would look to the streets for food. In the Piazza del Duomo, home to the city's grand cathedral, pigeons gather by the thousands to gobble feed dished out by tourists and pigeon-friendly locals. Yet half of Milan's hundred-thousand-odd pigeons don't eat on the streets. Instead they wake each morning and fly out to the farms surrounding Milan, where they spend the day feeding on grain before returning back to their city nests in the late afternoon.

While pigeons had our help in becoming the world's most abundant urban bird, others have to rely on their wits, and when it comes to brainpower few birds can match the corvids. The corvid family of birds, which includes crows, ravens and magpies, has the brainiest birds around, clever enough to rival apes and dolphins in the intelligence stakes. And their cleverness has helped them turn the city to their advantage, even if they can't pump out eggs anywhere near as fast as feral pigeons.

The jungle crows of Tokyo, which have relatively long beaks and dark gray plumage, are a prime example. They've figured out ingenious ways for stealing food from the bowls of dogs kept in backyards. Some crows land on dog kennels and drop objects onto the ground to distract the dogs from their meal. As the dog rushes over to investigate, the crow flies over to the bowl and scarfs the food while the pet is still busy sniffing the item. Another, more daring, strategy crows use is to creep up behind eating dogs and yank their tails. The birds then lead the enraged dog away from its bowl, out of the backyard, and onto the street. Then they fly back into the yard to eat the food while the hapless dog continues looking for the crow outside.

On the other side of the Pacific, the crows of Seattle have learned to use architecture to their advantage by deliberately chasing sparrows into windows to knock them out. It's not a perfect strategy, however. Sometimes the sparrows make a sharp turn just before hitting the glass and the pursuing crow slams into it instead.

Corvids have also become familiar with our trash. In Juneau, Alaska, a pair of ravens figured out how to dispense whipped cream out of an aerosol can. One would use its beak to spray the cream while the other ate, after which they would swap places.

Some crows even recognize the corporate brands amid our garbage. In one test, crows were presented with two brown paper bags filled with french fries. The only difference between the two bags was that one was plain while the other sported a McDonald's logo. Time after time the crows opted for the McDonald's bag first.

Crows also use automobiles to their advantage. In San Francisco, American crows work together to drive flocks of pigeons into high-speed interstate traffic, so that they get hit by cars and buses. The crows then feed on injured or dead roadkill pigeons. Never has the term "a murder of crows" seemed more apt.

The carrion crows of the Japanese city of Sendai have another roadside strategy. In autumn they like to eat walnuts but can't break the tough shells with their beaks, so they learned to crack the nuts by dropping them from a great height onto the hard road surface. It worked OK, but then the crows noticed that having walnuts run over by cars is even more effective and refined the strategy. Now they sit on power lines above intersections and drop the nuts into the path of the waiting traffic so the nuts get crushed when the lights turn green. Once the lights revert to red, the crows swoop down to safely retrieve the freshly cracked nuts.

Corvids may be the birds that understand how best to use roads, but other birds have also figured out that traffic can work to their advantage. Among them is the marabou stork, a strong contender for the title of the world's ugliest bird. No one will be asking these African storks, also known as the undertaker bird, to deliver babies anytime soon. They look as if they've escaped out of someone's nightmare. They stand five feet tall and have huge blue-gray wings, but when stomping around on the ground they hunch themselves up so their sharp swordlike beaks rest on the wobbly, inflatable sacs of bare pink flesh that dangle from their necks.

Their calls are a mix of chilling clattering noises and grunts, and their dark-gray legs usually appear white because they are covered in the stork's own excrement, which helps the birds stay cool in the hot sun. The bald scalps of their featherless heads help them stay clean when tearing flesh from the rotting carcasses that form much of their diet. Not that they only eat the dead. They often prey on other animals, swallowing live turtles whole and even taking down young flamingoes in the lakes of Africa.

They are graceful fliers though, so that balances things out.

The marabou stork's natural home is savannah and grassland, but they are common sights in many African cities. In the fast-growing Kenyan capital of Nairobi, marabou storks nest in the thorny fever trees that line the busy Uhuru Highway close to the Nyayo National Stadium. It's a handy spot for picking up roadkill or for paying a visit to the city's slaughterhouses. The storks also turn up at the miserable Dandora garbage dump on the edge of the city, where they join the estimated ten thousand people who spend their lives trawling through the filthy mountains of waste for anything they can eat or sell.

Though the birds' excrement has turned the sidewalk of the Uhuru Highway rusty white, the marabou stork is largely welcomed in Nairobi. Rather than seeking to expel them, the Kenya Wildlife Service regards them as unpaid cleaners, who help to keep the streets free from muck.

Birds do not just come to cities for the food. They also come for the weather.

Cities have powerful effects on the local environment, and one of the most startling is the urban heat island effect. This phenomenon can make city centers as much as twenty-two degrees Fahrenheit hotter than the rural areas surrounding them. The effect is the result of replacing vegetation and soil with buildings, roads, and sidewalks. First, the removal of vegetation means the cooling effect of the water vapor released by plants and the shade offered by trees is lost. Then there are the concrete and asphalt surfaces that replace the natural flora. These materials absorb rather than reflect sunlight. During the day they soak up sun rays, storing them as heat that is then released at night. It's like a battery that charges in the day and releases its energy at night.

Traffic, industry, and air conditioning also play a role, pumping out more heat, while buildings block out cooling winds. In dense city centers filled with skyscrapers, the heat island effect can be even greater, because glass windows concentrate the light onto the street below and the heat released at night becomes trapped, boxed in by buildings on all sides.

The urban heat island effect isn't universal. In fact, the exact opposite happens in cities like Phoenix and Abu Dhabi, where irrigation makes them cooler than the hot desert around them. But for most cities, the urban heat island effect is at work, dialing up the temperature.

The extra heat has a noticeable impact on life in the city. Plants flower earlier and insects become active earlier too—which is great news for the birds that eat them. In the wine-making city of Zielona Góra in western Poland, researchers found that black-billed magpies start building nests and laying eggs earlier than those outside the city, thanks to the supply of food and the warmth. As a result, the city's urban magpie population was growing three times faster than the rural population.

City lights produce similar effects, with blue tits laying eggs a day or two earlier in areas with streetlamps. Light also causes birds to start singing earlier in the morning and later at night, an effect that is more pronounced on cloudy days when more of the urban light is reflected back toward the ground.

So far, so good, then, for the urban birds. They can feast on our bird feeders, raid our trash, and forage on our dumps. They also get to enjoy a warmer climate and get to stay up later thanks to the lights. But these benefits come at a cost: noise.

Cities are noisy places, filled with the din of traffic, the sound of construction, and the bustle of people. Some areas are exceptionally noisy. Not least the Champs-Élysées in Paris, where the traffic thunders past at an ear-splitting eighty decibels. For urban songbirds, overcoming the blare is vital. If they can't make themselves heard above the traffic, they could miss out on attracting a mate, fail to hear their chicks crying for food, or not hear another bird's warning of a predator.

Songbirds have come up with different strategies for dealing with the noise. Some resort to singing when the city is quiet. In the Spanish city of Seville, house sparrows and spotless starlings sing early to avoid the rush-hour traffic. Blue tits, European blackbirds, and European robins do the same.

Others pump up the volume. One bird that does this is Australia's noisy miner, a gray-bodied bird with yellow patches next to its eyes that make its eyeballs look bigger than they really are. As their name suggests, these honeyeaters are loud birds at the best of times, but when they take up residence along the busy arterial roads of Melbourne, which carry more than five thousand vehicles a day, they get even louder. In some cases noisy miners drown out the traffic by letting out alarm calls at a whopping ninety decibels.

Traffic also forces birds to change their tunes. Most urban noise consists of low-pitch sounds, so birds often sing higher to avoid having their lower notes missed in the cacophony. It's a strategy favored by great tits, which also sing shorter and faster songs in cities.

But cities are not just loud, they get louder over time, as the male white-crowned sparrows of the Presidio of San Francisco know all too well. Since 1969 these birds, which despite their name have black and white stripes on their heads, have been trapped in a melodic arms race with the growing noise from the Golden Gate Bridge. To cope, the brown-winged birds have been singing higher and higher as they try to avoid being drowned out by traffic.

The resulting tune has changed so much that the sparrows no longer recognize the songs they sang back when hippies rather than techies roamed the San Francisco streets. When researchers played them recordings of their present-day songs, the birds reacted as if it was an intruding rival, but they paid no attention at all to the songs they sang in the 1960s.

Noise is not the only challenge for urban songbirds. The structure and architecture of cities plays havoc with their songs, which bounce off glass, get dulled by pavement, and echo around buildings. The sonic interference from the artificial surfaces and buildings means songbirds face the risk that their songs will get distorted, missed, or canceled out altogether.

To deal with urban acoustics, birds adjust their songs to take account of the artificial surfaces. Often their response reflects how high or low they usually sing. In Washington, DC, and Baltimore researchers examined how the songs of six songbirds changed in response to how built-up the local area was. They found that gray catbirds and Northern cardinals sang higher to avoid the low notes of their songs while higher pitched singers, like the American robin and house wren, went the opposite way, cutting back on the top notes to compensate for the effect of urban surfaces.

But as the white-crowned sparrows of San Francisco show, urban birds can't sit still. The city is constantly changing, and birds hoping to cash in on the food available in the city need to keep pace with an ever-changing environment. For some birds that challenge is just too much. "There's two very different sides to the story," says Kimball. "In order to create cities like L.A., we totally obliterated hundreds of square miles of habitat, some of it very specialized with very unique species. We destroyed it all. Some birds are habitat specialists and don't tolerate urbanization."

Others thrive for a while only to end up defeated. One such bird is the spotted dove, a pigeon-like bird with a dusty pink breast. Native to Southeast Asia, they were brought to Los Angeles in 1915 and soon became a regular sight around the city. "It became one of the most abundant birds in urban and suburban Los Angeles and beyond," says Kimball. "Then, starting in the 1970s, their populations just started dropping. People hardly even noticed until they were virtually gone by the 1990s. Now we just have a few little pockets of them here and there."

Why the spotted dove went from urban success story to near-extinction remains a mystery. Nest-raiding by crows is a possibility, disease another, but the truth is no one knows for sure. "Why were urban habitats so good for them and then suddenly, within a couple of decades, did they die out? And why did they die out when we still have mourning doves all over L.A.? Presumably they eat more or less the same things and have more or less the same predators, so why are mourning doves still common? Maybe the mourning doves are having the same problems, but there are millions more of them elsewhere in Southern California that are constantly recolonizing the city."

While birds like the spotted dove shine brightly but briefly in the city, for others it is nothing but a death trap.

09

THE CHICAGO BIRD MASSACRE

Saving Migratory Birds in Downtown Chicago

It's quarter past five in the morning and Chicago is dark and enveloped in fog. I'm waiting outside the Wrigley Building on North Michigan Avenue for Annette Prince, director of the Chicago Bird Collision Monitors. She's just called to say she's running late and suggests I check for injured or dead birds near the chewing gum giant's headquarters while I wait.

This is what the hundred or so Chicago Bird Collision Monitors do. Early every morning, while most of the city is asleep or getting ready for work, these volunteers are combing downtown streets looking for birds that have crashed into skyscrapers.

With time to kill, I figure what the hell and start scanning the sidewalk. It looks empty. The only signs of life are a few eager joggers, some night shift workers waiting for the bus home, and a homeless man, who is methodically checking the bins.

Oh, and the woman in the median of Michigan Avenue.

She stands out. Mainly because she's standing on the concrete surrounding the median's flower bed, singing a mournful hymn.

Her voice is beautiful but she looks deranged, her eyes glaring at the city as she belts out what sounds like a Hildegard of Bingen number to an imaginary audience. With her haunting vocal cutting through the mist, it all feels very gothic and it's about to get even more so.

Out of the corner of my eye I see something on the floor next to a ground floor window. I can't tell what it is from where I am; it might be a leaf or some litter. I head over for a closer look.

It soon becomes clear what it is: a dead bird about the size of a pigeon. Its yellow breast faces up to the sky, its black wings patterned with white lines. As I get nearer, I notice that its head is missing. Then, I see the ants.

Thousands of tiny ants are crawling all over the headless bird. Gruesome as the sight is, I'm kind of impressed that so many ants could eke out a life in this concrete corner of the city. For them the arrival of the dead bird must be like having all their Christmases come at once, a gift from the ant gods.

Just as I'm wondering where the bird's head is, I see it. It's twenty feet away resting upright in the middle of the sidewalk. A jogger runs right over it, missing the head with its scarlet crown and neck by less than an inch. She didn't even seem to notice it was there.

As I'm taking in this macabre scene, complete with ghostly mist and the eerie melody of the woman on the median, Annette calls me again. "Almost there," she says.

I tell her about the headless bird. "Do you have a bag?" she asks. "Er, no."

"Well, could you put it in your pocket then?"

"It's covered in ants," I protest. "Lots and lots of ants. I'm not going to put it in my pocket." In fairness, even if the ants weren't busy devouring it, I doubt I would have been up for having a decapitated bird in my pocket. The ants merely seal the deal.

Annette sounds a little frustrated at my unwillingness to collect the carcass, but it's not as if it's going anywhere. Unless those ants eat really fast.

Ten minutes later, Annette arrives. She's wearing a khaki photographer's vest over a bright green Chicago Bird Collision Monitors T-shirt and a tan baseball cap. In one hand she's holding a bird net and, in the other, a Whole Foods Better Bag filled with white paper bags, an assortment of binder clips, and some marker pens.

She checks out the body. "It's a yellow-bellied sapsucker," she says. It sounds like an insult but is actually a type of migratory woodpecker.

"This is most likely a peregrine kill—one of the peregrine falcons that live in the city. I don't think I want to take him because I'm not sure I want all these ants. I can see why you weren't going to take him with you. Good call."

She moves the body and head to a nearby flower bed that will now be the unfortunate bird's final resting place, and we set off to find more victims of the city.

We soon find another. I say we, but I mistook it for a leaf and carried on walking, until Annette called me back. It's a black-throated green warbler, a small bird with a yellow face and an olive smear that starts at the top of its head and runs down its back.

It's alive but dazed. It stands motionless at the bottom of the building. If this were a cartoon, there would be stars spinning around its head.

Annette crouches and creeps toward it. The bird is still staring vacantly into space when she brings her net down on it. The warbler barely responds as she scoops it into her gloved hand. Its beak is cracked.

"He has hit his head and broken his beak a little. His eye is swollen shut," says Annette as she shows me the bird. "Most of these birds have head trauma. See how the beak broke? It's like going through your windshield. His head really hurts right now; he'll have a concussion."

Annette takes out a paper bag and scrawls the date, time, and location on it in black marker before gently dropping the bird in and closing it with a binding clip.

"They are very unnoticeable because they are little compared to these gigantic buildings. It takes a whole sort of mindset to see them," she says when I marvel at how she spotted it. Right on cue, she immediately spots two more on the other side of the street.

As the morning progresses, we find more and more dead and injured birds. They are everywhere, crumpled or concussed on the sidewalks. It's nothing short of a massacre. We find an entire field guide's worth of birds. There are winter wrens, black-and-white warblers patterned like humbugs, hermit thrushes, indigo buntings with feathers the color of azure, and more yellow-bellied sapsuckers.

Over the years the collision monitors have found more than 150 bird species on the Chicago streets. They've even found rare species that bird watchers can spend their entire lives trying to see without success. "Someone called to say there's a dead bird on a bridge once and on these bridges there's generally nothing but pigeons, so we assumed it was a pigeon," Annette says. "It ended up being a very rare bird, the Holy Grail of bird watching—the black rail. It's like a little Easter egg chick. I've gone on so many bird trips looking for them, and 99 percent of bird watchers have never seen these birds because they are black and nocturnal and hide in marshes. The odds of seeing one are incredibly slim, so finding one on a bridge in Chicago was really astounding. But sad."

We find bats too. A silver-haired bat, which is named after the silver tips of its otherwise black fur, and an eastern red bat the color of ginger. "Not all volunteers pick up bats as bats have a risk of rabies," says Annette, lifting the red bat off the West Adams Street sidewalk.

Annette's been inoculated against rabies, although she would still need urgent medical treatment if she got bitten or scratched by a bat. The jabs merely buy her extra time to get treated. It's a risk she's willing to take, not least because she likes bats. "People just assume they are out of vampire movies or something like that, but they are gorgeous. Look! There's his little fangs!"

Anyhow, she adds, "the last person in Illinois who got rabies got it from a cow."

The two bats are both alive, but many of the birds are not so lucky. About half the birds we find are dead. Yet they still get bagged up all the same, because they are valuable for researchers, who have learned lots about bird migration patterns in the Chicago area from the bodies the collision monitors collect.

"There's a bird called the American woodcock. It's a game bird with a long beak," says Annette. "They thought all the birds moved up north where the males do these elaborate mating dances and the females pick the best and that it was at that point they try to nest." But the dead woodcocks the collision monitors found upended that theory. "When they looked at the females we get in the spring, many of them were already carrying eggs, so they must be breeding someplace further south and that indicates there are breeding grounds along their migratory path. That's something that would never have been discovered without having the birds in hand to see that the eggs were fertilized."

We're not the only ones out collecting birds today. Another twelve collision monitors are on patrol this morning. At one point we cross paths with one of them. He looks stressed. "One alive and four dead on the east side. I don't have time to bag them—I'm just literally throwing and running," he hurriedly tells Annette before hopping on his bicycle and racing off toward the Loop.

Then there are the phone calls. Annette is also handling the monitors' hotline, which Chicagoans can use to report sightings of fallen birds, and the *der-der-nu-nu* ring of her cell phone rarely stops. She's getting an average of one call every two minutes, and rush hour is only just starting.

The public isn't just calling, either. At one point a passerby hands us a McDonald's bag that he has used to pick up an injured Nashville warbler he spotted on his way to work. The janitors of Chicago's skyscrapers are also helping out. As we pass their foyers, they rush out to give us more bird-filled paper bags or to grab more bags from Annette.

"Most of the buildings are helpful—they are our eyes and ears," she says. Inevitably there are exceptions. "We've been told that one building's janitor has been putting live birds into the trash compactor. He won't save them for us and won't call us. Pretty horrifying."

Soon Annette's Whole Foods bag is overflowing with bagged birds, a few of which have overcome their concussion and are now fluttering and chirping in panic. With the bag and our hands full we put the search on hold and head to the monitors' van to offload them.

On the way I ask Annette how the monitors came to be. "It was founded in 2003, back when they were still leaving the lights on in the buildings," she says. "There were even more birds then. There were times when you could find a hundred birds at one building. One night they left the lights on at one of the more prominent buildings and they found a thousand dead birds there. Today, we will probably find a couple hundred, all told."

Annette, who is a speech therapist when she's not looking for birds on the streets, joined the group in 2004. "I didn't get into bird watching until later in life. I always thought that bird watching was a silly pastime where you got up far too early in the morning and looked around in the dark for birds. So now what do I do? I get up early in the morning and look in the dark for birds, so it's gone full circle," she laughs.

"I do it because I feel so bad for these birds that are making amazing migrations, traveling stupendous journeys from their wintering grounds to their summer homes and hitting these obstacles. It feels like a privilege to be able to do something to help these birds because they are so vulnerable. When these birds need help there's no one else to come to their assistance."

With the bag emptied we resume the search, but the rush hour is now in full flow and with it a new sense of urgency. As the roar of trucks, sirens, and cars fills the air and floods of commuters descend from the train lines above, the risk of injured birds being trampled or run over is rising fast.

Speed is everything and we're now running through the streets. "About 40 percent of what we find are dead, but about 60 percent are live," says Annette as we push through the crowds. "A good majority survive and get released if they get off the street before they are stepped on or otherwise attacked."

She stops suddenly. She's seen something across the street. "Bird! There!" she cries. "Alive, maybe?"

Annette shoots into the road, zig-zagging through the traffic. I scramble to keep up, panicked by the four lanes of traffic heading straight for me. But the bird, a dull brown-gray winter wren, is dead. "Everything is dead. Everything is dead. *Awww*," she says, deflated.

We soon see another bird in the road but, again, we're too late. It's already been crushed by the traffic. I hope it was dead by the time it hit the ground.

There are other dangers lurking in the streets for the birds that survive their collisions. As well as the peregrine falcon that took down this morning's sapsucker, the city's crows and seagulls see the dead and dazed birds as an easy breakfast.

Gulls and crows have even learned to track the collision monitors, using them to help find potential meals. "The crows and gulls are very smart. They will follow you. I've stopped to look for a bird and had a gull pull up and look at what I'm doing. There's a real understanding that we're pursuing what they are pursuing. If I'm fixed on something they turn their attention to it." They also go after the bats. "The crows and gulls will come and peck at the bats and eat them while they are still alive, and they scream. It's a really awful thing to see."

Not every predator has wings. There are feral cats, downtown rats, and hungry ants to contend with as well. "At one point we had a raccoon that moved into one of the plaza areas here, and every morning he would eat some of the birds."

The birds are often defenseless too, wrapped up tight in the spiderwebs they crash into as they fall down the sides of skyscrapers after hitting the windows. "We get an amazing number of birds all tangled in spider webbing," says Annette as she tries to pull strands of sticky web off of a black-and-white warbler. "Sometimes they fall down those buildings and brush all the cobwebs off, and you can't seem to groom them out. They are so wrapped up, the live ones can't get themselves free."

What is striking about the birds we find is that none of them are birds we expect to see in cities. There's not a single house sparrow, pigeon, starling, gull, or crow among them.

They are all migratory birds, and there's no shortage of them, because Chicago lies in the path of the Mississippi Flyway. The flyway follows the Mississippi River and is a major route for North America's migratory birds. About a third of the continent's bird species use the Mississippi Flyway, including 40 percent of waterfowl species.

But it does seem odd, nonetheless. Why can a pigeon navigate the city when a winter wren ends up crashing into something as obvious and static as a whopping great skyscraper?

One person trying to figure out the answer to this riddle is Graham Martin, the emeritus professor of avian sensory science at the University of Birmingham in England. Weather, he tells me, is a key factor. "These migrants tend to fly at many thousands of feet when migrating, so normally they are well out of the range of hazards like buildings and they fly over cities and we don't even know they are there. The danger seems to come when the weather changes and suddenly you get cloud cover coming in and the birds come down lower."

Birds appear to use the stars to guide them during migrations, and so once they are below the clouds, bright city lights often confuse them. "If they get caught in clouds they get disorientated and are attracted to pools of light," he says. "In misty, foggy conditions the illumination of cities can create a big pool of generalized light that they are attracted to. So the birds lose the moon and stars and basically don't know what they are doing and crash into buildings."

It happens a lot on offshore oil rigs in the North Sea, he says. "You can get quite big bird wrecks on the North Sea platforms because they are well lit. Under certain conditions birds will come down, get disorientated, and fly around and around the lights and eventually crash into the rig or the sea."

There are biological factors at play too. Birds just don't see the world in the same way we do. Because our eyes are in the front of our heads and there's a lot of overlap in what we see through each eyeball, we see the world as something that lies directly ahead of us. Most birds, however, have eyes on either side of their head, so even when they look ahead there's very little overlap between what they see with each eye, giving them a less complete picture of the world directly in front of them.

Also, their frontal vision seems to be about helping them accurately target nearby objects with their beaks rather than seeing what lies ahead. Instead, their sideways vision does most of the work in detecting their surroundings. Even then, the way they perceive the world during flight is more about spotting movement than detail. When in flight birds are looking for predators, prey, food, other members of their flock, and potential nesting sites, and as such when they are draw into cities by the lights they aren't looking ahead but to the sides.

Migrating birds are also flying fast because they have a long way to go and it is much harder to keep flying slowly, and since they are flying high they don't expect to bump into anything. It's like driving fast with poor brakes along a highway that you assume will be empty, while looking out the side window for interesting things and using the corner of your eye now and again to see what's ahead. In that situation it would be no surprise if you collided with a large obstacle in the road.

And this seems to explain why everyday urban birds, like pigeons, are so much better at making their way around built-up areas. They move slower, know the area, and expect to encounter obstacles. "Pigeons are local birds," says Graham. "They know where they are and get to know their patch. A new bird coming into an area could easily get disorientated and crash into something. Even so, I still get green finches, house sparrows, and pigeons flying into the window where I live, but that's probably when they are spooked by a sparrowhawk or something like that and think they are flying into cover when it's actually the reflection of the cover behind them."

For bats the problem is different, although the reasons why they crash into buildings are less well understood. Two theories exist, says Annette. First is that they mainly use their echolocation abilities when hunting and don't use it when migrating because they don't think it's needed. The other theory is that the urban surfaces distort their echolocation calls just as they mess with bird song, resulting in a fuzzy picture of the world around them and increasing the chances of them flying into something.

···ٜٜ·ٜ·●

By the end of my morning with the collision monitors they have filled four cars with bags of birds piled up in boxes that fill the trunks, back seats, and passenger seats. There's more than four hundred dead and injured birds in total, plus a few bats.

It's been a bad night for the birds, says Annette, but it's far from the worst. What's more, the birds they have recovered are merely the tip of the iceberg. Not only will the volunteers have missed some, but plenty never reach the ground and lie dead or dying on the balconies, awnings, overhangs, and tiered rooftops of buildings. They are the unlucky ones. No one will be coming to save them.

The annual death tolls are huge. Across the United States, an estimated six hundred million birds are killed by flying into buildings every year. Most of the deaths are due to collisions with residential and low-rise properties. High-rises account for just half a million, but there are far fewer skyscrapers out there and they have the highest kill rate of any building type.

For those hoping to help the birds, the focus is very much on how buildings can change. Many cities, Chicago included, have Lights Out programs that have helped make urban areas less likely to draw in migrating birds.

But some have gone further, and Toronto is the city that's been setting the pace. Since 2010 the Canadian city has required new buildings, aside from low-rise residential properties, to comply with its "bird-safe" design policies. These rules include using glass that mutes reflections or is patterned in a way that makes them more noticeable to birds and not putting rooftop gardens next to windows. In addition, only heritage buildings can have exterior lighting that points skyward.

Other cities have followed suit with rules of their own. Among them is Oakland, California, which requires developers to install timers or motion sensors that switch off interior lights so they can't be left on by accident and to avoid using mirrors in landscape design. San Francisco and the state of Minnesota have also introduced similar policies.

Architects are also picking up the baton. In Chicago, Jeanne Gang designed the eighty-two-story Aqua Tower on North Columbus Drive to be bird-safe by incorporating fritted glass with a gray dot pattern and undulating exterior terraces that make the skyscraper look like a cliff edge. "Each building has a pathology to it," says Annette. "It's all the elements combined. How it's designed, how the right angles are, and whether it's near something green," like a rooftop garden.

There are, however, difficulties in figuring out what works. Some have suggested that avoiding particular colors of light, such as red, can help but Graham believes the evidence isn't there yet. "Color doesn't seem to make a difference," he says. "There are people trying different color lights to see whether it makes a difference and there was a claim that it did, but I don't think it is very convincing at the moment."

One example is how people got hung up on the potential of applying ultraviolet patterns to glass because birds can see ultraviolet while we can't. "UV sensitivity in birds is very oversold," says Graham. "Their actual sensitivity to UV is really quite low. There's nothing special about it—it's probably more to observe plumages at close range than anything more. People have been playing around with UV markings on windows that are invisible to us but visible to birds, but that doesn't seem to have any effect. It's probably just light rather than anything specific."

Of course it is much easier to address the factors that attract birds when designing new buildings but, says Annette, existing buildings can be improved. "You can't fix an entire building, but our records show localized places on buildings where the strikes are occurring, and there are often simple or temporary measures you can do that significantly reduce the number of bird collisions," she says.

One such measure is moving vegetation away from windows. "Putting a green space that's attractive to birds right next to a glass window is like putting candy next to a swimming pool with no fence on," she says. "The kids come for the candy, fall in the swimming pool, and drown. You can't fix a whole building with multiple stories, but if there's anything you can fix it's having a green area right next to the window or plants inside next to the window. So that's what we try to persuade buildings to do. People aren't going to build buildings without windows in them."

And, she thinks, the building owners are generally up for trying to make cities safer for birds. "I don't think any of the buildings want to be hurting birds, and I think the Chicago skyline is spectacular on a beautiful day. It's just unfortunate that it's so deadly."

10

SUBURBIA CRAWLING

Bug Hunting in Raleigh Homes

Matt Bertone looks ready for a safari. He is wearing a khaki photographer's vest over his navy blue with white stripes polo shirt. The vest pockets bulge with equipment that includes a bunch of clear plastic vials, a handheld torch, and a pair of metal tweezers. Wrapped around his legs are black and yellow kneepads, and a headlamp is affixed to his shaven head. The final touch is the aspirator, the device that entomologists like Matt use to suck up insects. Its clear tubes are slung around his neck, the sucking end in easy reach of his mouth.

It is the outfit of a man who is about to search the Amazon for a new species of caterpillar, but there's no rainforest here. Instead, Matt is standing next to the breakfast bar in the open-plan kitchen of a suburban house in Raleigh, North Carolina.

It's an ordinary home. A silver kettle and wooden chopping board sit on the granite worktop. Pictures of the homeowners' kids are on display in the cupboard windows and a frying pan hangs from the range hood. At the far end of the room are sofas arranged around a flat-screen TV. The only plants here are in vases.

It is hard to imagine anywhere less like a rainforest, but looks can be deceptive. This might be a home, but it is also an ecological unknown. Scientists know more about life in the Amazon and deepest parts of the ocean than they do about the cave-like habitats that are our houses.

The ecology of the home is a mystery, a blank page yet to be written, and Matt, who works at North Carolina State University, and his colleague Michelle Trautwein of the North Carolina Museum of Natural Sciences have made it their mission to fill in some of the blanks. "Shall we find some bugs?" asks Matt. We nod, and he and Michelle get to work.

Matt flicks on the bright white light of his headlamp and homes in on the gas cooktop. He leans over it and sucks something up with his aspirator. He empties the find into the palm of his hand. "This looks like a shed skin of something," he says. He drops it into one of the vials, grabs his tweezers, and starts plucking more specks from the join between the work surface and tiled wall. I tell Matt that they look like nothing more than tiny pieces of fluff. "Actually, more often you pick up insects that you think are fluff," he replies, turning his attention to the small kitchen window.

"The windowsills are the best," he says, homing in on a crumpled insect. "Already, a huge crane fly." The crane fly is dead but well preserved. Its delicate wings with their network of black veins are undamaged as are the fly's long spindly legs, which bring to mind the tripods from H. G. Wells' *The War of the Worlds*. Matt adds it to the alcohol-filled vial.

Next, he spots a tiny, lifeless spider in the corner of the windowsill. "A cellar spider. It's a common one that we find on the first floors of houses. I bet there's one in every corner. And this, this is a little ichneumon wasp," he says, plucking up the insect next to the spider from the sill.

Ichneumon wasps are a very different type of wasp from the more familiar yellow-and-black picnic menaces. They are solitary parasites that plant eggs in the bodies of other arthropods so their larvae can eat their host alive from the inside out. The wasp Matt has found is jet black and the segments of its hook-shaped abdomen make it look armor plated. "This looks like it's from the subfamily Pimplinae," says Matt, whose expertise in insect identification makes him a rarity even among entomologists. "If it is, it might parasitize spiders. They could be in the home parasitizing things."

One type of parasitic wasp has been found time and time again in the Raleigh houses that Matt and Michelle have been surveying for their Arthropods of Our Homes project. Matt doesn't know exactly what species it is yet. Identifying insects down to species level is challenging at the best of times, and parasitic wasps are one of the toughest groups to classify. There are thousands of species, many are small, and they often look alike.

But Matt has a hunch. He thinks the most common parasitic wasp in Raleigh houses specializes in laying eggs in the eggs of cockroaches. "These wasps are really little—they have to be because they are egg parasites," he says. Too small to be our Pimplinae wasp, then.

While Matt has been sorting through the arthropods near the kitchen work surfaces, Michelle has been checking the living room window looking out to the backyard. She shows me her haul. One large shiny bluebottle and a smattering of tiny flies. "This big one's a Calliphoridae, possibly *Calliphora vomitoria*—a common trash-visiting and food-visiting fly, but, at the same time, there is this bunch of tiny gnats," she says. "We've got one, two, three, four . . . five, six. At least six different types of fly."

Flies, including mosquitoes, are the most common type of arthropod we share our homes with. They accounted for just over a quarter of all the species in the Raleigh houses. Beetles come next at 17 percent, followed by ants, bees and wasps at 15 percent. Spiders form the last big group, making up 14 percent of the finds. "We find more fly species associated with houses than any other group, but there's a lot of fly diversity," says Michelle.

To say there are "a lot" of fly species feels like an understatement. One in every ten known animals is a fly and it is believed that a great, great many more than the 150,000 known fly species are out there waiting to be discovered. "The two flies we find most often are the two people know about—the house fly and then the little fruit flies you see buzzing around your fruit. Both originated in Africa, just like we did. We dispersed around the world and they have followed us. There are house flies in old Egyptian mummy sarcophagi."

A good proportion of the flies are phorid flies, also known as humpback flies. They are tiny. The biggest are no more than six millimeters long. The smallest is *Euryplatea nanaknihali*, the world's smallest known fly. It measures a mere two-fifths of a millimeter long.

Another famous phorid fly—well, famous among entomologists at least—is *Megaselia scalaris*. "It is probably the most prolific insect on Earth," says Matt. "It seems to be everywhere around the world. It has even been found in an Antarctic research station. It feeds on everything: plants, fungus, paint, shoe polish. It's parasitic too. They are insane. Basically, if they can eat it, they will eat it."

And, as you might imagine for an insect that eats shoe polish, it doesn't care where it ends up. "Some were found alive in a snake that was preserved in formaldehyde in a jar," says Matt. "I've found papers about them infecting the lungs of a python that had pneumonia. They were in there eating the bacteria."

Other common household invertebrates are equally unfussy about what they eat. Not least, the wingless silverfish that often live in bathrooms, where they eke out an existence feeding on everything from wallpaper and shaving foam to dandruff and shampoo. "It takes silverfish years to mature because they eat things like glue, paper, and leather," says Matt. "They will eat really weird things that you don't think are digestible."

Insects like silverfish and book lice have a long history of living with us, says Michelle. "Book lice are these tiny little things and we see them in almost every house. An insect leg or a hair can feed a book louse for months. They are dwarfed by mosquito legs. They are not parasitic—they live off your detritus. They were probably doing that with our ape ancestors, so it goes back millions of years."

While some household arthropods date back thousands of years, others are more recent colonizers. "Some of them are a reflection of how our lifestyles have changed," she says. "So in living quarters of these houses in ancient Egypt there were dung beetles because human and animal waste was more closely associated with houses back then, whereas now we have got new species that are associated with indoor plumbing."

"I once found a dung beetle in my house," Matt volunteers. "Not sure what that says about my house."

One more of these modern arrivals are drain flies, a group of flies whose fuzzy fur makes them look like mini-moths. As their name suggests, they find the drains of modern homes a good place to live. Their larvae live inside the pipes, munching on the moist slime that builds up until they metamorphose into flies that live for a couple of days at most.

Or, at least, that is what they seem to be doing. Truth is, no one's actually done the science. "It looks like they are feeding on microbes in drains, but nobody's ever studied their biology or their evolution," says Rob Dunn, the associate professor of biology at North Carolina State University who dreamt up the Arthropods of Our Homes project with Michelle. "There does not appear to be a single scientific paper on them, other than enough to know that they exist."

The roots of the Arthropods of Our Homes project lie in another of Rob's studies, one that sought to find out what microbes live in homes. Like many of his studies, the microbes project was powered by citizen science with members of the public volunteering to have their homes swabbed for bacteria and other microscopic organisms.

After gathering all the samples from people's homes, Rob needed to give his army of volunteers something to do while he and his team pursued the time-consuming process of figuring out what bacteria they had found and analyzing the results. So he created a checklist of arthropods that people might find in their homes, e-mailed it to the volunteers, and asked them to report back on what they found in their game of creepy crawly bingo. One of the insects on the list was the camel cricket, a nocturnal brown cricket that gets its common name from its humped back. "I expected that people would find it as they sometimes turn up in basements, but that it wouldn't be that common," says Rob.

But when the results came in, something was up. The numbers saying, 'Yes, I have a camel cricket' were much higher than expected. Not only that, they were clustered geographically, rather than being dotted randomly across the country. Rob was puzzled. Maybe, he thought, people are mistaking something else for a camel cricket.

"There was this super-weird distribution. What we understood about these things is that they are a cave species and move into basements because they are like caves and that these crickets are all over North America. But when we mapped the results it was this weird smear on eastern North America. So we sent another e-mail saying send us a picture of it, because it's possible people were looking at a squirrel and thinking they were camel crickets or whatever."

When the photos came back, it became clear that the volunteers weren't mistaken. They had indeed found camel crickets in their basements, just not the one anybody expected. "Almost all of them turned out to be this invasive Japanese camel cricket. It looks similar but is a bit bigger and hoppier. It was known to be in the United States, but no one knew it had taken over basements across North America. I even had them in my own basement and didn't realize they were the Japanese ones."

The most visible difference between the two species is color. The back of the US camel cricket has a mottled appearance while its Asian counterpart has dark and light brown stripes. Japanese camel crickets also lack the spikes that are on the hind legs of the American species. These may sound like superficial differences, but they are just the obvious signs of the huge evolutionary gulf that exists between the North American and Asian camel crickets. "There's probably about twenty million years' difference between them. It's like thinking you have cats in the basement and you go and look and you realize it's wild African dogs. They are that different," says Rob.

After finding the surprise camel cricket lurking in the nation's basements, the idea for a deeper investigation into what is living in houses quickly took shape. Since then, Michelle, Matt, and the rest of the team have searched miles of baseboard and more than three hundred rooms in fifty Raleigh houses and collected more than ten thousand bugs.

Each house takes several hours to search and the researchers spend much of their time crawling around on the floor, which is why Matt wears kneepads on the job. "The longest was seven hours and that was me alone in an over three-thousand-square-foot, hundred-year-old house with three floors," says Matt, as he probes the utility room of the house, sucking up insects caught in the spider webs on the ceiling.

Even then, the searches are not as thorough as they could be. To protect people's privacy and save time, the team don't move furniture, check cupboards, or look behind fridges. They also stopped looking in light fixtures. "At the beginning we did, but light fixtures have as much diversity as a full house," says Michelle.

Perhaps surprisingly, people were more than happy to open their homes to the bug hunters. In fact, many were desperate to have them visit. "People were petitioning. They were like, 'How much can we pay you to come to our house? We've got the craziest bugs ever,'" recalls Matt. "It was like a competition, people saying, 'I've got more bugs than everybody else.'"

Yet no matter how unusual people think their creepy crawlies are, the reality is the bug count doesn't change much from home to home. Each property delivered a haul of about one hundred species. What's more, it doesn't seem to matter how much pesticide you spray or how often you clean. "You can't do anything about it," says Michelle. "It doesn't matter how much you spray. We are going to find a ton of stuff in your house if we come looking for it."

The volume of bugs in homes even surprises eminent biologists. Michelle tells me about the time that the famed American biologist and the world's foremost ant expert E. O. Wilson paid a visit to the North Carolina Museum of Natural Sciences. While he was there, Michelle showed him the bugs from one of the houses.

"Is this all from a house in a wood that kept its windows open?" he asked.

"No," replied Michelle. "This was a house that had a weekly cleaner. This is typical."

While regular cleaning and pesticide spraying doesn't seem to make much difference to bug diversity, having a dog does. Houses with dogs have consistently fewer species. Michelle's not sure why. It might be that dog owners vacuum more or that pets disturb the insects more, she guesses. But, for all we know, the pooches could be eating them.

First floor rooms boast the biggest range of arthropods, thanks to the regular influx of insects from the outside that either fly or get blown in by accident or are lured indoors by our lights. The attraction of artificial light explains why insects like sap-sucking leafhoppers are found in home after home.

For the bugs that spend their lives in our houses, the constant arrival of accidental visitors is a boon. "All those insects that come in accidentally get eaten by the spiders and other things," says Matt.

Spiders are especially well suited to life indoors, he adds. "There are plenty of spiders that live in homes and love traveling around homes. They are really good at living in dry environments because they can close up their bodies really well so that they don't lose a lot of moisture. That's why spiders can live in such arid regions.

They can also live for months without eating, a year without eating. They just have to be patient and see what comes along, so living in a house is fine for them, almost as much as living outside."

One spider that shows up regularly is the spitting spider *Scytodes thoracica*. One in ten of the Raleigh homes had these arachnids, which have bodies about the size of a grain of rice and sometimes live behind light switches. They are pale yellow with black splotches that become rings of black on their needlelike legs.

These spiders don't spin webs. Instead they are hunters that roam our houses in search of prey. Since their eyesight is poor, they rely on the sensitive bristles on their front legs to "smell" prey and so go on the prowl with their front legs held up so they can taste the air. After smelling a target, they close in and stop a couple of centimeters away before taking aim and shooting a mix of sticky webbing and venom that paralyses their victim. They also use this poisonous glue to defend themselves from predators and, sometimes, potential mates they mistook for a meal.

"The spitting spider has traveled around with us too. It's come from Europe," says Michelle. "Like a lot of these things they are covertly moving all over the planet, going for global domination without us having any idea."

Another, larger alpha predator of the home is the house centipede. Michelle calls it the "lion of the home" but Disney won't be making an animated picture about it anytime soon. Imagine all the traits about arthropods that freak people out and then put them together into one creepy crawly. Chances are you've pictured something close to a house centipede.

They can grow to two inches long but their fifteen pairs of long, spindly legs make them look twice as long. The last pair of legs is extra long, matching their drawn-out antennae and making it hard to tell its back from its front. Close up its face reveals a pair of sharp fangs for pincering prey and large jaws that look well designed for crunching hard exoskeletons. They move fast too. It seems like a creature that could cause nightmares and, judging by the panicked commentary on YouTube videos posted by those who have encountered these beasts in their homes, they probably do.

The house centipede is widespread, found across North America, Europe, and Asia, yet it remains one of the more mysterious members of the household ecosystem. House centipedes are understudied beasts. In the lab they eat everything from wood lice and cockroaches to earwigs and bees, but little is known about their behavior in our homes.

"If people really don't like an arthropod, we study it," says Rob. "People really don't like roaches—they are viewed as purveyors of disease, so we know a reasonable amount about them. Then, you've got bed bugs. Bed bugs are pretty well understood again. These things that really get to us, we will eventually learn about them in order to kill them. But this stuff that's there but neither deadly nor likable, nobody funds that. The house centipede just fits in this place where no one touches it."

And that's the crux when it comes to life inside our homes. No one is really studying anything more than the pests.

For all anyone knows, the bug life lurking in the freestanding houses of Raleigh are oddities. Would apartments and offices have more or less insects? Is the bug diversity in a house in the suburbs of Portland, Lisbon, or Perth different from that in Raleigh? We're a long way from knowing answers to these basic questions, let alone how all the bugs that live among us interact with each other.

But what the Arthropods of Our Homes project reveals is that our homes are more like jungles than we think. Beneath our feet is another, almost unnoticed world. One where unfortunate leafhoppers are hunted down by spitting spiders through carpet forests where book lice feast for months on fingernail fragments. A world where fly larvae feed beneath the plughole, cockroaches are terrorized by parasitic wasps, and invasive camel crickets quietly colonize basements.

It's a place we assume we know intimately but is every bit as unknown, fascinating and alive as the outside world.

Just as our houses look different when you're a bug, so do the streets, and for North America's ants the city is a battlefield. For more than 120 years, a war has been raging across the continent as native ants battle against a fierce invader: the Argentine ant. These dull brown ants reached the United States in the 1890s as stowaways on steamships delivering cargo from South America to New Orleans.

They are great at hitchhiking as they are unfussy about what they eat and where they nest, capable of settling down in places as unlikely as trash piles, bird nests, dishwashers, and bee hives. Their adaptable nature has taken them far since they got to Louisiana. By 1907 they had made it to California after hopping trains, and by 1999 they could be found in much of the southern and southwestern United States as well as in isolated patches as far north as Washington State.

For the native ants, the arrival of the Argentine ant was bad news. Very bad news. Argentine ants are warriors and have a zero tolerance policy to other ants in their vicinity. As they advanced, they wiped out other ants, which were slaughtered in the millions by the insect world's answer to Genghis Khan's Mongol hordes.

Only a few native ants have endured. Among them the winter ant, which protects itself from the marauders by spraying a toxic chemical on the ground to form a defensive barrier that delivers a quick and painful death to Argentine ants that try to attack.

But others have been forced into retreat: the wood-dwelling carpenter ant, the seed-eating harvester ant. Even the big-headed ant, which is such a successful invader in its own right that it has been called one of the world's hundred worst invasive species, can't stop it. When Argentine ants attack, big-headed ants abandon their nests and head off like refugees to find a new, safer place to live.

Key to the Argentine ant's ability to crush its opponents is its habit of building enormous super-colonies that house multiple queens and countless workers. The biggest of these colonies is in

Europe. It stretches for thirty-seven hundred miles, starting near the Italian city of Genoa before following the Mediterranean and Atlantic coasts all the way to the northeastern tip of Spain.

Such is the unity of the Argentine ants that if you take one from the European mega-nest and introduce it to the six-hundred-mile super-colony that runs from San Francisco to the Mexican border, it will integrate without a hitch. Most other ants would tear apart any ant from a different nest. Thanks to these super-colonies, Argentine ants have huge numbers on their side, allowing them to overwhelm other ants in battle and find food fast so their rivals go hungry.

But their success is not just down to numbers, super-colonies, or a catholic diet. The other advantage the Argentine ant has is us. Not only have our ships, trains, and trucks transported them around, but also the watered lawns of our cities and towns give them the moisture they need to thrive in otherwise unsuitable environments. As such, the expansion of the Argentine ant empire is closely tied to urban development. The number of Argentine ants increases almost exponentially with the extent of urbanization, and when they stray too far from us, they struggle to continue their otherwise relentless advance.

This ongoing war may seem inconsequential, a case of one ant replacing some other ants, but the fallout of this pint-sized conflict is causing wider damage. Many of the ants that are being exterminated help to disperse the seeds of local plants, and their loss has the potential to threaten the survival of these plants and, in turn, the animals that rely on them.

The California horned lizard is another victim of the ant war. These spike-encrusted reptiles were already struggling because of urban growth erasing their habitat, but the Argentine ants are upping the pressure. The lizard eats ants but needs a wide variety of species to thrive, and as the Argentine ant wipes out the opposition, the lizards are finding it harder to feed themselves.

The Argentine is not the only foreign ant invading the United States. In Texas, another more recent, and potentially more dangerous, arrival is threatening to bring down cities and space missions.

Tom Rasberry was the man who found them. Tom, a pest controller based in Houston, first spotted them in 2002 when a local chemical plant asked him to kill off a bunch of fire ants. They caught his eye because they were unusually small, about the size of a flea, and moved in wayward patterns rather than marching in orderly columns. Odd, he thought, before returning to the task of exterminating the fire ants with pesticide.

A year later the chemical plant called again. Ants, again? asked Tom. Yup, said the facilities manager. But on arriving at the plant he found no fire ants. Instead, the plant was swarming with millions upon millions of the flea-sized ants he spotted the year before.

They were everywhere, pouring into offices, zig-zagging across the parking lot and—most worryingly of all for a chemical plant— flooding into the electronics and causing them to short circuit. What the hell are they? wondered Tom as he tried to blast them out of existence with insecticide. Figuring that he needed an expert's input, he collected some of the ants and contacted Texas A&M University to see if its entomologists could tell him what it was.

The university's bug experts were equally puzzled. They made suggestion after suggestion, but each time they checked the ant didn't match. As the scientists tried to pin down exactly what the new ant was, Tom took to calling it the Rasberry crazy ant. Rasberry after himself, crazy in a nod to their chaotic movements.

The name stuck. Even after it was finally identified in 2012 as the tawny crazy ant *Nylanderia fulva*, the Rasberry crazy ant name refused to go away. "I don't know if I've soiled my family name or brought prestige to it," Tom told the TV show *Texas Country Reporter*.

By then it was clear that the Rasberry crazy ant was a serious problem. They might be small, but they are feisty. They have wiped out entire beehives as the bees can't stop their assaults because the crazy ants are just too small to sting. Fire ants face much the same problem when the crazy ants attack.

Then there is their habit of invading electronic equipment. The crazy ants like confined spaces and see electrical equipment as a good place to nest or look for food, and—since they are small—they have no trouble at all in getting into everything from desktop computers to cell phones.

Once inside the problems start. One of the ants will, inevitably, create a connection between the tracks of circuit boards and get electrocuted. As that individual dies she releases an alarm phero-mone, alerting the rest of the colony to an unspecific threat.

In response to the warning, the dead ant's sisters rally and head to the same spot ready for battle, only to get electrocuted themselves, accelerating the cycle until enough agitated ants get electrocuted to short the entire circuit.

The crazy ant's habit of getting electrocuted until they blow circuits has caused repeated shutdowns at chemical works in the city and panicked NASA, which has hired Tom to stop the ants from entering the Lyndon B. Johnson Space Center and destroying the computers that power its space missions.

But the Rasberry crazy ant is no longer just Houston's problem. They are spreading fast, aided by people inadvertently transporting them in their vehicles. By summer 2008 they had reached Orange County, Texas, on the Louisiana border. Four years later, their pres-ence had been confirmed in Louisiana, Mississippi, and Florida. With its ability to crush even the fearsome fire ant and its potential to wreck computers and electronics in hospitals, airports, power stations, and other critical facilities, the crazy ant may soon make the Argentine ant look like a welcome guest.

Invaders from foreign lands make for good headlines, but not every US city ant came from abroad. One of the most common in North

America is the odorous house ant, known to scientists as *Tapinoma sessile*.

In the country it is a meek species that lives a quiet life. The ants found small colonies in acorns that rarely exceed a hundred workers and adopt a rancher lifestyle, protecting aphids from predatory ladybugs and "milking" the aphids for sweet, sugary honeydew.

But, as the Bible passage goes, the meek shall inherit the earth. Or at least the city, for the urban hustle and bustle brings out the wild side of the odorous house ant. On reaching the city, the ants ditch the humble colonies they used to make and embrace the super-colony strategy of the Argentine ant, building networks of nests with multiple queens and more than ten thousand workers that seek to dominate the local ant world.

"It's gone from this rare ant that lived in acorns with one queen to this ant that takes over whole city blocks with hundreds of queens," says Rob. "My own house is surrounded by them. At first it was thought to be an evolutionary change. Nobody was quite sure what had caused it and it was talked about as a mutant."

But these are no mutants. The odorous house ant that conquers entire blocks and raids kitchens in search of sugary treats is exactly the same as those tending aphids in the woods.

Instead, they are powered up by the urban world. Buildings offer countless places to nest for an ant small enough to make an acorn its home, and the warmth and protection human structures offer allows odorous house ants to be active all year. There's also more food. Not only are cities full of human food but there are often high numbers of honeydew-excreting bugs like aphids and scale insects too.

Scale insects are strange creatures that act more like mussels or barnacles than insects. After finding a plant to feed on, they stick their proboscis in and use it like a drinking straw to suck the sap. They never move again. Some even shed their legs and antennae after finding a feeding spot, spending their lives drinking sap and covering themselves in protective wax.

Scale insects thrive in cities and one reason for this is the urban heat island effect. In Raleigh the willow oak trees in the hottest parts of the city have way more scale insects than those in the coolest zones. "In the warmest part of Raleigh the ground temperature is six degrees Celsius warmer than the coolest parts. For context that's about as much warming as we expect from climate change by 2070," says Rob, whose laboratory at North Carolina State University discovered the connection between the city's warmth and scale insect numbers. "What we're seeing in Raleigh is that the trees in those areas have thirteen-fold more scale insects. What is happening is these areas are getting warmer earlier and so speeding up the scales' metabolic activities so that they get bigger earlier in the year."

For the parasitic wasps that target scale insects this is a problem. "Because the parasitoids experience multiple temperatures when they fly around, their metabolism doesn't speed up as much, so by the time they go to attack the scales, the scales are already really big and so they can reproduce more," says Rob.

"It looks like these patches of heat are super important in affecting what's going on overall. It's interesting for us because, in general, we suck at making good predictions for what to expect with global warming, but in cities you have this terrific experiment where we've essentially simulated what we think conditions will be in 2070, and that's why we're looking at New York."

New York, and Manhattan especially, has become an object of fascination for Rob's laboratory. "New York's so cool," he says, eyes lighting up at the very thought. "The road medians on Broadway are super hot. They are surrounded by all these buildings and all the sunlight bounces off the buildings and can't get back up, so the ground heats up. These medians are like a foot of dirt on top of the subway and are this kind of fantastic futuristic ecosystem.

"Sixty percent of everybody now lives in cities, 70 percent is coming faster than anybody thinks, and the remaining 30 percent live in places that are not nearly so rural as we think. So in that regard the experience of walking down a street in Manhattan or Tokyo or some monster city in China is way more like our future experience of nature will be."

To find out what this ultra-urban future might mean, scientists from Rob's laboratory have been surveying the ants living in the road medians of Broadway to see what life might be like in a hotter future. Post-doctoral scholar Amy Savage has been leading the study. When we meet she is in the midst of crunching the data she has gathered after months of visiting New York and scrabbling around in the medians with her aspirator at the ready.

You must have gotten some funny looks doing that, I say. She nods. "One time I scared this woman. She was sitting at one of the tables on the median and looked up and there I was. I wasn't paying attention to her and she was like, 'Oh! What are you doing?' I said, 'I'm studying the ants.' Now sometimes people ask why and that's great because you can then talk about how ecology is happening everywhere, but this lady was like, 'All right. Whatever you want.'

"Another time a guy said, 'We don't like people being in the medians because they will hurt the plants but also because we put rat poison down every morning.' I was like, 'Oh. I've been sucking up the soil with my aspirator.'"

When not being interrupted by New Yorkers or sucking up poisoned soil, Amy has discovered some unusual things about the ants on Broadway. First, they are not the same ants as those living in the forested areas within city limits. "I thought we'd find everything that is in the medians would be in the parks and urban forests, but that's not what we're finding," she says. "We find things that are in the medians that you never see in the forest. The next step is to ask why, and so we're thinking about the idea of stress in the habitat and whether there's a relationship between stressful conditions and species."

Another curiosity is that the Broadway ants have different food preferences from other ants. "The story with ant diets is usually proteins versus sugars, and then there's some recent work showing that salty food is a requirement for some ants, so those ants do really well by roads because there's so much salt there."

Given this, Amy didn't expect to find anything unusual when she got around to testing the New York ants' food preferences. She set down five liquid baits: water, sugar water, salt water, an amino acid solution representing protein, and, for fats, some extra virgin olive oil. The water and olive oil were there as controls; it was the proportion of sugar, protein, and salt the ants went for that she wanted data on. The ants living in the parks behaved as expected, sipping at the sugar, protein, and salt options but—for the most part—living up to ants' reputation as sugar fiends.

But the Broadway ants didn't conform. "The pavement ants in the park, over 90 percent of the time they went for sugars, but in the medians there was this complete shift to the extra virgin olive oil. It wasn't just this one species. It happened with all the species. They all had this flip where they went for the fats in the olive oil. In the median almost all they went for was the oil."

Amy thinks the shift is because of the lack of other arthropods living in the medians and the steady supply of sugar passersby provide in the form of spilled soda and discarded New York–style pizza. "If you go to those medians on Broadway and turn over a rock, any rock, there are isopods everywhere: roly-polies, millipedes and these beetles called rove beetles. All of these species are really good at avoiding ant predation. So we have this hypothesis that median ants are just really hungry because there are few prey species available. They are able to get a lot of sugars from whatever is discarded, but if you think of it in evolutionary time, ants did not grow up with extra virgin olive oil, so they got their fats from grasshoppers and things like that, but there aren't any of those really fatty insects in the median."

The shortage of fats could, she says, be making the ants more aggressive predators, which might explain why the ants of Broadway are outcompeting rats for food. The ants' ability to outcompete the rats was first noticed when another researcher doing an unrelated study on the New York medians laid some traps for the rodents. "He was trying to trap rats with a trap with bait in it and had a heck of a time on the medians because the ants ate all of the bait before the rats could get to it," says Amy. "You think that an individual rat is so much bigger than an individual ant but, really, it's more reasonable to think of ants as a colony and the biomass of a colony can be big, although I'm not sure it would be as big as a rat's biomass. But ants are also super-efficient and active all the time, while rats are more active at dawn and dusk."

Rats might loom larger than ants in the minds of New Yorkers, but on these futuristic streets the ant may yet prove to be the real king of Manhattan.

TUNNELS OF THE BLOODSUCKERS

The Rats and Mosquitoes Lurking Under London

Paul Doumer arrived in Hanoi in 1897 burning with ambition. Fresh from a failed attempt to introduce an income tax while serving as France's finance minister, the Radical politician saw his new role as governor-general of Indochina as a chance to make his mark.

Until then, the French Empire had taken a hands-off approach to the colony. Previous governor-generals preferred an indirect approach to running the territory, but under Doumer that all changed. As far as he was concerned the place needed civilizing. He compared his mission to that of the Romans conquering the barbarians, and saw it as his duty to introduce the people of Indochina to the superior culture of France.

Doumer was ruthless in achieving this zealous goal. He deposed the local emperors, replacing them with figureheads who would do his bidding, and transformed Indochina's government into a highly centralized bureaucracy run almost entirely by the French. Keen to make the colony profitable, he imposed harsh taxes on the people and forced the nation's peasants into slavery so that a network of

181

highways, bridges, canals, and railroads could be built. To cap it all off, Doumer's government encouraged the Vietnamese to get hooked on opium, even opening stores to peddle the drug so it could reap the profits from creating a nation of addicts.

Doumer's actions caused deep resentment among the people of Indochina and helped sow the seeds for the Vietnam War. But as far as France was concerned he was doing fantastic work, and Indochina became the toast of the French Empire.

Hanoi was to be his crowning glory. He envisaged turning the ancient Vietnamese city into the epitome of an orderly, modern metropolis. To start the transformation, he built a whites-only residential neighborhood of luxurious villas and wide, tree-lined avenues connected by a thoroughly modern grid road network.

Naturally, this flashy new quarter of Hanoi was supported with a state-of-the-art sewer system. It was a far cry from the creaking drainage system the Vietnamese lived with, which did little more than pour raw sewage into the Red River and flood the streets with human waste in the monsoon season. The sewer was crucial to the new quarter. The role that rats and fleas played in the spread of bubonic plague had just been discovered, so the new whites-only sewers were designed to protect the French residents of Hanoi from an outbreak.

All was going well until the residents started reporting that rats were entering their homes through the indoor plumbing. It turned out the new sewers were infested with rats, which found them an ideal place to live thanks to the lack of predators and the convenience of having an underground network of tunnels to roam. Shortly after came the first cases of bubonic plague in the French quarter.

Unwilling to have his grand plan upset by mere vermin, Doumer ordered the rats be exterminated. So began the great rat massacre of Hanoi.

The massacre began in late April 1902 when the government sent in teams of Vietnamese rat catchers, who were paid in line with the number of rats they killed. It was dangerous and thankless work. The sewers were cramped, dark, and filthy places that housed not only rats but also spiders, flies, and snakes. Despite the challenge, the first week was a huge success. The rat catchers emerged from the sewers with thousands upon thousands of dead rats.

By early May nearly eight thousand rats had been killed, and the haul kept rising. By mid-June the rat catchers were bringing more than ten thousand dead rats to the surface every day. On one day their haul even topped the twenty thousand mark.

Not that this pleased the French residents, who now found their manicured streets were full of stinking Vietnamese rat catchers dragging around hundreds of dead rats. Soon the colonists were complaining about having to put up with the sight and smell of the rat catchers.

The rats, however, were down, not out. They quickly learned to avoid the rat catchers, and the numbers being caught began to plunge. At the same time the rat catchers were getting fed up and started demanding more money. After repeated strikes their pay was quadrupled, but by then they were struggling to deliver results. The rats, now wise to the rat catchers, were breeding faster than they could be caught.

Doumer's administration decided that if the rats were going to be defeated, they needed an army. So it told the people of Hanoi it would pay a bounty of one cent for every dead rat. Keen not to have mountains of dead rats dumped at their offices, the French told people to just bring in the tails.

The French imperialists must have felt rather pleased with themselves then, when people began turning up with thousands upon thousands of rat tails. But their glee was short-lived. Soon reports came in of tailless rats roaming the city. It turned out residents were chopping off the tails but letting the rats go free so they could keep breeding. Some enterprising people had even started breeding captive rats so they could profit from the tails.

Together the cunning of the rats and the people of Hanoi won

out. Thwarted, the French conceded defeat and scrapped the extermination program, and soon it was back to life as usual for the rats
beneath the city.

As Doumer's doomed extermination plan confirmed, rats are part
and parcel of city life, immovable and undefeatable. Rats have conquered cities the world over. Some have more, some have less, but
almost no city is rat-free.

While Southeast Asian cities like Hanoi are home to many species of rat, the streets of Europe and North America are dominated
by just two: the black rat, *Rattus rattus*, and the brown or Norway
rat, *Rattus norvegicus*.

The black rat, also called the ship's rat, is the rarer of the two, but
once upon a time it ruled the city. These velvet-furred rodents have
long been implicated as the vehicles that spread the plague-carrying
fleas that unleashed the Black Death, the twelfth-century pandemic
that wiped out more than one-third of Europeans.

How big a role the black rat played in the Black Death is dis-
puted. Some argue that the plague's rapid spread could only have
happened if the disease was transmitted person-to-person rather
than from flea bites.

What's not in doubt, however, is that black rats thrived in the
cities of old. They are capable climbers and could easily scale the
walls of timber buildings to nest in attics or thatched roofs, an ability that earned them yet another name: the roof rat.

But their reign has passed. As streets got cleaner and builders
swapped timber for brick, the black rat found the city less inviting.
The final straw was a challenger from the East.

Although it is called the Norway rat, the brown rat has nothing
to do with the Nordic nation. That name dates back to the rats'
arrival in England, which was blamed on Norwegian ships even
though the rodent is believed to have originated in northern China.

When the brown rat reached Europe and North America in the 1700s, it set to work usurping the black rat from its urban strongholds. The brown rats had evolution on their side. They are both larger and more aggressive than black rats and, crucially, they are burrowing rather than tree-dwelling rodents. So while the black rats were contending with new architecture that made it harder to nest in roofs, the brown rats found an abundance of basements and sewers to live in.

By the end of the 1800s, the brown rat had taken control of most North American and European cities. In Britain, the black rat nearly vanished altogether, ending up a rare sight outside of dockyards. They still cling on in warmer cities such as Phoenix, where they have gained a foothold in the Arcadia neighborhood, but the black rat's urban glory days are long gone.

Regardless of what species roams our streets, rats have many qualities that make them well suited to urban life, and one of the most important is that they are sex mad. Rats are promiscuous lovers with raging libidos, and adults can have sex twenty times a day. They are bisexual too, often mounting rats of the same sex. And all this sex results in lots of babies.

Rat pregnancies last just twenty-one days, and each litter produces eight to ten pups. And with the kids hitting puberty after sixty days, it doesn't take long before they are getting it on too. As a result, a single pair of rats can have up to fifteen thousand descendants in a single year. So it's just as well less than 5 percent live long enough to reach their first birthday.

Rats are also wary creatures. They avoid open spaces, preferring to run along walls where there is less chance of being spotted by predators like hawks or people. They also don't like change, preferring to retread the same routes night after night. If they find unfamiliar food they might nibble it, but they won't scarf it down until they are confident it is safe to eat. Same goes for the traps we lay for them. Rats will steer clear of traps when they first appear and tend to only pluck up the courage to investigate further when it has been sitting idle for a few days.

This combo of fearfulness and horniness makes them good at surviving in the city. The wariness makes them hard to exterminate, and even when they slip up it won't be long before a newborn pup replaces the unlucky individual.

Rats are expert cat burglars too. They can squeeze through gaps of just three-quarters of an inch in diameter and if a hole proves too small to get through they have the tools to make it bigger. The brown rat's sharp incisors are as hard as glass or a steel knife, so they are more than capable of chiseling their way through brick, mortar, and other materials if the need arises.

As London's chief sewer flusher, Rob Smith has seen the impact of their tunneling abilities many times. Rob has worked the sewers of the British capital for decades. He started his career by helping to build sewers more than forty years ago before switching over to maintaining them for the water company Thames Water.

There are plenty of sewers to maintain. London's eight million residents are served by thousands of miles of sewers that mix together modern drains, overwhelmed Victorian tunnels, and "lost" subterranean rivers that have long been buried beneath the streets.

Much of Rob's job involves getting rid of fatbergs, the stinking lumps of cold cooking fat, used wet wipes, cotton swabs, tampons, and other unsavory detritus that congeal in the sewers and block the tunnels. Every year Thames Water deals with forty thousand of these vile blockages.

The biggest fatberg to date was discovered in 2013 after nearby residents complained they couldn't flush their toilets. The fifteen-ton monstrosity took Rob and his team three weeks to blast apart with high-pressure jets of water.

Encounters with rats are par for the course when fighting fatbergs, Rob tells me over the phone, mere days before he hung up his gumboots for good and entered retirement. "The one that sticks in my mind was down through Leicester Square a few years ago. The fat was floating on top of the sewage and it was like the M1 for rats," he says, referring the motorway that links London and Leeds. "There were quite a few rats down there because they eat the fat and everything, so they had food and a means for getting from one area to another without getting into the sewage because they would cross over the top of the fat."

Rob decided to fix the fat problem by redirecting sewage from other parts of the network into the area for a weekend to flush it away. The following Monday morning Rob and his team headed into the sewers under Long Acre to see the results. "We went down and, in that particular sewer, the stairs are very much like you'd expect to see in a lighthouse or something: a spiral staircase, bricks, and Yorkstone slabs. Of course, all the rats had sought sanctuary in these side entrances and along the stairs. I think that was about the most rats I'd ever seen."

Having seen plenty of rats in their time, Rob and his colleagues weren't bothered. "They eye you from a distance," he says. "They will move out of the way and keep out of the light, so that you can just see their beady little eyes in the distance.

"There's three of us, sixteen or seventeen stone, quite big fellas with lights and making quite a lot of noise, and the rats start going down the stairs in front of us. Then they reached the point where they had no option but to go into the sewer and into the flow, and that's when they decided to come back up the stairs. So there was a bit of tap dancing going on, y'know."

Despite being good swimmers, London's sewer rats do all they can to avoid entering fast-flowing sewer water, which is dangerous even for them. "Very often if you get a snap storm, you find quite a few of Roland Rat and his friends turn up down at the works because they drown," says Rob, referring to the puppet that became a huge British children's TV star in the 1980s.

Fatbergs may be the problem that demands most of Rob's time, but the hard teeth of the rats mean they, too, threaten the city's sewers. "Believe it or not, they gnaw their way through brickwork. They can make their own access points and ingress points," he says. "A lot of the brick sewers rely on the ground around them to hold them in shape. So if you get rats digging around the outside of the sewer, it threatens the stability. In my twenty-odd years with Thames I've seen two or three points where rats have caused sewers, not to collapse, but to put the fabric of them at risk to the point that we've had to go down and do something about it."

Although sewers are not the only place city rats live, life under our streets is idyllic if you're a rat, as a Danish study discovered. The researchers examined the lives of rats living in two neighboring but unconnected sewer systems in the Copenhagen suburb of Kongens Lyngby.

They found a rat society that was peaceful and content. Intruder rats that ventured into the sewers were rarely attacked by those already living there as would normally happen when a rat enters another's territory. The sewer-dwellers lived longer too, lasting four rather than three months on average, and the smaller, drier pipes served as ideal nurseries for rats to raise their young.

In fact, none of the rats tracked by the researchers ever left the sewer they were born in. They weren't interested in the surface world. They didn't venture into it, and their distribution through the system bore no relation to whether there were houses or stores above them.

But it's unlikely they went hungry because in the sewer the food never stops coming. "There's a hell of a lot of food that goes into the sewer system," says Rob. "A lot of houses, especially the more upmarket places, and restaurants in London have got their disposal units. They just put the food in and it emulsifies it, and it goes out into the drainage system, and in places where you've got a fruit and veg market they hose it down and all the green stuff goes into the road gullies and then into sewers."

Londoners often imagine that the rats living in the city's underworld favor the aging Victorian sewers, but that's not the case. Although the Victorian portion looms large in the imagination, when Thames Water funded a study to see if rat hotspots were linked to the age of the sewers, all the hotspots turned out to be in the post-Victorian parts of the network.

Actually, a lot of what we believe about city rats is wrong, not least the oft-repeated claim that there's one rat for every person in New York City or that you are never more than six feet away from a rat in London.

These dodgy statistics date back to a survey William Richard Boelter conducted for his 1909 book *The Rat Problem*. Boelter asked people living on farms around England whether it was reasonable to assume that there was one rat per acre. Everyone he asked said yes or that there would be more than that. He didn't even bother asking anyone living in villages, towns, or cities, because he assumed that one or more rats per acre was a given in urban areas.

Having concluded on this flimsy basis that there was indeed one rat per acre, he noted that there were forty million acres of land in the UK and, therefore, forty million rats. By coincidence the population of the UK was about forty million people at the time, spawning the claim that there was one rat for every person. It may have been a bogus figure, but it was attention-grabbing, so newspapers and pest controllers kept reciting it until it stuck, and somewhere along the way it morphed into the claim that you are never more than six feet away from a rat.

In truth rats are nowhere near that common, even in cities. A more recent and more methodical estimate by the UK government puts the country's rat population at ten and a half million, of which just one-third live in urban areas.

Even in New York City, where rats loom large in people's imagination, the one rat per person claim doesn't hold up. The city's most thorough rat census dates back to 1949, when researchers concluded that there were quarter of a million rats in the five boroughs—well below the eight million Boelter's statistic suggested.

Although no one really knows how many rats live in the Big Apple today, even generous estimates based on reported rat sightings struggle to live up to the one-per-person claim. A crude estimate made by the news website *FiveThirtyEight* assumed that one in a hundred New Yorkers would report a rat when they saw one, that no rat would be seen twice, and that every sighting involved two rats. Apply that to the ten-thousand-odd sightings a year and that's two million rats in the city, one for every four people.

Equally surprisingly, city rats are less disease-ridden than their rural cousins. While it would go too far to call them clean, an Oxford University study comparing London rats with those from British farms found that country rats were dirtier.

The urban rats had lower levels of listeria, tapeworms, and roundworms. They were also less likely to have *Toxoplasma gondii*. This creepy protozan twists the brains of rats so they behave in ways that make them more likely to get eaten by cats, which are its final host, and it might be altering our minds too. About one in four people in the United States is infected with *T. gondii*, and it has been linked with increased risk of suicide and schizophrenia.

The rats were also free of the bacteria that cause the respiratory infection pseudomonas, which often thrives in hospitals. Even leptospirosis, the life-threatening disease rats are most associated with, was comparatively rare in the urban rodents. Only whipworms were more common in the city rats.

It seems that urban rats are less likely to get infected with these parasites because they have less contact with livestock excrement and, thanks to our own attention to hygiene, the rats living in the sewers are less exposed to parasites. As Rob tells me when I ask about the aroma of London's sewers: "It's not smelling of roses by any means, but it's not quite as bad as people think because they forget to factor into the equation the amount of water, soap, and scented perfume that gets washed into the sewer at the same time."

Of course being cleaner than rural rats is hardly a recommendation, and with their potential to damage sewers, spread disease, and gnaw through electrical cables there are plenty of good reasons why cities seek to keep these rodents under control.

But while London has opted to do no more to keep them at bay, Paul Doumer's dream of a rat-free city lives on elsewhere. Copenhagen has talked about eradicating rats by 2015 and New York has been experimenting with ways to sterilize its rats. So far just three large cities claim to be rat-free. The first two are Calgary and Edmonton in Canada, and both owe their lack of rats to the swift action taken in the 1950s to keep brown rats from entering the entire province of Alberta. The third is the Hungarian capital Budapest. It faced a tougher challenge: eliminating rats that had already conquered the city.

In 1970 Budapest was a city under siege, a place where Boelter's claim of one rat for each of its two million people actually held true. A third of properties were infested, including the whole of downtown, and each year the damage caused by rats was costing the city the equivalent of $40 million in today's money. In response the city declared all-out war on the rats and brought in Bábolna Bio, the pest control division of a state-controlled stud and chicken farm, to eliminate them.

What followed was a blitzkrieg. For almost two years Bábolna's extermination squads combed the streets, homes, factories, and sewers for rats. No location was left unchecked. The Communist government had required all citizens and businesses to open their doors to the pest controllers, and everywhere the exterminators went they laid down rat poison. By the end of the crackdown in December 1972, more than one and a half thousand tons of rodenticide had been spread over the city, and hundreds of thousands of rats were dead.

Since then Bábolna Bio, which is now privately owned, has been monitoring every site rats could use to recolonize the city, from railroad stations and markets to rivers and sewers, and acting fast to stamp out any rats that do show up. As a result Budapest has been near enough rat-free for nearly half a century. Today just one in every thousand Budapest properties gets a rat infestation every year. In comparison, three in every hundred homes and five in every hundred commercial properties in Britain have rats.

While Budapest proves that eliminating rats is possible, it is not an easy task, says Bábolna Bio's managing director, Daniel Bajomi. "Theoretically the same results could be achieved in New York or Paris too," he says, but it needs strong political will, a lot of money, and "a political system that ensures access to every premises."

And even then rats still cling on in small numbers. "Rats still live in the sewer system in minimal numbers," says Daniel.

Rats are not the only things living beneath cities. There are fungi in the sewer, for starters. "It's dark and dank, so it's the ideal environment for growing mushrooms and you do get some odd growths growing down there off the walls in a few places," says Rob. "We've got toads and frogs too, and some horrible little black flies that always manage to get in your eyes and your mouth whenever you have a deep breath."

Another resident of subterranean London is the mosquito *Culex pipiens molestus*, which first gained attention during the Second World War when it began feasting on people sheltering from German bombs in London Underground tunnels.

But *Culex pipiens molestus* is more than just another blood-sucking fly. It's actually a special underground form of the northern house mosquito, *Culex pipiens*, that can be found across the temperate zone of the Northern Hemisphere, from the northern half of the United States to Europe and onward, through Central Asia, to China and Japan.

Above ground the northern house mosquito behaves much like we expect mosquitoes to. The females need to feed on blood to develop their eggs, and while they much prefer to suck the blood of birds, if that's not an option us or another mammal will suffice, and they have no qualms about entering homes to find that vital meal. In fall, the females that are still alive enter diapause—a state of suspended animation that helps them survive until they reawaken in the spring.

But although it is the same species, the *molestus* form behaves very differently and is limited to dark, underground worlds like the London Underground, other metro systems, or the sewers. Unlike its brethren on the surface, *molestus* doesn't do diapause. Instead it is active year-round, cocooned by the largely constant temperatures of the urban underground, which is insulated from the winter cold and summer heat by the surrounding soil.

The *molestus* form also doesn't need blood. It can lay its first raft of eggs without feeding on an animal, a feat it can even manage when sugar is in short supply, which is often the case in the dark, flower-free underground. Instead it turns to blood when it hopes to lay more eggs and, since birds are rarely seen underground, *molestus* prefers mammal blood and makes rats, mice, and the occasional metro passenger its target.

Most of the time, the above- and below-ground forms of the northern house mosquito live separate lives. One roams the surface world, biting birds and the occasional person. The other buzzes around in the dark, laying eggs in stagnant pools of underground water and catching opportunistic blood meals from passing rats. So separate are their lives that the mosquitoes of the London Underground are genetically distinct enough from the mosquitoes living above ground to suggest the subterranean population originally entered the tunnels as far back as the late 1800s, when the deep Bakerloo and Central lines were being constructed.

The genetic differences don't stop at the surface. The mosquitoes may have colonized both the east-west Central line and the north-south Bakerloo line, but the only place these lines meet is at Oxford Circus station, and even then they are separated by a maze of escalators, stairs, and underground passageways. As such there's

little opportunity for the mosquitoes living on different Underground lines to meet, and over time that seems to have caused
their populations to become distinct through a process known as
genetic drift.

Genetic drift is about randomness and sampling error. Flip a
coin a thousand times and you should end up with an even split
where the result is half heads, half tails. But toss a coin ten times
and there's a good chance that you would get more heads than tails
because there is more chance of a disproportionate result when you
have a small sample.

A similar principle applies to the genetics of small, isolated
populations, like the London Underground mosquitoes. So when
Bakerloo line mosquitoes breed, some genes, quite randomly,
become overrepresented from one generation to the next. Over
time this random effect makes them less and less like the population on the Central line, where genetic drift may have led to
different genes being passed down.

As a result the isolated mosquito populations of the London
Underground become less and less like each other as well as distinct
from those on the surface. But when the above- and below-ground
forms of the northern house mosquito meet, the results can be
fatal.

One place this happened was in the villages west of Thessaloniki
in northern Greece, where open sewers and cesspits allowed the
usually isolated forms to interbreed. The fusion of underground and
overground mosquitoes created hybrids with a heightened taste
for the blood of both birds and mammals, as well as the ability to
survive winter by entering diapause.

In August 2010 these hybrids caused the first outbreak of the
West Nile virus in Greece, as the mosquitoes transferred the disease
from migratory birds to people. It became one of the largest-ever
outbreaks of the potentially deadly virus in Europe with more than
250 people infected and 35 dead.

It was not an isolated event. There's plenty of evidence suggesting that these hybrids caused the 1999 West Nile virus outbreak in New York that signaled the arrival of the disease in the Americas. Whereas in Europe the above- and below-ground forms rarely meet, in the United States, for reasons unknown, more than four out of ten northern house mosquitoes are hybrids. So when the virus reached New York, via bird or an infected person who caught it abroad, the mosquitoes were already well placed to spread it from bird to bird, bird to human, human to bird, and human to human.

Since then West Nile virus has spread across the United States, aided by migratory birds, hybrid northern house mosquitoes, and—in the South—their close relative *Culex quinquefasciatus*, the southern house mosquito.

Intriguingly, the *molestus* form that enabled these hybrids seems to be a recent development in evolutionary terms, emerging just ten thousand years ago. No one is sure why it came to be, but there are two theories. One theory is that a population of northern house mosquitoes got isolated during a glaciation. The other theory is that it developed in response to living alongside people, evolving to make the most of us and our settlements.

This latter theory is a startling idea, one that suggests cities may do more than just change the behavior of animals. Could it be that our cities are rewiring the very DNA of animals?

WEST SIDE ROACHES

NYC Cockroach Investigations and Bakersfield Kit Foxes

Mark Stoeckle's got mail: a small white envelope with his address at Rockefeller University scrawled on in black ink. He cuts it open and we look inside to find the squashed remains of a cockroach.

Mark gives it an approving nod. It's an American cockroach, and that's exactly the kind of roach he wants in his mail. For Mark, a geneticist at the New York City university, this is a regular occurrence. "They dribble in. Some days we might get none. Other days we get several."

The mail is just the start. People give him cockroaches wherever he goes. "I actually went to a meeting last night and someone gave me a plastic bag of cockroaches, and they were apologizing, saying, 'I tried to keep them alive.'"

Dead is preferred, Mark replied.

Mark's been collecting them too, scooping them off the Manhattan streets as he walks to and from his West Side home. "I carry a little plastic bag to collect them in," he says. "The morning is the best time to find them because, I think, the birds eat them and the ones you see out on the street in the day are dead while the ones at night are roaming around.

"I also went to some building supers in the neighborhood. The supers know where the cockroaches are and they were helpful. Some say we don't have any in our building, but that is sort of impossible for New York—if the building is connected to the sewer system, somewhere there are probably cockroaches."

What happens now? I ask, looking at the dead roach in the envelope. "I stick it in the freezer," he replies.

The freezer at Mark's laboratory is full of cockroaches, each stored in individual plastic vials with their origin recorded on them. Reassuringly, his roach collection is not a strange hobby but part of a *CSI*-style investigation into the genetics of New York City's most unwanted roommates.

It all began with sushi. "We've been doing projects with high school students for several years and, when my daughter was in high school, I had been working on DNA barcoding, which is a simple way of identifying species by their DNA," Mark explains. "My daughter had the idea that we could test sushi and so we did.

"We found a quarter of the fish in sushi was mislabeled, and the results got in the *New York Times* and on television. That gave us the idea that there are really interesting questions you could do with students where you could make real discoveries."

One of those high school projects tested the DNA of household bugs. It was supposed to be routine work, identifying everyday creepy crawlies, but one of the cockroaches didn't match the DNA records. Thinking that they may have found a new type of cockroach living in New York, they gathered more specimens and asked some experts to take a closer look. It wasn't a new species.

"They said that they are American cockroaches, but they were genetically distinct from what was in the database," says Mark.

That was enough to get Mark thinking about a new study, one that probed the genetic history of the Big Apple's cockroaches. To do this work he would need plenty of roaches, so rather than collecting them all himself, he asked the public to send in the bugs.

"We did a little investigating to see if it was OK to send them through the mail, and from what we found out it was OK," he says. "They are not officially pests, they are not on the quarantine list of the FDA, and they are not a protected species. They can contribute to asthma for some people and they can track things into food like a fly, but they don't carry specific blood-borne diseases. So it seemed an OK way to do it. We put it out on Facebook and talked to everyone we knew to see if we could get other people to collect cockroaches."

Soon Mark had a couple hundred cockroaches in his laboratory freezer, most of which came from the public, and more are arriving all the time. But he didn't want any old cockroach. Only the American cockroach would do.

The American cockroach isn't New York's most abundant roach. That title is held by the German cockroach. They are the ones most inclined to live in homes, where they lurk behind refrigerators and stoves.

Despite the name these roaches aren't German. In fact the Germans call it the Russian cockroach. But that name is wrong too, for these light-brown bugs are thought to have started out in Southeast Asia. Not that their point of origin matters much as they are so widespread now that asking where they came from is almost meaningless.

The American roach is the next most common species in New York and it is the biggest cockroach in the world. It's more of a sewer dweller than the German roach, although it also lives in prisons, hospitals, and other large institutions. Sometimes they visit apartments by coming up the drains, but this is rare.

The other five New York roaches are minor players, their numbers dwarfed by the hordes of German and American cockroaches.

There's the Oriental cockroach. It likes damp basements and the sticky insides of discarded soda cans. While the Oriental species likes it wet, the brown-banded roach is like a camel. It doesn't need constant access to water to get by, and so it can survive in drier parts of our homes, like bedrooms.

The Surinam roach is a digger and often lives in the soil of potted plants in Manhattan offices. In contrast, the speedy Australian roach prefers the outdoor life and regularly hangs around building perimeters.

The last member of the New York roaches is a newcomer. The Japanese cockroach was first discovered there in summer 2012, munching on poisoned bait inside a High Line rat trap. It took entomologists months to work out which of the world's four-thousand-plus cockroaches it was. The Japanese cockroach's ability to endure the cold should serve it well, but whether it can survive long enough to make it in New York remains to be seen.

Despite the options available, the American cockroach was the obvious choice for Mark's study. Not only had the previous study hinted that there was something to learn about the DNA of these roaches, but they were common enough to make them easy to find.

So it didn't take long before Mark had enough specimens to run the DNA tests. "It turned out that there are very distinct genetic types of American cockroach and these types are different enough that they are probably separated by a million or two million years, which means they probably came here from different parts of the world," he says.

"The biggest difference in the DNA of the types is 4 percent, so it's similar in magnitude to the difference between humans and chimps. There are certainly different species of warblers in North America that are less different than these cockroaches are."

What's more, these roaches don't mix. Each keeps to its own neighborhood. So the Upper West Side roaches are distinct from those scurrying around the Upper East Side, who are again different from those on Roosevelt Island. "To us they all look the same, but they are different and so they have to be staying in the neighborhood they were born in. Otherwise their DNA would be like a candy jar with everything mixed up in it. But it's not like that; it is like a series of candy jars."

Although Mark's tests show that the different ethnic groups of roaches don't mix, working out why is more difficult. One possibility is behavioral. Roaches are family oriented creatures. They recognize their own family members and prefer to stick together, using chemical communication to agree on where to rest and what to eat. They even get ill when alone.

"Cockroaches don't have the same complicated society that ants do, but they live in groups," says Mark. "That's a strange idea to me, to think of these cockroaches as these underground societies." It could be that these social bonds are keeping the cockroaches apart as they divide into the insect equivalent of the Jets and Sharks of *West Side Story*.

Another possibility is that the sewers and tunnels the different groups use are not connected, so they spend their lives completely unaware that other groups of roaches live just a couple of blocks away.

The genetic gulf between the New York roach tribes might be more attributable to where they first came from, but some cockroaches are having their DNA rewired by life around people. One of the most dramatic examples of this has been uncovered by biologists at North Carolina State University. After noticing that German cockroaches had, over a twenty-year period, stopped being attracted to the sugar baits of pest controllers, the university set out to discover why.

After unpicking the neural pathways of the roaches, they found that the insects had evolved an aversion to sugar. "What had happened is, essentially, that the taste receptors for sugar had been rewired so that sweet was now perceived as bitter," says Rob Dunn, head of the Dunn laboratory at the university.

Sugar-phobic roaches are not the only creatures exhibiting signs of evolutionary responses to urban environments. European blackbirds born in cities produce fewer stress hormones than those born in the forest, and this seems to have a genetic dimension, suggesting that being a chilled-out bird is helpful when living amid the hustle and bustle.

Then there are the subterranean river crabs of Rome. Italian scientists found the crabs in 1998 living in Cloaca Maxima, the stream that was turned into the main sewer of ancient Rome in the sixth century. Today, just three hundred feet of its length is exposed to the air and the water is no more than a few inches deep.

That the crabs were there at all was a surprise since the next nearest group of river crabs lives twenty miles away. More surprising still was that the underground crabs were not like their nonurbanized kin. The Cloaca Maxima crabs grow more slowly but live longer, eventually ending up 50 percent fatter than those found in streams and rivers elsewhere in the Mediterranean. These underground crabs also breed at a different time of year, a behavioral shift that suggests they could be on the long path to becoming a distinct species.

More familiar urban animals have changed too, says Rob. "Rats have undergone a lot of changes. It's not been super-well studied, but there have been a lot of behavioral shifts relative to their ancestors. So in cities they do this thing where they run along the walls. Their closest relatives, they don't do that."

Cities encourage the covert. For many urban animals, and especially pests like rats, the biggest danger they face is being discovered and then killed by us. "Historically, our approach to cities has been to kill stuff we don't like, and what that does is favor sneakier versions of those same species," says Rob. "So with rats it favors rats that run along the walls, and with roaches and bedbugs it favors ones that are resistant to insecticides and are then really hard to get rid of.

"So, on one hand, we've clearly experienced huge health benefits from trying to kill some of these things, and I am grateful to not be at much risk of the plague, but, at the same time, we've expended no energy on trying to figure out how to garden beneficial species.

"We have constructed a biome by default, and one of the questions that interests me is how could you garden a city for species that filter our air or that we find lovely or calming?"

The concept of biomes dates back to the formative years of the science of ecology when the botanist Frederic Clements floated the idea that communities of plants were "an organic unit" at a 1916 meeting of the Ecological Society of America.

The University of Illinois botanist took the idea further in 1939 when he and fellow ecology pioneer Victor Shelford published *Bio-Ecology*. In the book, Clements made the case that animals as well as vegetation were part of these organic units, which he was now calling biomes, and that these biomes were "superorganisms" with distinct characteristics.

The world's great landscapes are biomes, he argued. The tundra, the desert, the steppe, and the coniferous forest. They were all biomes, each with their own characteristic flora and fauna, and each containing myriad ecosystems.

Clements's claim that biomes were abstract superorganisms spanning hundreds, often thousands of miles, overstated the case, but he had hit on something profound. The biome concept stuck and became a central concept in ecology. Over the years other ecologists built on Clements's definition, adding environmental factors like climate and soil characteristics to the definition, but for the most part his original vision of biomes as collections of interrelated plants and animals endured.

For ecologists the biome was a useful concept, even if defining them precisely sometimes felt like hammering a square peg into a triangular hole. As well as being a convenient way to describe the world's wildlife, biomes help explain why similar species evolve in different parts of the world.

One example of this is the pronghorns of the Great Plains. Pronghorns are much like the antelopes of the Old World, but are actually more closely related to giraffes. The reason the pronghorn evolved to be much like the antelopes is that, despite residing on separate continents, they both live in a grassland biome and so face similar evolutionary pressures.

Yet fundamental to ecology as biomes are, the traditional definition only refers to natural habitats, acting as if people and cities do not exist. This oversight is causing some to question whether the traditional definitions still apply.

Leading the push for reframing biomes in light of human development is Erle Ellis, an environmental scientist at the University of Maryland. "The concept behind the classic view of biomes is that these global patterns are shaped by climate, terrain, and soils, that sort of thing, but mostly climate," he tells me over the phone from his office in Baltimore. "But when you look at the patterns now, they are not just shaped by climate. There's a huge amount of shaping going on from human activity. The most extensive one is agriculture: crops and pastures and range lands."

The idea that human influence was being overlooked came to him in the early 1990s when he went to rural China to study how the move from traditional to industrial farming altered the environment. "Place likes that, they are places that, since the last glacial, have not had a natural history. Humans have been using those landscapes for thousands of years and managing the ecology of the whole landscape. So it became obvious there was a lot of ecology that was essentially a human ecology, and my big question was how much of the Earth's ecology has been transformed by our activity, and I set out to answer that question."

The answer he arrived at was "almost all of it" and that—on land at least—natural landscapes have largely ceased to exist. In light of this he drew a new map of the world's biomes, one that replaced the traditional grasslands, tundra, and forests with eighteen "anthropogenic" biomes that represented the degree to which humans have altered the landscape. At one end there were the few remaining wildernesses, places like Antarctica. At the other end of the scale, the modern metropolis.

The city may be the most dramatic example of how we have changed the world, but agriculture is more significant, says Erle. "Urban areas do represent a very distinctive form of human transformed and sustained ecology, but it's important to understand that the urban areas are just a very, very small part of that global transformation. Urban areas are definitely less than 2 percent of ice-free land surface; they are not that extensive."

But can cities really be biomes? To fit that definition cities would need to have similar environmental processes and be home to similar communities of plants and animals regardless of where they are. It would mean that the ecology of Atlanta, Singapore, and Lagos have more in common with each other than the rural areas surrounding them.

That sounds far-fetched, but the evidence that this could be the case is growing. Take the example of Baltimore and Phoenix. On the face of it these cities sit in very different environments—Baltimore in the humid East, Phoenix in the arid West. But urbanization has altered their climates. Baltimore has become hotter than the surrounding countryside because of the urban heat island effect, while the construction of waterways has made Phoenix cooler. The net result is that air temperatures in Baltimore and Phoenix have become more similar.

Temperature is not the only thing that makes the two cities a closer match than their locations would suggest. The residents of Phoenix and Baltimore have similar gardening tastes, so they opt for the kind of lawns that can be seen in almost every American suburb. The result? Phoenix and Baltimore share similar green spaces with similar plant species.

Water systems also bring cities into line with each other. To build Miami, wetlands were drained, while the development of Phoenix saw the construction of lakes and canals. Now, when it comes to water, Miami and Phoenix are more like each other than the Everglades or Arizona desert.

The similarities between cities extend to fauna too. As we've seen, the animals that thrive in the urban world share common traits. The ability to keep a low profile is one, but urban animals also tend to be fast breeders with flexible behavior and diets. Just think of the stone martens of Berlin breeding faster than they can be killed, or the coyotes working out how to cross Chicago freeways or the red foxes learning to forage on Brighton Pier.

These animals are the garden weeds of the animal kingdom: adaptable, sneaky generalists that can overcome death by making lots of babies. This isn't just true of mammals. The most successful city birds are those with the most flexible behavior and an "I'll eat anything" attitude to life. Birds like pigeons and crows.

Size matters too. Larger animals like mountain lions, elk, and bears are more likely to be spotted and removed if they go too far into the city, while opossums and rats are small enough to slip past unnoticed. Bigger animals also have a harder time finding all the food they need in the city, and this principle applies as much at the level of tiny phorid flies as it does to cougars.

"The flies found in the center of the city tend to be small," says Brian Brown, the phorid fly expert who heads the entomology department at the Natural History Museum of Los Angeles. "You expect that with mammals. You expect that there are going to be deer and bears in the mountains but downtown not so much, because there is a limited resource base available for them. But it's also the case in the tiny one-to-three-millimeter-long flies."

Ecologists divide animals into two broad groups: K-selected and r-selected species. K-selected species are those whose numbers are limited by the amount of resources in the environment, animals like elephants and horses. In contrast, r-selected animals are limited by how much they can breed, and most of the successful urban animals fall into this group.

"The K-selected species are adapted to stable environments as it takes a few years for them to get big, whereas things that are small don't grow as much and can reproduce more," says Brian.

"The same principle operates at the level of small flies. So what we have living in downtown Los Angeles are fungus feeders largely and they are small species. The fungi they feed on are in the very perturbed environments like lawns and gardens that are constantly being disturbed, whereas the flies that live on gopher burrow and oak-associated fungi are going to be found in the mountains."

Add to this our tendency to spread species like the European starling or spitting spider around the world, and the animal life of far apart cities becomes increasingly similar. More evidence is needed, especially from cities outside the most developed nations, but what already exists suggests that urban areas are a biome and, uniquely, one that is almost entirely manmade.

As Rob suggests, that raises an interesting question. Since we control, shape, and design the urban biome, can we mold cities into something that fosters the wildlife we want rather than just a gathering spot for animals that are sneaky, smart, and sex-crazed enough to make it their home?

It's an idea some people are already experimenting with.

. . . ꙮ . •

It's an unexpectedly sunny October day in Chicago, a final hurrah of summer before the cold sets in, and Seth Magle is giving me a tour of the Nature Boardwalk at Lincoln Park Zoo.

The boardwalk's path snakes around the edge of a b-shaped pond within the grounds of the zoo. On either side of the path are clumps of tall, thin grasses and, among them, a smattering of delicate flowers. The calm water offers a clear reflection of the city skyline and, as we walk, we catch glimpses of the Lake Michigan shoreline that lies just across the road from the zoo.

"This used to be just a concrete-lined pond where they did paddle boats," says Seth. "But then the zoo, some years ago, decided they wanted to renovate it as a native urban pond prairie ecosystem.

They reseeded the whole thing and threw out all the concrete. All of these plants are native Illinois prairie plants that attract certain arthropods and birds."

As we pass under a small bridge that arches over the narrow of the pond, Seth points to the small ledges above us. "These are for cliff swallows," he says.

Elsewhere along the path are strategically placed birdhouses. "Those are for black-capped chickadees because they are cavity nesting birds and we don't have a lot of cavities out here. We've built them in such a way that the aperture size excludes house sparrows but allows black-capped chickadees. That's been very successful."

The pond also teems with life. Fish can be seen moving beneath the surface, and shiny dragonflies flit around near the bulrushes lining the water's edge.

At the southern end of the pond, there's a small island peppered with trees. "You'll probably see some turtles around the island," says Seth. "We introduced painted turtles, but red-eared sliders and snapping turtles have found their way here on their own. We suspect that the red-eared sliders may have had help, since people buy them as pets and then let them go."

One unexpected resident of the Nature Boardwalk is the black-crowned night heron, a stocky wetland bird with dark red eyes and black feathers that run from the top of its head and down the back of its otherwise white and gray body. These birds, which feed on fish and aquatic invertebrates, are an endangered species in Illinois, yet there is a thriving colony of them in Lincoln Park.

"The heron started showing up right around the same time as we renovated this area. We did have a small colony before that, but every year they are coming and nesting in larger and larger numbers right here in the heart of Chicago, which gives you an example of how you can conserve a rare species even in an urban landscape."

The boardwalk is only the most visible example of Lincoln Park Zoo's urban wildlife work. As well as creating a slice of Illinois prairie in the heart of Chicago, the zoo's Urban Wildlife Institute is busy piecing together the ecology of the city.

Seth is the institute's director, and his path into urban ecology was the result of sloth. "I feel like most people in wildlife studies have a very inspiring story of what got them started," he says. "You know, they saw a bald eagle perched on a tree during a hike or they woke up and realized that the rattlesnake was their spirit animal or something. My own story is born out of laziness.

"When I was an undergraduate at the University of Colorado, we had to do a project where we had to watch an animal for a few hours and write down things about its behavior. Well, the apartment building I lived in in Boulder had a prairie dog colony living across the street. So I thought that would be perfect as I could virtually see them from my window and they were awake during the day and were not going anywhere."

His professors were unimpressed with his plan to watch the tan-colored rodents. "I went to my academic advisor and said, 'Hey, what's going on with all these urban prairie dogs that I see everywhere?' He said, 'Oh, I don't know. Why would anyone want to know that?'"

Undeterred, Seth headed to the university library to check the scientific literature for information about the urban lives of black-tailed prairie dogs. There was nothing.

"I realized, 'Wait, really? No one knows anything? These animals live fifty feet from where I sleep. How can no one know anything about them?' That just blew my mind. So I asked some very basic questions, the sort of things people were asking about animals in the wild in the early 1900s, and ended up turning that project into a masters thesis and then a PhD."

Initially, Seth thought there would be little difference between the prairie dogs of urban Colorado and the wild, where the activities of these burrowing rodents changes the vegetation and soil in ways crucial for everything from sagebrush and burrowing owls to pronghorns. "I thought they would influence diversity in the same way and that their populations would function the same, but that wasn't true at all. We found that they lived in ten times the density that they did in natural landscapes, that they didn't really migrate between colonies as much as they should, so their genetics were peeled back, and they didn't change the bird community in the same way as they did on the prairie."

Seth's prairie dog study is ongoing, but now it is just one of the projects underway at the Urban Wildlife Institute, which has also been studying the effect of relocating groundhogs and nonlethal ways of keeping city rabbits under control.

The institute's flagship project is the biodiversity monitoring study. Its goal is to build as complete as possible a picture of wild Chicago. "We've set up over a hundred field stations. They initiate right over there in downtown Chicago and travel out west, southwest, and northwest," says Seth, as we plant ourselves on a bench overlooking the boardwalk pond.

At each field station are motion cameras that take snaps of passing animals and alcohol-filled "pitfall" traps to catch spiders and insects. The team also holds regular bird counts at each station. As with the prairie dogs, the results have confounded expectations. "When I look back over my body of work so far, the recurrent thread is that things didn't turn out the way I thought they would," says Seth. "Things were very different with the prairie dogs, and we're finding more or less the same thing here.

"One of the things we really expected to find in our data was that we would see fewer deer in sites where we see coyotes. Well, not true at all. The sites that have deer tended to also have coyotes.

"We think it's just that habitat is so limited and resources so limited that if you're a deer trying to decide where you are going to browse, you may have coyotes in your patch but leaving involves going across several roads and highways. It's a hazardous journey and it's uncertain if you will find another patch, and even then that patch may have coyotes too."

This, he explains, is not how deer and coyotes behave in more natural habitats. "We have this thing there called the 'ecology of fear' where the deer move around and coyotes sort of track them. But that's not how it works in urban systems."

Eventually the institute hopes to build a model for how urban ecosystems work that can explain how the wild residents of cities interact with one another, whether that's how coyotes and red foxes fight for territory or the influence of particular plant species on local birdlife.

That model is some way off, but Seth's hope is that by understanding these systems better, we can start using cities to protect species we value. "In the long term we want to have a thorough conservation strategy that can conserve all types of species," he says. "To do that we need to learn to manage human-wildlife conflict in urban areas, so we can use these areas as part of our strategy for conserving species."

The idea of using cities as places of conservation divides urban ecologists. "There is a schism between people who think all we can do is focus on managing the species that move into cities and the people who feel that we can use cities as an important component of conservation if we change the way we build our cities. I fall into the latter camp.

"I think that taking the view that cities are an evil, that anything that happens in the city is unimportant, is quite short-sighted, because I don't see any trends that we're going to stop urbanizing the world."

Besides, he adds, we're running out of options. "Our rate of finding land to preserve is dwindling, so at some point we're not going to have any more preserves. But we will always have more city."

The Nature Boardwalk at Lincoln Park Zoo may be a deliberate attempt at conservation within the city, but even when we don't act, urban areas are supporting many threatened species. The rebound in the number of peregrine falcons across the world is largely due to their success in cities, and as we've seen, Los Angeles has more Mexican red-head parrots than the part of Mexico they originated in, while the city of Jodhpur helped Rajasthan's Hanuman langurs endure drought.

Stockholm golf courses are also helping at-risk species. Close to two-thirds of the Swedish capital's golf courses boast bird and insect diversity equal to or better than that within nature reserves and can attract declining species like red-headed woodpeckers.

One shining example of urban conservation is the city of Bakersfield, California, which is helping the San Joaquin Valley kit fox survive. This rare sub-species of kit fox has been facing extinction due to habitat loss but, somewhat ironically, has found refuge in Bakersfield, where they live in shipping yards, parks, golf courses, and undeveloped land.

Life in Bakersfield is good for these small buff-furred desert foxes, which look as if they evolved to be muses for Japanese anime artists with their short snouts and their extra big pair of ears that keeps them cool in the heat. There are fewer predators to worry about, plenty of sites for dens, and a steady supply of human food, insects, and ground squirrels to eat. All of which has led to the kit foxes of Bakersfield living longer and breeding more than those outside the city.

The kit foxes rarely cause problems for people, either. They are quiet and rarely knock over trash cans. Their most heinous crime is nothing more serious than occasionally stealing golf balls during play. That and getting themselves tangled up in soccer nets.

Their fox cub looks and lack of antisocial behavior has won them plenty of supporters. Some Bakersfield residents have taken it upon themselves to defend the foxes, stopping people from disturbing the animals and even installing artificial dens on their property for them to use.

The urban kit foxes have also rallied the locals to their wider cause. Most residents who have seen the kit foxes now support efforts to protect them, compared to 40 percent of those who haven't had a firsthand encounter. By fueling support for their conservation and maintaining their population, the Bakersfield kit foxes could prove crucial in helping the sub-species survive both in the city and beyond.

The idea of using cities for conservation is, however, easier said than done. The Mexican red-head parrots might be abundant in Los Angeles, but what's the point of shipping them to northeast Mexico to rebuild the original population if the problems that caused their decline there remain? But having cities that act as life rafts for troubled species does at least offer a potential means of doing that.

Of course urbanization itself has pushed out plenty of species, a good proportion of which now face extinction, but the realpolitik of the situation is that cities are not going to vanish or stop growing unless there's some cataclysmic nuclear war. We might not be able to reverse the damage already done by urbanization, but that's no reason not to use cities to supplement our wider efforts to help struggling species, especially when there's plenty of evidence suggesting that they can do this.

The reasons to use our cities in this way don't just stop with maintaining biodiversity. Having urban areas that are more wild-life friendly makes cities and towns better places to live in. Urban wildlife can sometimes be irritating or messy and, in cases like the leopards of Mumbai, genuinely scary, but for the most part these unexpected encounters with the animals among us are positive, a cheering reminder that we are not alone and that our cities are far from sterile or divorced from nature. It's hard not to have your day brightened by a glimpse of a bushy-tailed fox running down the street or a flock of monk parakeets flying across the skyline or a wild boar with piglets in tow holding up traffic.

Their presence might even make us healthier. More and more studies are finding connections between contact with nature and better mental health or reduced stress levels. Some studies even suggest that more exposure to nature can improve children's school grades.

Working out how we can engineer wilder cities is tricky, though. Urban ecology has gone understudied for many years and, as Seth's work shows, much of what we know about how ecosystems function in the wild or in rural areas just doesn't apply in cities. More funding for urban ecology research is going to be needed before we understand city environments well enough to really start designing cities that encourage wildlife effectively.

But that research need not be confined to the halls of academia. The efforts of groups like the Chicago Bird Collision Monitors have, through their dedication and studious recording of bird strikes, proven the effectiveness of Lights Out programs and helped both architects and urban planners make cities more bird-friendly. Citizen science studies, like Mark's cockroach investigation and the Arthropods of Our Homes project, offer people a way to learn about what animals live around them while also helping to increase our wider understanding of urban wildlife. From bird counts to indoor bug hunts, universities, animal charities, and natural history museums are running citizen science initiatives that can involve everyone.

But while our understanding of urban wildlife is incomplete, we already know that some approaches to fostering urban wildlife work. One approach with plenty of evidence behind it is the creation of green or brown roofs. The idea of creating rooftop wildlife gardens started in Germany back in the 1970s, and the worldwide movement that followed has plenty of success stories to tell. In the Swiss city of Basel, where green roofs are now compulsory on new flat-roofed buildings, these rooftop gardens have become home to significant numbers of rare beetles and spiders. Brown roofs of crushed brick and concrete also take much of the credit for the return of the black redstart, a robin-sized bird with gray-black plumage, to London.

Yet the full potential of green roofs has yet to be realized, says Clare Dinham, brownfield conservation officer at the British arthropod conservation charity Buglife. "The odd green roof here and there will provide some habitat, but it's limited," she says. "However, if you do it on a great scale then it can become really important."

The potential is huge. If a small number of brown roofs in London can bring back the black redstart, just imagine what a city full of green and brown roofs could achieve. And what if we embraced Berlin's long-held vision for "coherent greenery" and started linking green roofs and green spaces together via green walls? We could also think about the Bakersfield kit foxes and cliff swallows in Lincoln Park Zoo and create artificial dens and nesting sites for the wildlife we want to encourage in our parks and yards.

But before we can do any of this, we've first got to stop thinking of cities as barren, anti-nature zones. This environment we've built, this urban biome, is teeming with life, but all too often we just blank it out. "I was in a meeting just yesterday and a woman was there from another zoo, and she made this statement that 'I love it when kids come to the zoo. For many of them it's the first time they've ever seen a wild animal,'" Seth tells me as we sit on that bench looking out over Chicago.

"I just had to stand up and say, 'That's not true! They have all seen squirrels, they have all seen pigeons, and the fact that you don't think of them as wildlife does not mean they aren't wildlife. It's just that you are so attuned to them being around, you no longer think of them as wildlife.'"

And as I sit with Seth, I see the evidence all around us. The cliff swallows under the bridge. The rare black-crowned night heron standing in the water. The squirrels scampering up the trees. And out there in the city, beyond the zoo, there are crows hunting dazed indigo buntings on the streets, ants nesting under the sidewalks, spitting spiders roaming apartments, pigeons pecking at crumbs, and coyotes snoozing unseen in the bushes.

The city is alive. The wild is here, right on our doorstep, in our streets and inside our homes.

All we have to do is open our eyes.

ACKNOWLEDGMENTS

A great many people made this book possible, not least my ever-supportive husband Jay Priest, my fantastic agent Isabel Atherton, and Yuval Taylor and the rest of the Chicago Review Press team.

Thanks also to my sister Jade for joining me in Berlin, Tom Homewood (and his assistant Ben Milne) for the illustrations, and my German interpreter, Nancy Chapple.

A big thank you also goes to all of the people who generously shared their time and expertise as I delved into the world of urban wildlife: Vidya Athreya. Daniel Bajomi. Steve Baldwin. Carol Bannerman. Eric Barna. Liz Barraco. Matt Bertone (with further thanks for the edits). Brian Brown. Adrian Diaz. Scott Diehl. Mohammad Dilawar. Hoang Dinh. Clare Dinham. Rob Dunn. Erle Ellis. Mark Fagan. Captain Jeffrey Fobb. Omar Garcia. Jane Griffin Dozier. Dallas Hazelton. Derk Ehlert. Mason Fidino. Blair Fyten. Kimball Garrett. Stan Gehrt. David Gummer. Paul Hetherington. Lila Higgins. Wes Homoya. Bryan Hughes. Kate Kuykendall. Garry Lafaille. Liza Lehrer. Judy Loven. Seth Magle. Graham Martin. Anne Maschmeyer. Shane McKenzie. Holly Menninger. Zeeshan Mirza. Alex Muñoz (who needs an extra thanks for making my trip to Miami so productive). Armando Navarrete. Maria Németh. Gilda Nuñez. Miguel Ordeñana. Justin O'Riain. Gregory Pauly. Will Peach. Annette Prince. Curt Publow. Gregory Randall. Ian Rotherham. Tiffany Ruddle. Amy Savage. Dawn Scott. Laurel Serieys. Sarah Sharpe. Vincent Sheurer. Rob Smith. Ruth Smith. Vernon Smith. Angela Speed. Mark Stoeckle. Michelle Trautwein. Jill Turner. Wilfredo Valladares. Tim Webb. Paul Wilkinson. Mary Winston. Karen Wise.

REFERENCES

1. Hot Tub Snakes

Albert, Josh. "*Pituophis catenifer.*" Animal Diversity Web, University of Michigan, 2008. http://animaldiversity.ummz.umich.edu/accounts/Pituophis_catenifer.

Argos, Greg. "Javelina Encounters in Phoenix Area on Rise." CBS 5 KPHO, January 7, 2014. www.kpho.com/story/24390727/javelina-attack-womans-dog-encounters-on -the-rise.

Arizona Game and Fish Department. "Living with Javelina." Accessed August 20, 2014. www.azgfd.gov/w_c/urban_javelina.shtml.

BBC News. "Fox Lived in the Shard Skyscraper at London Bridge." February 24, 2011. www.bbc.co.uk/news/uk-england-london-12573364.

Best, Jessica. "Man Discovers a Fox in His Bed After Rolling Over to Give His Girlfriend a Cuddle." *Mirror*, August 27, 2013. www.mirror.co.uk/news/weird-news/man-discovers -fox-bed-after-2227937.

Channel 4. "A Short History of the Urban Fox." Accessed August 20, 2014. www.channel4.com/programmes/foxes-live-wild-in-the-city/articles/all/a-short -history-of-the-urban-fox.

Devenish-Nelson, Eleanor. "Sarcoptic Mange in Red Foxes: The Role of Fox Behaviour." Mammal Research Unit, University of Bristol. Accessed August 20, 2014. www.bio .bris.ac.uk/research/mammal/fox_mange.html.

Gehrt, Stanley D., Seth P. D. Riley, and Brian L. Cypher, eds. *Urban Carnivores: Ecology, Conflict and Conservation.* Baltimore: Johns Hopkins University Press, 2010.

Harris, Stephen. "Culling Urban Foxes Just Doesn't Work." *New Scientist*, February 20, 2013. www.newscientist.com/article/mg21729050.200-culling-urban-foxes-just -doesnt-work.html.

Hough, Andrew. "Twin Girls in Hospital After Fox Attack at London Home." *Telegraph*, June 6, 2010. www.telegraph.co.uk/news/uknews/7807232/Twin-girls-in-hospital -after-fox-attack-at-London-home.html.

Martin, Emer. "Fox Attacks Man, Woman and Cat at Their Home in South London." *London Evening Standard*, July 10, 2013. www.standard.co.uk/news/london/fox -attacks-man-woman-and-cat-at-their-home-in-south-london-8699892.html.

Mills, David. "Mugged by a Fox for a Stick of Garlic Bread." *News Shopper*, March 9, 2012. www.newsshopper.co.uk/news/9581004.Mugged_by_a_fox_for_a_stick_of_garlic_bread.

Texas A&M University–Kingsville. "What Is a Javelina?" Official website, May 6, 2011. www.tamuk.edu/about/what_is_a_javelina.html.

2. Voodoo Chickens

CBS Miami. "Python Attacks and Kills 60-Lb Husky." September 10, 2013. http://miami .cbslocal.com/2013/09/10/python-attacks-and-kills-60-lb-husky.

Enge, Kevin M. "FWC Bioprofile for the Argentine Black and White Tegu (*Tupinambis merianae*)." Florida Fish and Wildlife Conservation Commission, September 2006. Available at Florida Invasive Species Partnership, www.floridainvasives.org/Heartland /links/TeguBioprofileSep2006.pdf.

Gingell, Fred. "*Iguana iguana*." Animal Diversity Web, University of Michigan, 2005. http://animaldiversity.ummz.umich.edu/accounts/Iguana_iguana.

Hamacher, Brian, and Keith Jones. "13-Foot Python Found in Hialeah Homeowner's Shed." NBC 6 South Florida, August 6, 2013. www.nbcmiami.com/news/13-Foot -Python-Found-in-Hialeah-Homeowners-Shed-218365901.html.

Hutt, Katherine. "Gang Violence Tarnishing Little Haiti." *Ocala Star-Banner*, August 13, 1996.

Maza, Erik. "Miami's Chicken Busters Are No More." *Miami New Times*, February 16, 2010. www.miaminewtimes.com/2010-02-18/news/miami-s-chicken-busters-are-no -more.

Munzenrieder, Kyle. "Snail Mucus Swallowing Leaves Religious Followers Sick." *Miami New Times*, March 11, 2010. http://blogs.miaminewtimes.com/riptide/2010/03 /snail_mucus_swallowing_leaves.php.

Scheub, Harold. *A Dictionary of African Mythology*. Oxford: Oxford University Press, 2000.

3. The Great Sparrow Mystery

Anderson, Ted R. *Biology of the Ubiquitous House Sparrow: From Genes to Populations*. New York: Oxford University Press, 2006.

Balmori, Alfonso, and Orjan Hallberg. "The Urban Decline of the House Sparrow (Passer domesticus): A Possible Link with Electromagnetic Radiation." *Electromagnetic Biology and Medicine* 26 (2007): 141–151.

Boersma, P. Dee, S. H. Reichard, and A. N. Van Buren, eds. *Invasive Species in the Pacific Northwest*. Seattle: University of Washington Press, 2006.

Breitwisch, R., and M. Breitwisch. "House Sparrows Open an Automatic Doors." *Wilson Bulletin* 103 (1991): 725–726.

Brockie, R. E., and Barry O'Brien. "House Sparrows (Passer domesticus) Opening Autodoors." *Notornis* 51 (2004): 52.

Brook, R. K. "House Sparrows Feeding at Night in New York." *Auk* 90 (1973): 206.

Broun, Maurice. "House Sparrows Feeding Young at Night." *Auk* 88 (1971): 924–925.

Crick, Humphrey Q. P., Robert A. Robinson, Graham F. Appleton, Nigel A. Clark, and Angela D. Rickard, eds. *Investigation into the Causes of the Decline of Starlings and House Sparrows in Great Britain*. British Trust for Ornithology Research report 290 (July 2002).

Encyclopedia of Life. *Invasive Species: Starlings Podcast*. iTunes podcast, January 24, 2013.

Feare, Christopher. *The Starling*. Oxford: Oxford University Press, 1984.

Grinnell, Joseph. "The English Sparrow Has Arrived in Death Valley: An Experiment in Nature." *American Naturalist* 628 (1919): 468–472.

Homan, H. Jeffrey, Howard R. Channing, Judy S. Loven, Erin E. Meredith, Scott A. Stippich, and Carl A. Voglewede. "Movements and Site Use of European Starlings Wintering in Indianapolis, Indiana." Unpublished paper, USDA-APHIS-WS National Wildlife Research Center, 2008.

Kalmus, H. "Wall Clinging: Energy Saving by the House Sparrow Passer domesticus." *IBIS* 126 (1984): 72–74.

Martin II, Lynn B., and Lisa Fitzgerald. "A Taste for Novelty in Invading House Sparrows, Passer domesticus." *Behavioural Ecology* 16 (2005): 702–707.

Matthews, John. *Complete American Armoury and Blue Book: Combining 1903, 1907 and 1911–23.* Baltimore: Clearfield Company, 1991.

Potts, G. R. "Urban Starling Roosts in the British Isles." *Bird Study* 14 (1967): 25–42.

Robbins, Chandler S. "Introduction, Spread, and Present Abundance of the House Sparrow in North America." *Ornithological Monographs* 14 (1973): 3–9.

Robinson, Robert A., Gavin M. Siriwardena, and Humphrey Q. P. Crick. "Size and Trends of the House Sparrow *Passer domesticus* Population in Great Britain." *IBIS* 147 (2005): 552–562.

Shaw, Lorna M., Dan Chamberlain, and Matthew Evans. "The House Sparrow *Passer domesticus* in Urban Areas: Reviewing a Possible Link Between Post-Decline Distribution and Human Socioeconomic Status." *Journal of Ornithology* 149 (2008): 293–299.

Singh, Madhur. "Heroes of the Environment 2008: Mohammed Dilawar." *Time,* September 24, 2008. http://content.time.com/time/specials/packages/article /0,28804,1841778_1841782_1841791,00.html.

Summers-Smith, J. Denis. "Changes in the House Sparrow Population in Britain." *International Studies on Sparrows* 30 (2005): 23–37.

———. *On Sparrows and Man.* Guisborough, UK: Thersby Group, 2005.

4. Street Hunters

Associated Press. "Wild Boar Attack Leaves Four Injured in Berlin." *Guardian,* October 30, 2012. www.theguardian.com/world/2012/oct/30/wild-boar-attack-berlin.

Berlin Senate Department for Urban Development and the Environment. "The History of Berlin's Urban Green Space." Official website. Accessed August 20, 2014. www .stadtentwicklung.berlin.de/umwelt/stadtgruen/geschichte/en/stadtgruen/index.shtml.

Braun, Stuart. "In Gritty Berlin, Green Space Plays a Surprisingly Large Role." DW, April 12, 2011. www.dw.de/in-gritty-berlin-green-space-plays-a-surprisingly-large-role /a-14983881.

Carter, Kimberlee. "*Martes foina.*" Animal Diversity Web, University of Michigan, 2004. http://animaldiversity.ummz.umich.edu/accounts/Martes_foina.

Chinitophd. "Raccoons in Germany: A Matter of Fashion . . ." *The Amazingly Normal Adventures of El Chinito* (blog), October 4, 2012. http://chinitophd.wordpress .com/2012/10/04/raccoons-in-germany-a-matter-of-fashion.

Chu, Henry. "Unfortunately for Germany, It's a Wonderland for Raccoons." *Los Angeles Times,* September 26, 2012. http://articles.latimes.com/2012/sep/26/world/la-fg -germany-raccoons-20120927.

Fashion Encyclopedia. "Raccoon Coat." Accessed August 20, 2014. www .fashionencyclopedia.com/fashion_costume_culture/Modern-World-1919-1929 /Raccoon-Coat.html.

Gehrt, Stanley D., Seth P. D. Riley, and Brian L. Cypher, eds. *Urban Carnivores: Ecology, Conflict and Conservation.* Baltimore: Johns Hopkins University Press, 2010.

Gross, Justin, Françoise Elvinger, Laura L. Hungerford, and Stanley D. Gehrt. "Raccoon Use of the Urban Matrix in the Baltimore Metropolitan Area, Maryland." *Urban Ecosystems* 15 (2012): 667–682.

Herr, Jan. "Ecology and Behaviour of Urban Stone Martens (*Martes foina*) in Luxembourg." PhD thesis, University of Sussex, 2008.

Kotulski, York, and Andreas König. "Conflicts, Crises and Challenges: Wild Boar in the Berlin City—A Social Empirical and Statistical Survey." *Natura Croatica* 17 (2008): 233–246.

Lachat, Nicole. "Stone Martens and Cars: A Beginning War?" *Mustelid & Viverrid Conservation*, October 1991, 4–6.

Local, The. "Stone Martens Are Coming for Your Car." July 16, 2009. www.thelocal.de /20090716/20633.

Mösken, Anne Lena. "Park der Mauern." *Berliner Zeitung*, June 13, 2009. www.berliner -zeitung.de/archiv/auf-dem-frueheren-todesstreifen-liegt-berlins-bunteste -gruenflaeche---doch-es-gibt-streit-um-die-zukunft-park-der-mauern,10810590 ,10645814.html.

Nicholson, Esme. "In Berlin, a Boar of a Story." *NPR*, November 20, 2012. www.npr.org /2012/11/06/164435055/in-berlin-a-boar-of-a-story.

Project Waschbär. "Allgemeine Angaben." Accessed August 20, 2014. www.projekt -waschbaer.de/allgemeine-angaben.

Ridgley, Heidi. "The Boar Wars." *National Wildlife*, April 1, 2006. www.nwf.org/news-and -magazines/national-wildlife/animals/archives/2006/the-boar-wars.aspx.

Robertson, Joanna. "The Battle for Berlin's Gardens." BBC Radio 4, August 7, 2010. http://news.bbc.co.uk/1/hi/8892623.stm.

Schulz, Matthias. "Raccoon Invasion: Germany Overrun by Hordes of Masked Omnivores." *Spiegel Online*, August 3, 2012. www.spiegel.de/international/germany /germany-overrun-by-raccoon-invasion-a-847847.html.

Somaskanda, Sumi. "Berlin Fights Boar Wars, as Wild Swine Swagger Through City Streets." *Washington Times*, May 12, 2011. www.washingtontimes.com/news/2011 /may/12/berlin-fights-boar-wars-as-wild-swine-swagger-thro.

Spiegel Online. "Furry Interloper: Berlin Hotel Unsure How to Deal with Raccoon Guest." June 16, 2008. www.spiegel.de/international/zeitgeist/furry-interloper-berlin-hotel -unsure-how-to-deal-with-raccoon-guest-a-559949.html.

Walker, Marcus. "In Berlin's Boar War, Some Side with the Hogs." *Wall Street Journal*, December 16, 2008. http://online.wsj.com/news/articles/SB122937877627908421.

Wickline, Kristin. "*Sus scrofa*." Animal Diversity Web, University of Michigan, 2014. http://animaldiversity.ummz.umich.edu/accounts/Sus_scrofa.

5. Romancing Coyotes

Brown, Justin L. "The Influence of Coyotes on an Urban Canada Goose Population in the Chicago Metropolitan Area." Master's thesis, Ohio State University, 2007.

Chicago Tribune. "So This Coyote Walks into a Quiznos . . ." April 4, 2007. http://articles .chicagotribune.com/2007-04-04/news/0704040747_1_coyote-anne-kent-bina-patel.

Cook County, Illinois, Coyote Project. "The Coyote-Wildlife Relationship." Official website. Accessed August 20, 2014. www.urbancoyoteresearch.com/Relationship_to _other_wildlife.htm.

Dell'Amore, Christine. "City Slinkers." *Smithsonian Magazine*, March 2006. www.smithsonianmag.com/science-nature/city-slinkers-12208091.

Gehrt, Stanley D., Seth P. D. Riley, and Brian L. Cypher, eds. *Urban Carnivores: Ecology, Conflict and Conservation*. Baltimore: Johns Hopkins University Press, 2010.

Lloyd, Robin. "How Birds Can Down a Jet Airplane." LiveScience, January 15, 2009. www.livescience.com/3239-birds-jet-airplane.html.

McCoy, Nicole H. "Economic Tools for Managing Impacts of Urban Canada Geese." Human Conflicts with Widlife: Economic Considerations paper 12 (2000).

Metz, Rachel. "Coyotes Take to City Streets." *Wired*, February 2, 2006. http://archive
    .wired.com/science/discoveries/news/2006/02/70136.

6. Thieves in the Temple

Bamford, Helen. "Infamous Baboon Put Down." IOL News, March 26, 2011. www.iol
    .co.za/scitech/science/environment/infamous-baboon-put-down-1.1047651.
———. "Infamous Fred Remembered." IOL News, April 3, 2011. www.iol.co.za/news
    /south-africa/western-cape/infamous-fred-remembered-1.1051260.
———. "Two More Baboons Put Down." IOL News, July 23, 2011. www.iol.co.za/news
    /south-africa/western-cape/two-more-baboons-put-down-1.1104580.
Barilla, James. *My Backyard Jungle*. New Haven: Yale University Press, 2013.
BBC News. "Monkeys Attack Delhi Politician." October 21, 2007. http://news.bbc.co.uk
    /1/hi/world/south_asia/7055625.stm.
Express India. "Deputy Mayor Bajwa Falls Off Terrace, Admitted at Apollo ICU." October
    21, 2007.
Gentleman, Amelia. "Monkeys in the Parks, Monkeys in the Palace." *New York Times*,
    November 14, 2007. www.nytimes.com/2007/11/14/world/asia/14delhi.html.
Gosling, Melanie. "Of Baboons and Humans . . ." IOL News, September 22, 2008.
    www.iol.co.za/news/south-africa/of-baboons-and-humans-1.417333.
Grimes, Stephanie. "Looting Baboons Raid South African Apartment." *Las Vegas Review-
    Journal*, December 11, 2013. www.reviewjournal.com/news/looting-baboons-raid
    -south-african-apartment.
Harris, Gardiner. "Indians Feed the Monkeys, Which Bite the Hand." *New York Times*, May
    22, 2012. www.nytimes.com/2012/05/23/world/asia/fed-by-indians-monkeys
    -overwhelm-delhi.html.
Hartley, Aziz. "Man Dies After Baboon Shoves Him." IOL News, June 1, 2009. www.iol
    .co.za/news/south-africa/man-dies-after-baboon-shoves-him-1.472609.
Hindu, The. "Deputy Mayor Dies After Fall from Terrace." October 22, 2007.
    www.thehindu.com/todays-paper/tp-national/tp-newdelhi/deputy-mayor-dies-after
    -fall-from-terrace/article1934364.ece.
Hoffman, Tali S., and M. Justin O'Riain. "Monkey Management: Using Spatial Ecology
    to Understand the Extent and Severity of Human-Baboon Conflict in the Cape
    Peninsula, South Africa." *Ecology and Society* 17 (2012): 13.
Huffington Post. "Baboon Ambushes Woman Carrying Groceries in Cape Town, Makes Off
    with Veggies." September 20, 2013. www.huffingtonpost.com/2013/09/20/baboon
    -ambushes-woman-groceries-cape-town-veggies_n_3957474.html.
Jaman, M. Firoj, and Michael A. Huffman. "The Effect of Urban and Rural Habitat
    and Resource Type on Activity Budgets of Commensal Rhesus Macaques (*Macaca
    mulatta*) in Bangladesh." *Primates* 54 (2010): 49–59.
Kaplan, Bentley S., M. Justin O'Riain, Rowen van Eeden, and Andrew J. King. "A Low-Cost
    Manipulation of Food Resources Reduces Spatial Overlap Between Baboons (*Papio ursinus*)
    and Humans in Conflict." *International Journal of Primatology* 32 (2011): 1397–1412.
Kumar Dash, Dipak. "Ban On, Langurs Out of Monkey Business." *Times of India*, February
    7, 2013. http://timesofindia.indiatimes.com/city/delhi/Ban-on-langurs-out-of-monkey
    -business/articleshow/18374810.cms.
Monkey Thieves, episode "Coming of Age." National Geographic Channel. Posted on
    YouTube by XiveTV, July 9, 2013. http://youtu.be/ZeE0Y8ENnjg.
Pandey, Geeta. "Delhi Metro in Monkey Business." BBC News, August 2, 2006. http://
    news.bbc.co.uk/1/hi/world/south_asia/5238626.stm.
Southwick, Charles, and M. Farooq Siddiqi. "India's Rhesus Populations: Protectionism
    vs. Conservation Management." In *Monkeys on the Edge: Ecology and Management of*

Long-Tailed Macaques and Their Interface with Humans, edited by Agustín Fuentes and Michael D. Gumert. Cambridge: Cambridge University Press, 2011.

Times of India. "JMC Fails to Curb Monkey Menace in City." May 19, 2009. http:// timesofindia.indiatimes.com/city/jaipur/JMC-fails-to-curb-monkey-menace-in-city /articleshow/4549587.cms?referral=PM.

Vlahos, James. "Howl." *Outside*, January 28, 2009. www.outsideonline.com/outdoor -adventure/nature/Howl.html.

Vyawahare, Malavika. "A Conversation With: Delhi's Wildlife Warden." *New York Times*, May 23, 2012. http://india.blogs.nytimes.com/2012/05/23/a-conversation-with -delhis-wildlife-warden.

Waite, Tom A., Anil K. Chhangani, Lesley G. Campbell, Lal S. Rajpurohit, and Surendra M. Mohnot. "Sanctuary in the City: Urban Monkeys Buffered Against Catastrophic Die-Off During ENSO-Related Drought." *EcoHealth* 3 (2007): 278–286.

Yeld, John. "William the Baboon Trapped and Killed." IOL News, July 7, 2010. www.iol .co.za/news/south-africa/william-the-baboon-trapped-and-killed-1.489119.

7. The Lion of Hollywood

Agence France-Presse. "Leopard Filmed Snatching Dog from Mumbai Home." NDTV, June 27, 2013. www.ndtv.com/article/cities/leopard-filmed-snatching-dog-from -mumbai-home-385026.

Athreya, Vidya, and Vidya Venkatesh. *Mumbaikars for SGNP 2011–2012*. Forest Department & Centre for Wildlife Studies report (2012).

BBC News. "Leopard Dies from People Attack." January 18, 2007. http://news.bbc .co.uk/1/hi/world/south_asia/6274415.stm.

BBC Two. "Leopards: 21st Century Cats." First broadcast August 8, 2013.

Beckmann, Jon P., Leslie Karasin, Cecily Costello, Sean Matthews, and Zoë Smith. *Coexisting with Black Bears: Perspectives from Four Case Studies Across North America*. Bozeman, MT: Wildlife Conservation Society, 2008.

Beier, Paul, Seth P. D. Riley, and Raymond M. Sauvajot. "Mountain Lions (*Puma concolor*)." In *Urban Carnivores: Ecology, Conflict, and Conservation*, edited by Gehrt, Stanley D., Seth P. D. Riley, and Brian L. Cypher. Baltimore: Johns Hopkins University Press, 2010.

Bhagat, Simit. "Spotted: Ajoba's Trek from Malshej Ghat to National Park." *Times of India*, June 30, 2010.

Bhattasali, Amitabha. "Leopard in Deadly Attack in Indian City of Guwahati." *BBC News*, January 9, 2012. www.bbc.co.uk/news/world-asia-india-16473569.

Bidkar, Manoj, and Siddharth Gadkari. "Big Cat's Big Adventure." *Pune Mirror*, July 13, 2010.

Biswas, Partha Sarathi. "City Anchor: Leopards Thrive Unnoticed in Human-Populated Area." *Indian Express*, February 22, 2013. http://archive.indianexpress.com/news/city -anchor-leopards-thrive-unnoticed-in-humanpopulated-areas/1077943.

Davidson, Neil. *The Early History of "Non-Lethal Weapons."* Bradford Non-Lethal Weapons Research Project occasional paper 1 (December 2006). www.bradford.ac.uk/acad/nlw /research_reports/docs/BNLWRP_OP1_Dec06.pdf.

Groves, Martha. "Scientists Track Cougar's Wild Nightlife Above Hollywood." *Los Angeles Times*, October 4, 2013. www.latimes.com/local/la-me-griffith-park-lion-20131005 -story.html.

Hindu, The. "Girl Falls Prey to Leopard in Mumbai." July 17, 2012. www.thehindu.com /news/national/other-states/article3646930.ece.

Kertson, Brian N., Rocky D. Spencer, and Christian E. Grue. "Cougar Prey Use in a Wildland-Urban Environment in Western Washington." *Northwestern Naturalist* 92 (2011): 175–185.

KOLO 8. "Mountain Lion Cornered in Downtown Reno." August 24, 2012. www.kolotv
.com/home/headlines/167312605.html.
Lenin, Janaki. "Sugarcane Leopards." *Current Conservation* 4, no. 4 (2010).
Maharashtra Pollution Control Board. *District Environmental Atlas of Pune District*. MPCB,
2006. http://mpcb.gov.in/relatedtopics/PuneDEA_Annexure%20I.pdf.
McKenzie, John A. "The Demographic and Nutritional Benefits of Urban Habitat Use by
Elk." Master's thesis, University of Guelph, 2001.
NDTV. "Leopard Sighting Triggers Panic, 30,000 People Under House Arrest." December
26, 2011. www.ndtv.com/article/cities/leopard-sighting-triggers-panic-30-000-people
-under-house-arrest-160816.
9News. "Dumpster-Diving Bear Caught on Camera." August 1, 2013. www.9news.com
/story/local/2013/08/01/1870876.
Ordeñana, Miguel. "What's on P22's Menu?" Urban Carnivores, September 24, 2013.
www.urbancarnivores.com/miguels-blog/2013/9/24/whats-on-p-22s-menu.
Southeast Lifestyle. "Bears in Urban Areas (Health Information)." Accessed August 20,
2014. www.selifestyle.com/Bears.html.
Thaxton, Zach. "Mtn. Lion Snatches Dog Being Walked on Leash Near Broadmoor."
KOAA 5, March 19, 2013. www.koaa.com/news/mtn-lion-snatches-dog-being-walked
-on-leash-near-broadmoor.

8. Singing a Different Song

Arroyo-Solís, A., J. M. Castillo, E. Figueroa, J. L. López-Sánchez, and H. Slabbekoorn.
"Experimental Evidence for an Impact of Anthropogenic Noise on Dawn Chorus
Timing in Urban Birds." *Journal of Avian Biology* 44 (2013): 288–296.
Avian Welfare Coalition. "Frequently Asked Questions About Monk Parrots (*Myiopsitta
monachus*), Also Known as Quaker or Monk Parakeets." Official website. Accessed
August 20, 2014. www.avianwelfare.org/issues/forum.htm.
Badger, Emily. "Sparrows Actually Change Their Tune to Sing over the Noise of the City."
Atlantic Cities, April 4, 2012. www.theatlanticcities.com/neighborhoods/2012/04
/sparrows-actually-change-their-song-sing-over-noise-city/1667.
Barrett, David. "Bel Air Fire." Los Angeles Fire Department Historical Society. Accessed
August 20, 2014. www.lafdmuseum.org/bel-air-fire.
Bittner, Mark. *The Wild Parrots of Telegraph Hill*. New York, NY: Three Rivers Press, 2004.
Chonghaile, Clar Ni. "Kenyan Rubbish Dump Offers Little Money for Much Misery."
Guardian, September 18, 2012. www.theguardian.com/global-development/2012
/sep/18/money-misery-nairobi-dandora-dump.
Clucas, Barbara, and John M. Marzluff. "Coupled Relationships Between Humans and
Other Organisms in Urban Areas." In *Urban Ecology: Patterns, Processes, and Applications*,
edited by Jari Niemelä, Jürgen H. Breuste, Glenn Guntenspergen, Nancy E. McIntyre,
Thomas Elmqvist, and Philip James. Oxford: Oxford University Press, 2011.
Dobson, Roger. "Twitter in the City: The Urban Life of Birds." *Independent*, January 31,
2011.
Dowling, J. L., D. A. Luther, and P. P. Marra. "Comparative Effects of Urban Development
and Anthropogenic Noise on Bird Songs." *Behavioral Ecology*, 2011. http://beheco
.oxfordjournals.org/content/early/2011/11/11/beheco.arr176.full.
Environmental Protection Agency. "Urban Heat Island Basics." In *Reducing Urban Heat
Islands: Compendium of Strategies*. EPA, October 2008. www.epa.gov/heatisland
/resources/pdf/BasicsCompendium.pdf.
Frey, Corinne M., Gergely Rigo, and Eberhard Parlow. "Investigation of the Daily Urban
Cooling Island (UCI) in Two Coastal Cities in an Arid Environment: Dubai and Abu
Dhabi (U.A.E.)." *ISPRS Archives* 36, part 8/W27 (2005).

Garrett, Kimball L. "Population Status and Distribution of Naturalized Parrots in Southern California." *Western Birds* 28 (1997): 181–195.

Garrett, Kimball L., Karen T. Mabb, Charles T. Collins, and Lisa M. Kares. "Food Items of Naturalized Parrots in Southern California." *Western Birds* 28 (1997): 196–201.

Gehrt, Stanley D., Seth P. D. Riley, and Brian L. Cypher, eds. *Urban Carnivores: Ecology, Conflict and Conservation.* Baltimore: Johns Hopkins University Press, 2010.

Groffman, Peter M., Jeannine Cavender-Bares, Neil D. Bettez, J. Morgan Grove, Sharon J. Hall, James B. Heffernan, Sarah E. Hobbie, et al. "Ecological Homogenization of Urban USA." *Frontiers in Ecology and the Environment* 12 (2014): 74–81.

Haag-Wackernagel, Daniel. "The Feral Pigeon." Research Group Integrative Biology, Institute of Anatomy, University of Basel. Accessed August 20, 2014. http://anatomie .unibas.ch/IntegrativeBiology/haag/Culture-History-Pigeon/feral-pigeon-haag.html.

Human Planet, episode "Cities: Surviving the Urban Jungle." Directed by Mark Flowers. First broadcast by BBC One, March 3, 2011.

Humphries, Courtney. *Superdove.* New York: Smithsonian Books, 2008.

Jerzak, Leszek. "Synurbanization of the Magpie in the Palearctic." In *Avian Ecology and Conservation in an Urbanizing World*, edited by John Marzluff, Reed Bowman, and Roarke Donnelly. Norwell, MA: Kluwer Academic Publishers, 2001.

Johnston, Richard F., and Marián Janiga. *Feral Pigeons.* Oxford: Oxford University Press, 1995.

Lowry, Hélène, Alan Lill, and Bob B. M. Wong. "How Noisy Does a Noisy Miner Have to Be? Amplitude Adjustments of Alarm Calls in an Avian Urban 'Adapter.'" *PLoS One* 7 (2012).

Martin, Glen. *Game Changer: Animal Rights and the Fate of Africa's Wildlife.* Berkeley: University of California Press, 2012.

Marzluff, John. *Gifts of the Crow: How Perception, Emotion, and Thought Allow Smart Birds to Behave Like Humans.* New York: Atria, 2013.

Marzluff, John, and Tony Angell. *In the Company of Crows and Ravens.* New Haven, CT: Yale University Press, 2008.

McDonald, Michele. "Sparrows Change Their Tune to Be Heard in Noisy Cities." George Mason University, April 2, 2012. http://newsdesk.gmu.edu/2012/04/sparrows.

Mosca, Alexandra Kathryn. *Green-Wood Cemetery.* Charleston, SC: Arcadia Publishing, 2008.

Most, Madison. "The Concrete Jungle: Uncovering the Mystery of Wild Parrots in Southern California." Havasi Wilderness Foundation, October 25, 2012. www.havasiwf.org/the-concrete-jungle-uncovering-the-mystery-of-wild-parrots-in -southern-california.

Niemelä, Jari, ed. *Urban Ecology: Patterns, Processes, and Applications.* Oxford: Oxford University Press, 2011.

Nordt, Anja, and Reinhard Klenke. "Sleepless in Town—Drivers of the Temporal Shift in Dawn Song in Urban European Blackbirds." *PLoS One* 8 (2013).

Pilipili, Oscar. "Marabou Storks, a Fortune or Nuisance?" Standard Digital, February 6, 2009. www.standardmedia.co.ke/?articleID=1144005945&pageNo=1.

Rogers, Simon. "Every Train Station in Britain Listed and Mapped: Find Out How Busy Each One is." *Guardian*, April 25, 2013. www.theguardian.com/news/datablog/2011 /may/19/train-stations-listed-rail.

Sacchi, Roberto, Augusto Gentilli, Edoardo Razzetti, and Francesco Barbieri. "Effects of Building Features on Density and Flock Distribution of Feral Pigeons *Columba livia* var. *domestica* in an Urban Environment." *Canadian Journal of Zoology* 80 (2002): 48–54.

Thompson, Clive. "How Loud Is It?" *New York Magazine*, July 12, 2004. http://nymag .com/nymetro/urban/features/noise/9456/index1.html.

Toronto Zoo. "Marabou Stork." Official website. Accessed August 20, 2014. www.torontozoo.com/explorethezoo/AnimalDetails.asp?pg=618.

Vulture Territory. "Marabou Stork." Accessed August 20, 2014. www.vulture-territory
.com/marabou.html.
Yamac, Elif, and Cihangir Kirazli. "Road Effects on the Breeding Success and Nest
Characteristics of the Eurasian Magpie (*Pica pica*)." *Ekoloji* 21 (2012): 1–10.

9. The Chicago Bird Massacre

American Bird Conservancy. "Minnesota and Oakland, Calif. Adopt Bird-Friendly Building
Requirements." Media release, June 26, 2013. www.abcbirds.org/newsandreports
/releases/130626.html.
Audubon Minnesota. *Bird-Safe Building Guidelines*. Saint Paul, MN: Audubon Minnesota,
2010.
DeBare, Ilana. "Oakland Adopts Bird-Safe Building Measures." Golden Gate Birder,
June 16, 2013. www.goldengateaudubon.org/blog-posts/oakland-adopts-bird-safety
-building-measures.
Fatal Light Awareness Program. "Toronto Becomes World's First City to Mandate Bird-
Friendly Buildings." Media release, October 28, 2009.
Loss, Scott R. "Bird-Building Collisions in the United States: Estimates of Annual
Mortality and Species Vulnerability." *Condor* 116 (2014): 8–23.
Martin, Graham R. "Understanding Bird Collisions with Man-Made Objects: A Sensory
Ecology Approach." *IBIS* 153 (2011): 239–254.
Niemelä, Jari, ed. *Urban Ecology: Patterns, Processes, and Applications*. Oxford: Oxford
University Press, 2011.

10. Suburbia Crawling

BBC News. "Ant Supercolony Dominates Europe." April 16, 2002. http://news.bbc.co.uk
/1/hi/sci/tech/1932509.stm.
Brand, Jacqueline. "*Scytodes thoracica*." Animal Diversity Web, University of Michigan,
2013. http://animaldiversity.ummz.umich.edu/accounts/Scytodes_thoracica.
Brown, Brian V. "Small Size No Protection for Acrobat Ants: World's Smallest Fly is a
Parasitic Phorid (Diptera: Phoridae)." *Annals of the Entomological Society of America*
105 (2012): 550–554.
Buczkowski, Grzegorz. "Extreme Life History Plasticity and the Evolution of Invasive
Characteristics in a Native Ant." *Biological Invasions* 12 (2010): 3343–3349.
Diaz, Ryder. "Argentine Ants March Through Bay Area." *San Jose Mercury News*, March 12,
2013. www.mercurynews.com/ci_22767106/argentine-ants-march-through-bay-area.
Gotzek, Dietrich, Seán G. Brady, Robert J. Kallal, and John S. LaPolla. "The Importance
of Using Multiple Approaches for Identifying Emerging Invasive Species: The
Case of the Rasberry Crazy Ant in the United States." *PLoS One* 9 (2012). http://
urbanentomology.tamu.edu/pdf/Gotzek%202012.pdf.
Hölldobler, Bert, and Edward O. Wilson. *The Ants*. Berlin: Springer-Verlag, 1990.
Holway, David A., Andrew V. Suarez, and Ted J. Case. "Role of Abiotic Factors in Governing
Susceptibility to Invasion: A Test with Argentine Ants." *Ecology* 82 (2002): 1610–1619.
Lewis, J. G. E. *The Biology of Centipedes*. New York: Cambridge University Press, 2007.
Meineke, Emily K., Robert R. Dunn, Joseph O. Sexton, and Steven D. Frank. "Urban
Warming Drives Insect Pest Abundance on Street Trees." *PLoS One* (2013).
Meyers, Jason Michael. "Identification, Distribution and Control of an Invasive Pest
Ant, *Paratrechina* sp. (Hymenoptera: Formicidae), in Texas." PhD diss., Texas A&M
University, 2008.
Moffett, Mark W. "Supercolonies of Billions in an Invasive Ant: What Is a Society?"
Behavioral Ecology 23 (2012): 925–933.

Mooneyham, Katlin. "Camel Cricket Cliff Notes." *Your Wild Life* (blog), March 9, 2012. www.yourwildlife.org/2012/03/a-cliff-notes-guide-to-camel-crickets.

Nauman, Jennifer S., Patricia A. Zungoli, and Eric P. Benson. "Entomology Insect Information Services: Argentine Ants." Clemson Cooperative Extension, Entomology Insect Information Series, 2004. http://media.clemson.edu/public/esps/pdfs/hs42.pdf.

Rasberry, Tom. "Crazy Rasberry Ants Getting Close to Louisiana." Personal blog, August 18, 2008. http://crazyrasberryants.blogspot.co.uk/2008/08/crazy-rasberry-ants-getting -close-to.html.

Ricks, Winston. "*Scutigera coleoptrata.*" Animal Diversity Web, University of Michigan, 2001. http://animaldiversity.ummz.umich.edu/accounts/Scutigera_coleoptrata.

Schwenkmeyer, Dick, and Brad Hollingsworth. "*Phrynosoma coronatum*: Coast Horned Lizard." San Diego Natural History Museum. Accessed August 20, 2014. www.sdnhm .org/archive/fieldguide/herps/phry-cor.html.

Spicer Rice, Eleanor. *Dr. Eleanor's Book of Common Ants.* iBook. Raleigh: North Carolina State University, 2013.

———. *Dr. Eleanor's Book of Common Ants of New York City.* iBook. Raleigh: North Carolina State University, 2013.

Suarez, Andrew V., David A. Holway, and Ted J. Case. "Patterns of Spread in Biological Invasions Dominated by Long-Distance Jump Dispersal: Insights from Argentine Ants." *PNAS* 98 (2001): 1095–1100.

Texas Country Reporter. "Rasberry Crazy Ant." Posted on YouTube, March 9, 2010. www.youtube.com/watch?v=NgpCXGsC6PU.

Trautwein, Michelle. "The Exoskeletons in Your Closet." *North Carolina Naturalist,* Winter 2012.

Wiegmann, Brian M., and David K. Yeates. "Diptera: True Flies." Tree of Life Web Project, November 29, 2007. http://tolweb.org/Diptera.

Williams, Matt. "Crazy Ants Harmful to Texas Governments' Computers." *Government Technology,* December 31, 2008. http://www.govtech.com/health/Crazy-Ants -Harmful-to.html?topic=117677.

Wong, Kate. "Argentine Ants Threaten Californian Horned Lizards." *Scientific American,* February 27, 2002. www.scientificamerican.com/article/argentine-ants-threaten-c.

11. Tunnels of the Bloodsuckers

Bajomi, Daniel. "Budapest Rat-Free for More Than Thirty Years." *International Pest Control* 44 (2002): 318–319.

Ballingall, Alex. "The Race to Go Rat-Free." *Maclean's,* September 13, 2011. www.macleans.ca/society/life/rat-race.

Barnett, S. Anthony. *The Story of Rats: Their Impact on Us and Our Impact on Them.* Crows Nest, Australia: Allen & Unwin, 2001.

Battersby, Stephen A., Robin Parsons, and Joanne P. Webster. "Urban Rat Infestations and the Risk to Public Health." *Journal of Environmental Health Research* 1 (2002). www.cieh.org/JEHR/urban_rat_infestations.html.

BBC News. "Black Rat Back in the UK." May 7, 1999. http://news.bbc.co.uk/1/hi /uk/337680.stm.

Bourne, John. "The History of Rat Control in Alberta." *Agri-Facts,* October 1, 2002. www1.agric.gov.ab.ca/$department/deptdocs.nsf/all/agdex3441/$file/682-1.pdf.

Byrne, Katharine, and Richard A. Nichols. "*Culex pipiens* in London Underground Tunnels: Differentiation Between Surface and Subterranean Populations." *Heredity* 82 (1999): 7–15.

Carter, Claire. "Britain's Biggest 'Fatberg' Took Three Weeks to Remove." *Telegraph,* August 6, 2013. www.telegraph.co.uk/finance/newsbysector/utilities/10224854/Britains -biggest-fatberg-took-three-weeks-to-remove.html.

Chalabi, Mona. "The Quest to Count City-Dwelling Rats." *FiveThirtyEight*, March 17, 2014. http://fivethirtyeight.com/datalab/rats-its-hard-to-calculate-urban-vermin.

Channon, D., E. Channon, T. Roberts, and R. Haines. "Hotspots: Are Some Areas of Sewer Network Prone to Re-infestation by Rats (*Rattus norvegicus*) Year After Year?" *Epidemiology & Infection* 134 (2006): 41–48.

Ciota, Alexander T., Pamela A. Chin, and Laura D. Kramer. "The Effect of Hyrbidization of *Culex pipiens* Complex Mosquitoes on Transmission of West Nile Virus." *Parasites & Vectors* 6 (2013): 305.

Cohen, Jennifer. "Can We Stop Blaming Rats for the Black Death?" History.com, August 18, 2011. www.history.com/news/can-we-stop-blaming-rats-for-the-black-death.

Cottrell, Robert C. *Vietnam: The 17th Parallel*. New York: Infobase Publishing, 2009.

Davis, David E., and W. T. Fales. "The Distribution of Rats in Baltimore, Maryland." *American Journal of Hygiene* 49 (1949): 247–254.

Encyclopædia Britannica Online. "Paul Doumer." Accessed August 20, 2014. www.britannica.com/EBchecked/topic/170268/Paul-Doumer.

———. "Vietnam." Accessed August 20, 2014. www.britannica.com/EBchecked/topic /628349/Vietnam.

Farajollahi, Ary, Dina M. Fonseca, Laura D. Kramer, and A. Marm Kilpatrick. "'Bird Biting' Mosquitoes and Human Disease: A Review of the Role of *Culex pipiens* Complex Mosquitoes in Epidemiology." *Infection, Genetics and Evolution* 11 (2001): 1577–1585.

Fonseca, Dina M., Nusha Keyghobadi, Colin A. Malcolm, Ceylan Mehmet, Francis Schaffner, Motoyoshi Mogi, Robert C. Fleischer, and Richard C. Wilkerson. "Emerging Vectors in the *Culex pipiens* Complex." *Science* 303 (2004): 1535–1538.

Gomes, Bruno, Elias Kioulos, Anna Papa, António P. G. Almeida, John Vontas, and João Pinto. "Distribution and Hybridization of *Culex pipiens* Forms in Greece During the West Nile Virus Outbreak of 2010." *Infection, Genetics and Evolution* 16 (2013): 218–225.

Hanson, Anne. "Rat Teeth." Rat Behavior and Biology, January 25, 2004. www.ratbehavior .org/Teeth.htm.

———. "Wild Norway Rat Behavior." Rat Behavior and Biology, October 29, 2003. www.ratbehavior.org/WildRats.htm.

Hebblethwaite, Cordelia. "Turning London's Fatbergs into Power." Public Radio International, April 15, 2013. www.pri.org/stories/2013-04-15/turning-londons-fatbergs-power.

Jennings, Eric T. *Imperial Heights: Dalat and the Making and Undoing of French Indochina*. Berkeley, CA: University of California Press, 2011.

Johnston, B. Lynn, and John M. Conly. "West Nile Virus—Where Did It Come from and Where Might It Go?" *Canadian Journal of Infectious Diseases* 11 (2000): 175–178.

Kassim, Nur Faeza A., Cameron E. Webb, and Richard C. Russell. "Is the Expression of Autogeny by *Cluex molestus* Forskal (Diptera: Culicidae) Influenced by Larval Nutrition or by Adult Mating, Sugar Feeding, or Blood Feeding?" *Journal of Vector Ecology* 37 (2012): 162–171.

Milius, Susan. "Little Mind Benders." *ScienceNews*, January 26, 2013. www.sciencenews .org/article/little-mind-benders.

New Zealand BioSecure Entomology Laboratory. "*Culex pipiens* Complex." New Zealand BioSecure, May 31, 2007. www.smsl.co.nz/site/southernmonitoring/files/NZB /Culex%20pipiens%20pallens%20-%20profile%20May%2007.pdf.

Office for National Statistics. "London's Population Was Increasing the Fastest Among the Regions in 2012." ONS, October 17, 2013. www.ons.gov.uk/ons/rel/regional-trends /region-and-country-profiles/region-and-country-profiles---key-statistics-and-profiles --october-2013/key-statistics-and-profiles---london--october-2013.html.

Pritchard, Charlotte. "Are You Never More Than 6ft Away from a Rat?" BBC News, December 17, 2012. www.bbc.co.uk/news/magazine-20716625.

Public Health. "Rat-Free City." Special edition, no date.

Rappole, J. H., and Z. Hubalek. "Migratory Birds and West Nile Virus." *Journal of Applied Microbiology* 94 (2003): 47–58.

Robich, Rebecca M., Joseph P. Rinehart, Linda J. Kitchen, and David L. Denlinger. "Diapause-Specific Gene Expression in the Northern House Mosquito, *Cluex pipiens* L., Identified by Suppressive Subtractive Hybridization." *Journal of Insect Physiology* 53 (2007): 235–245.

Sakai, Mike. "City Confirms Roof Rats Invade Northeast Mesa Neighborhood." *East Valley Tribune*, September 13, 2012. www.eastvalleytribune.com/local/mesa/article _a32930d0-fdf6-11e1-9153-0019bb2963f4.html.

Sullivan, Robert. *Rats: A Year with New York's Most Unwanted Inhabitants.* London: Granta Books, 2005.

Vann, Michael G. "Of Rats, Rice, and Race: The Great Hanoi Rat Massacre, an Episode in French Colonial History." *French Colonial History* 4 (2003): 191–203.

12. West Side Roaches

Antani, Kartik, and Amanda Burgeson. "*Blattella germanica.*" Animal Diversity Web, University of Michigan, 2011. http://animaldiversity.ummz.umich.edu/accounts /Blattella_germanica.

Ark in Space (blog). "The Pronghorn—the American Almost Antelope." October 16, 2011. www.arkinspace.com/2011/10/pronghorn-american-almost-antelope.html.

Bonanos, Christopher. "Six-Legged Freak." *New York Magazine*, January 26, 2014. http:// nymag.com/news/features/cockroaches-2014-2.

BugLife. *Creating Green Roofs for Invertebrates: A Best Practice Guide.* BugLife, no date.

Clements, Frederic E., and Victor E. Shelford. *Bio-Ecology.* New York: John Wiley & Sons, 1939.

Colding, Johan, and Carl Folke. "The Role of Golf Courses in Biodiversity Conservation and Ecosystem Management." *Ecosystems* 12 (2009): 191–206.

Dunn, Rob. "Has a New 10-Legged Species Evolved Beneath Rome?" *Scientific American*, June 14, 2012. http://blogs.scientificamerican.com/guest-blog/2012/06/14/has-a-new -ten-legged-species-evolved-beneath-rome.

Ellis, Erle C. "Anthropogenic Transformation of the Terrestrial Biosphere." *Philosophical Transactions of the Royal Society A* 369 (2011): 1010–1035.

Ellis, Erle C., and Navin Ramankutty. "Putting People in the Map: Anthropogenic Biomes of the World." *Frontiers in Ecology and the Environment* 6 (2008): 493–447.

Encyclopædia Britannica Online. "Cloaca Maxima." Accessed August 20, 2014. www.britannica.com/EBchecked/topic/121939/Cloaca-Maxima.

Gehrt, Stanley D., Seth P. D. Riley, and Brian L. Cypher, eds. *Urban Carnivores: Ecology, Conflict and Conservation.* Baltimore: Johns Hopkins University Press, 2010.

Grant, Gary. "Extensive Green Roofs in London." *Urban Habitats* 4 (2006): 51–66.

Groffman, Peter M., Jeannine Cavender-Bares, Neil D. Bettez, J. Morgan Grove, Sharon J. Hall, James B. Heffernan, Sarah E. Hobbie, et al. "Ecological Homogenization of Urban USA." *Frontiers in Ecology and the Environment* 12 (2014): 74–81.

Jones, Steve. *Darwin's Ghost: The Origin of Species Updated.* New York: Ballantine, 1999.

Maller, Cecily, Mardie Townsend, Anita Pryor, Peter Brown, and Lawrence St. Leger. "Healthy Nature Healthy People: 'Contact with Nature' as an Upstream Health Promotion Intervention for Populations." *Health Promotion International* 21 (2006): 45–54.

Niemelä, Jari, ed. *Urban Ecology: Patterns, Processes, and Applications.* Oxford: Oxford University Press, 2011.

Partecke, Jesko, Ingrid Schwabl, and Eberhard Gwinner. "Stress and the City: Urbanization and Its Effect on the Stress Physiology in European Blackbirds." *Ecology* 87 (2006): 1945–1952.

Rodriguez, Gladys. "*Blatta orientalis*." Animal Diversity Web, University of Michigan, 2001. http://animaldiversity.ummz.umich.edu/accounts/Blatta_orientalis.

Rosiere, R. E. "Biome." In *Range Types of North America*. Tarleton State University, 2013. www.tarleton.edu/Departments/range/Literature%20Review/biome.htm.

Shefferly, Nancy. "*Cynomys ludovicianus*." Animal Diversity Web, University of Michigan, 1999. http://animaldiversity.ummz.umich.edu/accounts/Cynomys_ludovicianus.

Stetson, Brad. "*Periplaneta americana*." Animal Diversity Web, University of Michigan, 2001. http://animaldiversity.ummz.umich.edu/accounts/Periplaneta_americana.

Stoltz, Martin. "Tenacious and Abundant: A Guide to the Cockroaches of New York." *New York Times*, April 24, 1994. www.nytimes.com/1994/04/24/nyregion/tenacious-and -abundant-a-guide-to-the-cockroaches-of-new-york.html.

Wada-Katsumata, Ayako, Jules Silverman, and Coby Schal. "Changes in Taste Neurons Support the Emergence of an Adaptive Behavior in Cockroaches." *Science* 340 (2013): 972–975.

Walker, Matt. "Why Cockroaches Need Their Friends." BBC Nature, May 2, 2012. www.bbc.co.uk/nature/17839642.

INDEX

233

ABOUT THE AUTHOR

Tristan Donovan is a nonfiction author and freelance journalist and editor. Born in London in 1975, he planned to become an ecologist before getting distracted by journalism. Since then he has contributed to numerous newspapers, magazines, and websites, including BBC News Online, the *Times* (London), *Stuff*, *Community Care*, the *Guardian*, and *Kotaku*.

He is the author of *Replay: The History of Video Games* and *Fizz: How Soda Shook Up the World*. That playing too many video games while drinking too much soda featured heavily in his childhood is just coincidence.

He lives in Lewes, East Sussex, in the UK with his husband and two ham-obsessed dachshunds.